I've Got This Round

OTHER BOOKS BY MAMRIE HART

You Deserve a Drink

I've Got This Round

More Tales of Debauchery

MAMRIE HART

A PLUME BOOK

PLUME

An imprint of Penguin Random House LLC
375 Hudson Street
New York, New York 10014

LIBRARY OF CONGRESS CATALOGING-IN-PUBLICATION DATA

Names: Hart, Mamrie, 1983– author.
Title: I've got this round : more tales of debauchery / Mamrie Hart.
Description: New York : Plume, 2018.
Identifiers: LCCN 2017048891 (print) | LCCN 2017058195 (ebook) |
ISBN 9780399576805 (ebook) | ISBN 9780525533603 (hardback) |
ISBN 9780525536529 (signed edition)
Subjects: LCSH: Hart, Mamrie, 1983– | Actors—United States—
Biography. | Entertainers—United States—Biography. | BISAC:
BIOGRAPHY & AUTOBIOGRAPHY / Personal Memoirs.
Classification: LCC PN2287.H27 (ebook) | LCC PN2287.H27 A3
2018 (print) | DDC 791.4302/8092—dc23
LC record available at https://lccn.loc.gov/2017048891

Printed in the United States of America
1   3   5   7   9   10   8   6   4   2

Penguin is committed to publishing works of quality and integrity.
In that spirit, we are proud to offer this book to our readers;
however, the story, the experiences, and the words
are the author's alone.

For my Pussy Posse

Contents

CONTENTS

I've Got
This Round

Introduction

THE DAY AFTER my first book, *You Deserve a Drink*, came out, I was sitting down for lunch surrounded by my "team," comprised of my manager, agents, editor, and PR people, the whole ridiculous shebang. As I sipped my midmorning martini, I thought to myself, *Well, look at you, Miss Hart. A few years ago, you were begging people to come to your comedy show in this neighborhood, watching them throw your flyers in the trash can two seconds after you handed it to them.* Now, you're sitting here all fancy. Enjoy it, girl. You've earned it.* But before I could break into a choreo'd number to "I'm Every Woman"† in my head, I was snapped out of my daydream.

"So, what are we thinking for the next book?" one of the suits

---

* If I ran out, I would just delicately pick up the unused pile of flyers from the top of the bin like when George Costanza ate that éclair out of the trash because it was still pristine.
† Obviously, the Whitney version from the *Bodyguard* soundtrack. I love that whole album. I used to rock out hard to "Queen of the Night" as a nine-year-old, having no idea I was just scream-singing about being a prostitute.

asked me. I froze like I'd just realized I was sitting at a table of T. rexes. *Next one?* I thought. *This one has been out for twenty-four hours.* Then another spoke up: "Yes! When can we expect a follow-up?"

I gulped down that lemon drop with a plastered-on smile, nodding and looking attentive, while internally, I was losing it. *Those were all my stories!* I thought. *It took me thirty-one years to collect them! I don't have anything left to tell! Besides, most of them happened in my early twenties. I'm in my thirties now! I don't have that kind of energy anymore!*

But when a huge publishing company named after a flightless bird wants another book, you say YES. When I got back to LA, where I had been living for about a year, I wondered how I was going to pull this off. *Well, lots of authors fabricate stories for their books. Maybe I can just make some up? That's not that bad, right?* Of course it's bad! There's nothing I hate more than listening to someone tell a story and knowing that they are exaggerating. Back to the drawing board. *Maybe I can just leave the business entirely? Retire at the top of my game!* I took a ~~shot~~ deep breath.

This wasn't me. I am not a person who is scared of challenges. My motto has been and always will be "**fuckin' prove it**."

It's true. Whenever someone in my life says they want to do something, I say, "Well, fuckin' prove it." This can be as simple as someone saying they are going to belly flop into a pool or make out with someone at a bar, to bigger things like going back to school or finally writing that movie idea they've told me the plot of eight hundred times.

I needed to heed my own advice. I needed to **fuckin' prove it**.

So, I did! For the next year and a half, I actively sought out the weirdest and funniest adventures I could find. Luckily, I can make YouTube videos from the road, and I avoid going on auditions at all costs, so getting out of town was actually feasible. I'd adventure in a new city, and then my sunglasses-on, hungover self would write up the tale on the plane home, so as to not forget any details. But this book isn't just stories of random boozy adventures and wacky celeb run-ins. See, while I was off acting like a free spirit, indulging in those overpriced plane spirits, I was also dealing with a major turning point in my life: the end of a decade-long relationship.

Initially, I thought I'd keep the breakup out of this book. Hell, what better way to deal with an emotional earthquake than pretending it's not happening and getting the hell out of town, right? Turns out, you can't leave those feelings. They are your constant carry-on.

As I was writing, I realized I couldn't just tell you about my wild night in Paris and leave out the fact that I was bawling like an idiot! Or pretend like my summer of mayhem wasn't in part due to being single and also living alone for the first time in my adult life! I went into the writing process for this book expecting it to be an easy follow-up. Another collection of random debauchery, except this time in my early thirties. But, turns out, when I sat at that table sipping that 'tini in Rockefeller Center, I wasn't just about to start a new writing project. I was about to start a new chapter in my life, and that's what I've documented here. Between the travel and the life-changing circumstances, this book is my *Eat, Pray, Love*, except it would be more accurately titled *Drink, Drink, Drink*.

This book is the closest thing I've had to a diary since the Hello Kitty one I kept in the fifth grade, which I used to write thorough reviews of spin the bottle, and it's by and large the most vulnerable I've ever been in public. Which at first made me hesitant. But it's like they always say: you can't spell "vulnerable" without "all rub even." By "they," I mean me looking at an online anagram generator, but weirdly enough, that phrase actually ties the book together nicely. I started off solid like a rock, threw myself into a tumbler of mayhem, and came out feeling polished and smooth, ready to skip along any tough waters that come my way. Wow, did I just invent a beautiful metaphor?

SOMEONE. CALL. OPRAH.

I really do hope you enjoy this collection. I hope it makes you laugh on a beach somewhere, or say "Oh Lawd-a-mercy" on a crowded subway train, or allows you to feel a little bit better about your own transitions in life. And if it doesn't, have no fear: I always have a drinking game incorporated to help give you a nice buzz during the process. So drink every time I . . .

1) mention a canceled TV show
2) name a snack item you could buy at 7-Eleven
3) reference a chain restaurant
4) use a slang term for a reproductive organ

And also, like the first book, I am instituting a safe word for anyone related to me reading this. Trust me, it's for your own good if you want to be able to look me in the eyes again at a future family function. In the first book, the safe word was "rutabaga," so why don't we stick to the root-vegetable theme and make this book's safe word "KOHLRABI!"? Why? Because I have never used that word in a conversation, and also 'cause it kind of looks like "cool rabbi." Like a rabbi that would bust out a rap at a bris.

Now, you've bought the book, you know the drinking game

rules, you know the safe word, and I've fully prepped you to get into this thing, so there's only one thing left to do . . .

FUCKIN' PROVE IT.

I even got this obnoxiously large neon sign made to remind myself of this motto. To anyone passing by, my living room looks like a Barbie brothel.

The Poc-oh-no's

A DISCLAIMER: Every good relationship I've had has started with honesty . . . and usually a long night of drinking and creating memories that could be used as future blackmail. But since they wouldn't let me duct-tape a fifth of tequila to every copy of this book, I'll just stick with being truthful instead. SO: This chapter, out of the entire book, is the longest. Most authors wouldn't do this. Most authors would kick off their book with a snack of a story. Something to whet the appetite. Like an amuse-bouche at a fancy restaurant or a mini Snickers in your car before Chili's. But that's not my style. I respect you too much to start you off with a quick bang. I wanted our first time to be slow and attentive and leave you satisfied. That said . . . let's get into some trouble, y'all!

Reader, if there's something you need to know about me, it's that I often get very obsessed with **very** dumb things, one of these things being comically large items. Nothing makes me happier than larger-than-life gags: giant whoopee cushions;

water towers painted to look like food items; roadside attractions, like the world's largest ball of twine. This love for colossal crap started early, thanks to a creative local business in my hometown. Where I grew up, in Podunk, North Carolina, there were only a few businesses in town: some gas stations,* a VHS rental/tanning bed salon hybrid, and, situated right by the town's only intersection, a silk-screening shop that took care of all your sports uniforms and fund-raiser T-shirt needs.

Now, I'm no marketing exec, but one would think that the best way to advertise this last business would be to put some jerseys in the window. Ya know, show the people driving by the best examples of your work. But not this place. Instead, they filled their window with a ginormous pair of bright orange granny panties, at least four feet wide, that read "Home of the Whopper" across the ass. It killed me, and still does. To this day, it's my go-to visual to make me laugh, like Peter Pan's happy thought to fly. Home of the Whopper. SMDH.

But despite all the oversize goods I've been around in my day, there has always been one giant thing I've yet to find. My comically large holy grail . . . no, but seriously, it is a grail, because I'm talking about a giant champagne glass.

Let me take you back. When I was just shoulder high to a titmouse, I saw a commercial for a romantic resort with a couple in a tub shaped like a massive champagne glass. I couldn't believe my freshly diagnosed nearsighted eyes! What a sight to behold. This couple was happier than an eighties Newport cigarette ad, heads cocked back, laughing as bubbles swirled all around them.

---

* One that I have recently been told has karaoke on Thursdays. That's right. Karaoke at a BP gas station.

I immediately fell in love with that scene and that tub. I know what you're thinking:

1) WTF does "shoulder high to a titmouse" mean? Stay tuned for more confusing Southern colloquialisms!
2) What kind of child fantasizes about going to what is clearly a lovers' resort?

THIS one. I was a weird child who wanted to be an adult by about age eight. While other kids were decorating their Barbie Dreamhouse or out in the yard playing hide-and-seek, I had a different routine. I would sit at my dining room table, ordering "Vodka Vavooms" from an invisible waiter, which was really just cran-grape in a martini glass. Then I'd take that 'tini to the roof of my dilapidated barn, imagining it was a sexy rooftop bar,* drinking, and puffing away on a small twig as if it was a Capri cigarette.

This is all especially strange because neither of my parents ever drank or smoked while I was growing up. Despite this, I was basically a four-two Samantha Jones in the making, and so naturally, when I saw that commercial, I felt I had to go. I even asked to visit the resort as a birthday gift, which looking back is amazing—a kid begging her mom to take her to a place that is obviously made for people to have lots of sex? She said no and, I'm assuming, started researching youth-size chastity belts.†

Now, twenty-five years later (ouch), I found myself wondering

---

* Pretty sure I called it the BARn, which is brilliant and a business I should probably open immediately.
† My poor mom. While most kids made a list of toys, I was straight-up circling items in a Frederick's of Hollywood mailer. Look, don't call lingerie a "teddy" like the toy bear and adorn silky pastel outfits in rhinestones and feathers if you don't want a weird eight-year-old pining after them like they are "adult costumes."

if I had just imagined this commercial as a kid. That is, until one night when I was at a bar, ~~socializing with friends~~ scrolling through my Instagram feed. There, in a pic drenched in likes, was a shot of my friend Alan, down on one knee, proposing to his girlfriend, in front of the *very* champagne tub from my memory!

It existed! Hallelujah! I was elated. Obviously for my friend finding true happiness in another human but also because this meant that I had not made up this place in my li'l horny brain *and* that it was still open for business.

In no time, I was texting Alan:

Congrats on the engagement yada yada yada where on Earth is that champagne glass?!

Thanks Mame-dog. It's in the Poconos, at a resort called Cove Haven. It's amazing, you gotta go!

Cove Haven, huh? It sounded like a short-lived *Days of Our Lives* spin-off. But then he sent the website. I clicked the link and scrolled through, mouth agape like a preteen boy seeing his first nudie mag. It was **glorious**. Not only were there elaborately themed suites, but there were multiple bars, performances every night, laser tag, archery, you name it. There was so much adrenaline coursing through my veins that I momentarily blacked out, and when I came to, I had a Visa in my hands and booked a champagne suite for Martin Luther King Jr. weekend, one month away. MLK had a dream, and so did I. A dream to have my own dreams atop the circular bed that was prominently featured on the resort's home page.

I knew the perfect person to take with me: my dear friend and former camp counselor buddy, Hayley. Now, those of you who read my first book might remember Hayley from a few chapters, particularly the one where we ate mushrooms and I kept accidentally setting my faux fur coat on fire with my cigarettes at a Flaming Lips concert. Long story short: I was so out of my gourd that night that I thought the greatest way to ring in midnight would be to pour all our bottles of bubbly into a tub and hop in before it struck twelve. Glamorous in theory, but in reality, it was just a girl tripping balls while sitting in four inches of cold André. Not my finest moment.

But this would be so full circle. This wouldn't be a couple of idiots in their early twenties sitting in a birdbath of grocery store champs! This would be two idiots in their early *thirties* lounging in a giant bubble bath champagne glass! So I texted her with my plan.

Fuck yeah, Mamie!!! she texted back. I need this soooo bad. And she did. Hayley is a mom and a wife, and her husband had just been through a major health scare. In other words, Mama needed a weekend of debauchery out of North Carolina. I knew she'd be the perfect copilot, too. Hayley should be illegal in most states, 'cause that woman is a firecracker. Seriously, I consider myself to be an exuberant, charismatic person, but Hayley makes me look like a baked potato with a wig on.

The plan was in motion. I would fly out from LA and meet her at the closest airport to Cove Haven, in lovely Wilkes-Barre,* Pennsylvania, before heading to our luxurious weekend of love.

Three weeks later and there I am, waiting for Hayley in the arrivals area, happy that my weed gummies passed as gummy vitamins[†] through security despite them being skunky as hell. But

---

* A hyphenated town name? How progressive of you, PA!

† I just want to give a special shout-out to the genius who realized they should start making boring old vitamins into gummies. I am still waiting for the day that they make gummy birth control. It may be the only way I'll remember to take it regularly.

that wasn't the only thing skunky at baggage claim. "Mamie Rocket!!!!" Hayley screamed from across the room. She was rocking a new hairdo of shaved dark sides and a bleached-out coif on top, like an edgy Pepé Le Pew. She started barreling toward me, and I say "barreling" because she had clearly drank about a barrel of whiskey on her Detroit layover.

We embraced like I was a soldier coming home from war, Hayley lifting me off the ground and spinning me in 360s.*

"Are you ready for the weirdest weekend ever?" I asked.

We piled into our rental, which might as well just have been a go-kart with a car shell on top of it. I can't remember the exact make or model, but something makes me think it was called a Dust? Which was fitting because every time there was a breeze, it felt as though the car was levitating. We were literal Dust in the Wind, and I was terrified. But there was no time to worry about being blown off the road in this wind sock of a car. I had my ride and my ride-or-die chick beside me, and we were about to undergo Operation: Acquire Alcohol.

There are few things I know about Pennsylvania besides the fact that the scenery can get *real* monotonous as you are driving through the state. But here are a couple of nuggets I know that will hopefully help you in bar trivia one day:

1) Bret Michaels, the lead singer of Poison and the person whose scalp might be detachable—he's been hiding it under a bandana for thirty years—is from there.
2) Steelers fans are intense.

---

* We were both bases in cheerleading back in our day, so never underestimate our brute strength.

3) Buttloads of Amish people.
4) The alcohol laws are crazy strict.

That last fact was the only thing that mattered to me in that moment. In Pennsylvania, you can only buy wine and liquor in sanctioned stores, which were surely closed by this hour. We were tired and jetlagged, and the thought of having to seek out different storefronts for booze made me want to drive into downtown Scranton and quietly pull brown bags of Mad Dog out of sleeping bums' hands. But rather than die by the hand of a vagrant's shiv that night, I called the resort and put it on speaker.

"Cove Haven, this is Barbara, how can I help you?" The woman's voice was so calming, so relaxed. Meanwhile, I responded with the fervor of a woman who'd just been locked up in Thailand for drug trafficking and was allotted ten seconds on the phone with her lawyer. There was no time for punctuation.

"Hi my name is Mamrie Hart and I am checking into a champagne suite tonight I'm on the way there from the Wilkes-Barre Airport and so we won't get there till eleven and I need to know if I can buy wine to be put in the room before it's too late and also what time does the bar close?"

"Slow down, Miss Hart," she replied sweetly. It was a bold move to assume I was single, considering where I was staying for the weekend. Perhaps the desperation to get liquored up in my voice gave it away? "The bar is open till one A.M. And yes, we'd be happy to do that for you. Would you like red or white?"

"Umm, I guess a bottle of each? No. Make it two bottles of red and one white? Wait, no. Two of each . . . and a bottle of champagne."

"Let me get this right—you want two bottles of white, two bottles of red, and one bottle of champagne?" I looked at Hayley, who was doing "bring it home" hand signals like a damn third base coach.

I could sense the judgment in Barb's voice, so I combatted it with my ultimate weapon: my Southern charm. "Five bottles total would be wonderful, Barbara. And thank you in advance for your warm hospitality and impeccable customer service. Looking forward to seeing you shortly." I am 90 percent sure she had her hand pressed to her chest from being so flattered before hanging up the phone.

Hayley and I spent the next hour catching up on life as I drove through the light snowfall. The farther we drove, the more we realized that we were in the middle of *nowhere*, passing town after town of abandoned businesses and sketchy gas stations.

"Is that it?" I asked, pointing to a massive red heart-shaped sign in the distance. We pulled up closer and, sure enough, the sign read "Cove Haven." "What do you think the next-door neighbors think of this place?" Hayley said, nodding toward the yard across the street covered in broken lawn tools and a rusted-out kids' bouncy horse.

I turned into the gate. The driveway was so dark, it could've been surrounded by water, or a rainforest, or a single-file line of escaped convicts, and we would've had no idea. After what seemed like forever, we pulled up to the check-in center, which from the outside had all the glamour of a senior center, and ran in as fast as we could out of the cold. Who knew that Pennsylvania would be so freezing in January?!*

The interior was not much of an improvement. We walked on the old-school carpeting, past the fake champagne tub filled with packing peanuts, to meet the sweet, smiling face of Barbara. "Welcome to Cove Haven!" she said as we strutted in.

---

* Anyone with a rudimentary grasp on weather, probably.

"You two are the last guests to check in. We're fully booked this weekend." I was taken aback. I didn't realize that so many people still even came to this place. Were they here ironically? Maybe the word had gotten out among Brooklyn hipsters about this frozen-in-time novelty just a few hours away from NYC.

We grabbed the keys to our suite from Barb and hightailed it up the road. As we passed one drab brick building after the next, I started to get nervous. There was not a soul in sight, despite Barb saying they were fully booked. Finally, Hayley broke the tension. "Mamie,* be honest with me, is this an extremely complicated murder plot? 'Cause you could've just killed me at home, in that case. I sleep *very* hard."

"Oh come on," I said, trying to keep the faith. "I'm sure everyone is just passed out from making sweet, sweet love all day long." I forced a smile as we continued driving through what looked like a desolate community college, with row after row of redbrick, ranch-style buildings that looked to be from the seventies. Finally, we spotted our building number and pulled in without saying a word. An abandoned shed with police tape lay on its side in front of us.

What the fuck have I gotten us into? I thought. *I've taken my friend away from her adorable daughter and husband, promising a ridiculous adventure, and this is where we're staying?* This place was just plain **creepy**. And this is coming from someone who understands middle-of-nowhere weirdness—after all, I hail from an area that is the home of Andy Griffith and has a huge OxyContin problem. The Land of Opie and Opiates!†

"Let's just check out our room," I said hesitantly as I stepped

---

* Hayley is the one person besides my mom who calls me Mamie. I love it. It sounds like I'm from the 1800s, living on the prairie and hoping I get an orange and a penny for Christmas.

† How is this not on a welcome billboard as soon as you enter my home county? I gotta run for office.

out of the Dust, which immediately raised up as if it had hydrau-
lics on it like a hooptie in a Snoop Dogg video. The snow was
falling harder now, and the grounds were eerily quiet. I thought
at any moment we'd hear the breathy "ha ha ha"s of a slasher
movie and a deranged serial killer would come out of the toppled
shed. Being brutally murdered would be bad enough, but everyone learning I was found in the parking lot of this place with
Hayley? That's a son-of-an-obituary way to go.

I slid the key card through the slot on the painted red door,
which was peeling harder than a redneck's back after the first
sunburn of the summer. We held our breath as we opened the
door slowly, scared of what we might find. But as soon as our
eyes adjusted to the red lightbulb–only lighting, our fears dissolved. **IT WAS MAGNIFICENT.**

The living room was all eighties furniture all the time, with
a small fireplace and a glass-enclosed hot tub room. There were
rose petals scattered across the floor, luxurious red drapes, and
the pièce de résistance: the champagne tub. It was almost too
much to take in all at once. We instantly started jumping up and
down and running around the room, like Kevin McCallister
when he first realizes he's "Home Alone."

"There's a red leather massage table and little sauna down on
a level below the hot tub!" Hayley yelled. "There's mirrors and
twinkly lights above the bed!" I screamed down from the third
floor, as I grinned at my reflection from the mirrored ceiling. I
looked to the unbelievably eighties red bedside table to see our
five bottles of wine, lined up perfectly like cans on a fence about
to be shot by a BB gun. Beside it was a welcome card and one of
those classic heart-shaped boxes of chocolates that's bordered
with lace—you know, the kind that your high school boyfriend
gifts you on Valentine's Day along with a single red rose from a

gas station, thinking it's a fair trade for a hand job. I immediately ripped open the box. Could these be vegan? Was that realistic in rural PA? Nope! *Veganism be damned!* I thought to myself, as I popped one in my mouth. I was on vacation!

After we were fully winded, we piled on the bed, cracking open our sparkling wine. "Cheers," I said, lifting my glass to Hayley. "To what will no doubt be a fever dream of a weekend." And with that, we clinked glasses, downed the bottle, popped a weed gummy, and headed down to the nightclub. If we were lucky, we'd be able to catch the second set from the cover band. Oh, did I fail to mention that Cove Haven has not one but *two* entertainers booked every single night? Their schedule had hypnotists, magicians, local bands, and every nighttime cruise ship activity your heart could desire. My only regret was that we hadn't made it out in December to see the Trans-Siberian Orchestra cover band.

The nightclub felt like walking into that box of chocolates. The walls were coated in rich red wallpaper; the barstools were red; the bar itself was red. We grabbed one of the tables for two that lined the curved wall facing the stage. Around us, tuxedoed waitresses took orders as couples danced to the cover band's rendition of "Drops of Jupiter" by the United States's most underrated band, Train.* I wondered for a moment if our Dust had actually run off the road on our way here and "Cove Haven" was just a weird dream I was having while in a coma. Before I could tell this theory to Hayley, our waitress approached.

"Hey, girls, I'm Maureen. What can I get you tonight?" Good ol' Maureen had a Helen Hunt vibe and sounded exactly like Molly Shannon.

---

* Don't you dare try to act like you don't like Train. You might think you don't, but I guarantee if there was a GoPro in your car and "Hey, Soul Sister" came on, you would know all the words and you would have a delightful time singing them.

"I'll take a double vodka soda," I said. "Make that two!" Hayley agreed as we continued observing the premises, watching the couples slow dance to all the top smooth jams of the early aughts.

One double turned to two, two to three, and by the time we were liquored up enough to invite our waitress to sit down with us, our table had more doubles than Wimbledon.

"Maureen, give us the scoop on this place," Hayley asked between sips. We'd already learned that Maureen had been working at the resort for more than twenty years, so surely she had the dirt. "Yeah, what's the deal with this place?" I asked. "I mean this as a compliment, but it feels like we just walked into a David Lynch fuck palace that hasn't had any renovations in fifty years."

Maureen laughed. "I don't know why they don't put any money into upgrading it. But people keep coming back, so if it ain't broke, don't fix it."

I pointed to a group of couples taking shots at the bar. "Be honest, Maureen. Is this a big swingers' destination? Did those couples just meet tonight? Oh! Or are they all just dudes here with their mistresses?"

"Oh, them? I don't know what happens behind closed doors, of course, but they didn't meet tonight. Those couples have been coming here together for years." Apparently, Cove Haven was known for its repeat customers. Maureen even told us about a couple who had come there on their honeymoon in 1965 and still returned every year on their anniversary. She pointed to an old woman sitting by herself. "Her husband passed away a few years back, but she still comes on their anniversary every year." Hayley and I aww'd so loud that we could've made that eighty-year-old whip her head around if it weren't for the band playing Santana featuring Rob Thomas's "Smooth" so loudly.

I glanced back at the dancing couples, they looked so sweet.

Everyone gazing into each other's eyes lovingly, men dipping their wives and sneaking in little butt pats as the wives giggled. Meanwhile, from their point of view, we were just two wastoid Statler-and-Waldorfs from the Muppets, coming there to raise hell and make fun of everyone. It was like getting up and giving a roast of a toast at your friend's wedding, ragging on all their exes, and then the next person gets up and reads a sonnet, making you look like a real grade A-sshole. Little pangs of guilt filled my stomach, so I took a big sip of vodka to try to drown those suckers.

Maureen continued, "Yep. It's pretty sweet. We call those couples *Forever Lovers*."

"We want to be Forever Lovers!" Hayley and I shouted in unison. Maureen laughed. "I'm so happy you're here for a few days! You two gals are fun!" We felt instantly comfortable, and those pangs started to fade away. We weren't being judged for being judgy! And the longer we were there, the more charmingly perfect the place felt.

The night kept on, and so did we. When we moved from the table to the bar, we met our second-favorite person, Mike the bartender. He kept the drinks flowing and didn't complain one bit that he was staying there later than normal, which is the opposite of how I would've acted if that happened to me back when I was bartending. Put it this way: You know that Snapchat filter that makes you looks normal, but as soon as you open your mouth, bats fly out and you become a demon? That is what you would've seen IRL if you dared sit at my bar after I had started wiping it down.

But not Mike! Mike was such a good sport that he bought us a round of shots to apologize for the ~~swingers~~ couples at the end of the bar who had asked me if I was a witch. In their defense, I was going through a new hat phase, and what was fashionable in

LA must've looked to a dude in a Steelers windbreaker like I was Stevie Nicks on her way to a goat sacrifice.

We stayed until they had to legally shut down the bar. We were drunk and blissful, calling out, "Mike, we love this place! We love you! We love Maureen!" as we stumbled out. There we were, back in the flurrying snow on the eerily quiet grounds. Besides Mike, we must've been the only people awake in the whole place. We had a choice: optimism or pessimism. We could look at our glass as half empty, or fill that mothafuckin' champagne glass tub half full!

The next few hours can only be describe as a hazy, crazy, honeymoon turned funnymoon.* We ran around our room butt naked to all the jams we would make our campers listen to back in the day. We pressed our ears up against the walls to see if we could hear our neighbors. An hour in, we had destroyed the box of chocolates and were getting to the end of the wine. We laid on the bed doing dancing routines into the mirrored ceiling. "Fuck. We are going to be so hungover tomorrow," I said, shoveling the last truffle into my mouth as Hayley sat on the floor opening the fourth bottle of wine. "Mamie, I got a plan. Let's jusss sweat out all the toxins in the hot tuuuuub." I looked down at her. Her eyes were half open. Bish was at half-mast, but she had a point. If we just steeped ourselves in the hot tub for an hour, we could sweat out a chunk of our hangover. . . . Bikram that shit! It was science! (Or at least science for two idiots at five A.M.)

We hobbled down the stairs, and before I could dip a toe, Hayley cannonballed right in. She emerged from the water screaming. "It's not a hot tub! I repeat! It's not a hot tub. It's a

---

* How the hell *Funnymoon* isn't a 2003 movie starring Topher Grace and Drew Barrymore is beyond me.

pool, and it's *freezing*!" Before I could tell Hayley I wasn't feeling a polar bear plunge, she pulled me in. It felt like what I imagine coaches feel after a big victory when the team pours ice-cold Gatorade over their heads. Why someone would make the world's tiniest heart-shaped pool instead of a hot tub was beyond me, but I had stopped looking for rational explanations here at the Cove.

For the next hour, we performed tiny synchronized swimming routines until we were tuckered out and our hands were prune-y. The day had been a long journey, and I was finally ready to call it a night. We put on our pj's and crawled into the bed. As tired as I was, Hayley was even more so, as evidenced by this pic I took in the ceiling mirrors. In the words of 2 Live Crew, she was "face down, ass up, that's the way we like to fuck"–ing passed out.

Star added so you don't see Hayley's bare ass.
Although, it is a star of an ass if I do say so myself.

———

THE NEXT MORNING was shockingly not a struggle. Why? Because we slept right through it. One P.M., however, came at me hard. It felt like there was a pocket-size Property Brother perched on each ear, thrusting a sledgehammer at my temples like it was demo day. I let Hayley keep snoozing as I ventured out to find us coffee. Outside looked like a winter wonderland, or at least a wonderland of brick buildings covered in two inches of snow. Magical! I walked past the restaurant that was shaped like the Colosseum and the outdoor bar (closed for winter) called Tan-Lines, with its heart-shaped sign of a butt in a thong, before finally ducking out of the cold into Spooner's, the café/pool hall/basketball courts building.* There was even a woman in the corner taking orders for caricature drawings. I sidled up to the bar to get some coffees to go and, lo and behold, Mike was behind the bar again. If I hadn't known any better, I would assume Mike and Maureen were either the only two people who worked there, or they were both sets of triplets who rotated shifts.

Back in the room, I attempted to rouse Hayley. "Mamie, I just threw up, like, four times," she said miserably from under the covers. I spent the next hour cuddled up in the living room on the first level, reading my book, and watching Hayley occasionally get up and head to the bathroom to do her thing. One would think that while building a place meant specifically for banging that they might throw in some soundproof walls, but nope, I could hear her every breath as she was puking her guts out. It was like being on a very romantic vaca with the chick from *The Exorcist*.

---

* For those of you who get uncomfortable when a building serves only three purposes, don't worry. There was also mini golf, archery, and roller skating in the basement.

After an hour of her bathroom-to-bed relay, it looked like everything was finally out of her system, so I convinced Hayley to hop in the car and come with me to a local greasy dive a few miles away from the resort. Whenever I'm hungover and the holy trinity of Advil–Club Soda–Water doesn't work, there's only one thing to do: fry, fry again.

When we got to that hole-in-the-wall, I knew what had to be done and ordered the best hangover options: "We'll take fried zucchini sticks, fries, fried pickles, and onion rings, please."

Just the mention of food made an audible shift in Hayley's stomach. It sounded like the closing grunt Tim Allen makes in the opening credits of *Home Improvement*. It was loud. Quizzical, even. "Where is your restroom?" Hayley asked with fear in her eyes.

"Down the hall, second door on the left. But I'm warning you—" Hayley was off before the waitress could finish her sentence, so I was the only one that got to hear, "It's pretty icky."

Hayley came back a few minutes later and said she wasn't touching any of the food. As an avid member of the Clean Plate Committee, I considered finishing all the food myself. At a Mexican restaurant in college, I once ate a three-pound burrito just for the free T-shirt. So, I knew I was capable of pounding this grub, but without a fully functioning live audience, I didn't see the point. We headed back to the resort, and Hayley somehow looked worse than when we left. Not even the TanLines sign, in all its giant-butt glory* could make her smile.

We curved past the roundabout and started up the hill to the champagne suites when Hayley threw her arm in front of me. "Mamie, pull over," she said with her hand over her mouth. To

---

* Oh my god, winter would've been a perfect time to throw those Home of the Whopper panties on that bad boy.

our right, a wholesome young couple walked down the hill hand in hand. "Oh shit, wait just a sec to get past these—" It was too late. Hayley flung open the door and released the beast just steps away from the horrified-looking couple's sensible shoes. This couple had the type of innocence you see only on those TLC shows where couples wait until they are married to kiss. Their mouths were agape until the girl's small mouth eventually peeped, "Oh no."

I covered my face with my hands. Hayley waved at the couple and slammed the door shut. "Drive!" she said, ducking down onto the floorboard. I stepped on the gas, and we peeled off, laughing to the point of wheezing the whole way up back to the suite. The cry-laughing stopped only when it made Hayley cough enough that she was back in the bathroom. She came out shaking her head.

Hayley slept through the overcast afternoon while I got some much-needed R&R, watching TV and vegging out. When dinnertime rolled around, I shook her gently. "Hey, sleepyhead. I'm going to go have dinner. Do you have it in you to join?"

"I can't do it. I'm sorry." I assured her it was okay and headed out on my own, hearing her call, "But let me know if they have anything good," as I closed the peeling door. Cove Haven was back to being dark and quiet as I walked down the snowy path to the Colosseum restaurant. As soon as I entered, I knew it was gonna be awkward. *Every single* table was filled with couples. It was Noah's ark up in that piece. Look, I am a girl who is totally okay to do things by myself. I love going to get a drink in solitude; I prefer to go to the movies solo so the only people I have to violently shush are strangers. But I am big enough to admit that rolling up to that host stand and saying, "Table for one," in this situation was embarrassing.

The hostess sat me, and I immediately tried to order a glass of wine off her. "Sorry, I can't get stuff from the bar, but a waitress will be over in just a sec," she said with pity in her eyes, looking at me as if my husband and I had broken up in our suite and I was just waiting for the next bus out of there. As I sat there, I took inventory of the room. The bar was a huge heart shape. Another display champagne tub, like in the welcome center, was dead center in the lobby, filled with packing peanuts to give the illusion of bubbles. Every table was a two-top, with a lovey-dovey couple enjoying their buffet bounty. I've never seen so many people feed each other bites of food.*

"Where's your sidekick, sweetie?" I looked up to see a smiling Maureen standing in her tux and holding an order pad. "Maureen!" I exclaimed. "I'm so happy to see you! I feel like a loser eating by myself, but Hayley hit the bottle a *little* too hard, and now she's cooped up in bed sick."

"Aww, don't feel like a loser," she assured me. "People eat here by themselves all the time."

I stared at her blankly. "Besides Forever Lover widows?"

Maureen laughed. "Yes, besides widows! Now what do you want to drink?"

I gave her my order (a glass of red wine the size of a champagne tub) and headed to make myself a plate. Pasta, mashed potatoes, rolls. My plate was whiter than a Trump rally.

Just as I was digging into my plate o' carbs, the hostess sat a couple down at the table next to mine. She walked away only to reveal that, of fucking course, the couple Hayley had almost puked on was gazing lovingly across the table at each other. I

---

* I've never understood how feeding someone is sexy. I am not a baby; I can hold the fork. Also, I don't want you accidentally scraping your metal fork on my teeth. They are ~~fucked up~~ unique enough, thank you.

immediately hid my face with my wineglass to avoid being spotted but also to make it less obvious that I was *completely* eavesdropping on them.

Within seconds, I realized, *holy shit*, this couple was on their honeymoon. In fact, their wedding had been only twenty-four hours prior! I listened to them swoon over each other, talk about how great of a dancer her dad was, and how both of them got teary during the best man's speech. It was the purest thing I'd ever spied on! I finished my last bite of baked potato (yes, I had mashed *and* baked, don't come for me) and started to make my exit. This was not easy, seeing as it was a packed house and the tables were bumped up beside each other. I had to decide: Was I sliding out with my butt lingering over their plates? Or my crotch? I went crotch.

But just as I was skimming past their salt and pepper shakers, I was stopped by Maureen.

"I know your friend's sick as a dog, but I fixed her up a plate just in case she gets her appetite back," she said with a smile, handing me a to-go box. I looked down at the couple, whose blissful grins had morphed into blank stares as I thanked Maureen and continued past their table. I walked about two feet away before turning back and leaning down to them to say, "The wedding sounded beautiful. Congratulations." Hell, at least now they would have a honeymoon memory besides a whole bunch of missionary-style sex.

The next and final morning, Hayley woke up bright-eyed and bushy tailed. We were ready to make the most out of our last day at Cove Haven, determined to do all the activities. We roller-skated! We played basketball while roller skating! We mini golfed while roller skating! The only thing we couldn't do was take our roller skates out on the ice-skating rink, but don't think we didn't try.

We made some poor bastard who was just trying to romance his girlfriend take approximately ninety pics of us.

As the sun began to set, we knew we had to get on the road. But before we left, we had to stop and say good-bye to Maureen and Mike. "You two better come back!" Mike told us, while exchanging info and big hugs. "Yes!" Maureen added. "If you two are going to be Forever Lovers, this has to be a tradition!" And we knew it would be. Maybe with less vomiting on newly-weds, but a tradition no less.

We drove away from the resort just like every couple does—completely in love. But in our case, it was with Cove Haven itself. Completely and unironically in love. Sure, she might be a little old for us, and idiots might say she needs a face-lift, but we thought she was just perfect. I'll never forget that first trip to Cove Haven. And something tells me they weren't forgetting us anytime soon. We were burned into their memories . . . although according to the caricature drawing I had made of us, they will remember us as a random news anchor with a strong jawline and Cuba Gooding Jr.

A Forever Lovers duo for the ages.

Starr-Spangled Manners

RALPH WALDO EMERSON, the godfather of transcendentalism, once said, "Life is a journey, not a destination." Why do I bring this up?

A) Because I want to prove that I'm actually educated.
B) Such was the case on my way to meet Hayley that fated MLK weekend.

You guys, I should've known that I was going to have a *time* in Pennsylvania because just getting there was a story in and of itself. Let me back up.

As you'll find out over the course of this book, I fly **a lot**. I think in 2016, the longest I went without flying was three weeks. This means I'm generally pretty calm and prepared when it comes to air travel. When I have a layover, I don't run around scrambling to find my next gate or stuff my gullet with the nearest shitty wrap. When I deplane, I know exactly how long it's going to take me to get to my connecting flight and where I'm stopping to eat. Flying Virgin in San Francisco? You better believe I'm getting grilled artichokes and a cucumber martini at Cat Cora's restaurant.* JetBlue out of JFK? You know I'm hitting up that greasy food court pad thai but pairing it with a crisp pinot grigio from the tapas place.

So, yes, I fly all the damn time. And while I might fly like a bird, I usually drink like a fish while doing so. As far as I'm concerned, airports are like international waters. Time zones don't exist. When you saddle up to a bar, you have no idea if the guy to your right is about to get on his first flight ever, which is why he opted for that thirty-six-ounce Blue Moon, or if he needs a little hair of the dog because motherfucker is on Shanghai time.

These rules apply on the plane, too. If my feet are thousands of feet off solid ground, you best believe I'm ordering a cocktail no matter what time of day it is. And you can forget it if it's an international flight! I've considered bringing my stewardess an Ace bandage wrist protector for how often I'm gonna make her hoist up that big-ass magnum of merlot to refill my cup. But there was never a time I wanted a hard kick of vodka to my face more than on my flight to meet Hayley.

Picture this . . .

It was maybe a hair past six A.M., and after dragging my sleepy self through security, we were finally boarding. I had upgraded my seat to economy coach (what can I say? I had had a good year) so I could relax and stretch these German gams. I quickly realized that relaxation was not on the docket when I glanced at my seatmate. There she was, rocking some major

---

* Cat Cora is an Iron Chef on the Food Network who is known for her Southern drawl and rampant drinking, aka me with knife skills.

leftover makeup from the night before* and a bedazzled sweat suit that looked like she let a few cars run over it before putting it on. This woman had headphones on that were blasting horrible techno so loudly that I wondered if she was actually deaf. Regardless of this, the real problem was that she was in my seat.

"Oh, excuse me," I said, pretending to double-check the seat number on my ticket. She took her time taking out the headphones, the cabin filling with her pulsating beats. "Are you also in 8B?" This sweet routine of looking surprised instead of just saying, "Bitch, you're in the wrong seat," had become one of my favorite airplane acting exercises, along with pretending to feel guilty when I have to make the aisle seat get up to let me use the bathroom.

"Yeah, I'm the window seat, but I need a tray table," she replied brusquely. I looked at the window seat, positioned beautifully behind the emergency exit row, with no seat in front of it. Unlimited legroom all in exchange for one of those awkward pullout tray tables? I'll take it!

"Oh, okay. I don't mind the window," I said, waiting for her to acknowledge how chill I was being, or at least ask if this arrangement was okay. Naturally, this never happened, so I just made myself comfy. I stretched out my legs, buckled my seat belt, looked to my right, and saw exactly why a work surface was so important for this person.

She had her laptop and supplies spread out everywhere like she was renting 8B as a personal office space. Her long nails (minus one, RIP right-hand ring finger) were clicking away on her keyboard, and it was already driving me crazy. I never knew someone

---

* Hey, I am the queen of sleeping in makeup. But not rolling to a flight the next morning, pretending like those aren't your fake eyelashes from the night before. Like anyone glues tarantulas onto their eyes at six A.M.?

could produce such volume just by simple keyboard taps. It was like she had microscopic microphones under each pointy claw.* Seriously, the nails were filed into such sharp tips, she could sit at a bar and spear an olive from four stools down. They were sharper than the tiny forks you use to dip fondue! I digress.

Before I could block out with my headphones the assault-rifle sounds of her typing, a business-looking skeeze of a man rounded out our row with the aisle seat. Now, I know I sound extremely judgmental in this chapter, but I am just going to say fuck it and really give you my inner snarky thoughts. This suit-wearing dude had such a smirk on his face when he saw this woman that it just made me think . . . well . . . have you ever looked at a man and just known he hires hookers? That "hey, whatever happens on my business trip is business, and my wife, Sheila, doesn't need to know a thing about it" look? The kind of guy who flirts with the babysitter while his baby is in the room or compliments how nicely his best friend's daughter is filling out? That was this guy.

He immediately struck up a conversation with her, and I immediately wanted to crawl into a hole. But instead I did the mature thing: I put in my headphones, hit Play on my favorite playlist, then turned the volume all the way down so I could eavesdrop on their convo.†

"Hi, I'm Robert," the skeeze said, offering his hand for a shake, which was risky since his hand was basically coming in hot to shake five pocketknives. "I'm Starr, two Rs," she replied.

---

* I'm sorry, I know the nail-art culture is a big deal these days, and I am all for getting in there with a magnifying glass and painting the cast of *Game of Thrones* on each digit to celebrate the season premiere, but I can't handle the claw nails. Unless you are Lady Gaga and can pull off the look with an assistant doing your daily tasks, why have them? How. Do. You. Wipe?!

† I also used this fake-out technique when I walked late at night in Brooklyn, as if some dudes plotting to rape/murder me were going to have a loud conversation about it first since they saw I had headphones in.

Of course her name was Starr with two *R*s. The woman was a star. A fiery, giant ball of a gas. I watched Starr shake his hand before immediately returning to her work. And here's where I'm going to go ahead and take this opportunity to bust out my first KOHLRABI! Please and thank you.

I sat there wondering, *What the hell kind of business does this mess have to attend to at the ass crack of dawn?* So I decided to take a peek at her laptop. Turns out, it was actual ass cracks.

There, on Starr's laptop, was a screen laid out like a grid, full of little squares of girls doing webcam sex videos. I KID YOU NOT. This woman was watching porn. Amateur porn. Private-room porn. A grid of nine small squares of women were on display, performing into their low-res webcams. It looked like a really low-budget, porn version of the *Brady Bunch* opening.

I wasn't the only one who noticed. When Robert saw the screen, his face lit up so bright, you would've thought that Starr's laptop had a giant Kardashian-style LuMee case on it.*

"Ladies and gentleman," the soothing voice of the flight attendant purred though the speaker. *Oh yes,* I thought to myself, *normalcy. I remember it well.* I leaned into the sound of her voice, tilting my head like a cat wanting to be pet. "We are going to begin our taxi to the runway if everyone could just make sure their bags are slid all the way under the seat in front of them, their tray tables are put away, seats are upright, and your seat belt is securely fastened." This did not sit well with Starr, who let out the most exaggerated, exasperated sigh this side of teenagehood, an exhale so strong a tsunami of coffee-and-

---

* For those of you who don't know what a LuMee case is because you actually use your phone for more important things than selfies, a LuMee case basically has a ring of light all around it. It gives you not only flattering and perfectly lit selfies but also extreme shame when someone catches you having a photo shoot in the produce section of Trader Joe's with what is essentially a mini lighting kit.

buffalo-wing-flavored-Pretzel-Crisps breath knocked me in the face. Something told me that Starr had stayed out all night and brushed her teeth in the airport bathroom with the corner of her pink hoodie.

Luckily, she had her new bestie Robert to keep her entertained and to interview her as we took off and reached cruising altitude. I closed my eyes as to up the "I'm not eavesdropping" ante and listened to my new favorite podcast, *The Bobby and Starr Hour.*

"So, what do you do for work?"

Gimmie a break, Bobby! I thought to myself. *She's clearly a surgeon. A pediatric surgeon who just really loves to watch girls strip on top of mismatched bedding and piles of clean clothes they've yet to fold.* I kept my trap shut and continued listening. Apparently, Starr was leaving LA from one of the world's biggest porn conventions. She was *super* close to selling her live-streaming porn website to one of the big dogs in the porn world, because according to her, they only had Eastern European girls, and she was the only one with "all the American bitches." Currently, she had to watch her girls in their private rooms to make sure they didn't do anything against the rules. Which occasionally they would, but Starr, ever the classy lady, would put her hand up to block the screen when one of them indeed got out of line.

Look, I'm not being a hater for a girl getting out and being entrepreneurial, no matter what the profession. In the words of our Lord and Savior, Beyoncé, who run the world? Girls! And I believe that. I simply wish that this particular girl had also run her tracksuit through the wash cycle before being in such tight quarters.

As soon as the ~~doctor~~ drink cart rolled up, I knew I needed a little something to get me through the rest of the flight with these clowns in tow. "I'll take a coffee with Baileys," I said sweetly to the flight attendant. Based on the look of sympathy she gave me, word of the woman watching porn must have spread to the flight attendant corridor. I half-expected her to mouth, "Wink twice if you need saving," like I was a kidnapping victim.

But that wasn't the crazy part. The crazy part was that as soon as the word "Baileys" left my mouth, Starr did a straight up–cartoon double take at me. The look of disgust on her face was as if I had just ordered a stem-cell latte. I'm sorry, but this woman who was explaining erotic asphyxiation to Bobby* was judging *me*?! What, like, I'm the freak because I'm having a drink at six A.M.?

That's when the thought hit me: OH MY GOD, I'M HAVING A DRINK AT SIX A.M. I am drinking at six A.M. to go spend the weekend at a lovers' resort in the Poconos. *Maybe I am the gross one in this row*, I thought to myself. *Maybe I'm the one who should reevaluate my life choices.* As I lifted up my hand to tell the flight attendant to cancel my order, I looked down to see Starr pointing out her site's top searches, which were, naturally, "anal" and "bondage." I was transfixed watching her letter opener of a nail pointing to the sidebar of keywords that would make Jenna Jameson cringe. It felt like an episode of *The Twilight Zone*. If I would've looked out the window, surely there would've been a gremlin attacking the wing of the plane.

"Yes?" the flight attendant finally asked, noticing my now-frantic waiting.

"Oh," I said, smiling, "I'll also take a Bloody Mary." Starr's jaw dropped, and I'm pretty sure her clip-in extensions fell to the

---

* Like he didn't know. Pffffft. Yeah right, Bobby boy.

floor from the way her head jerked toward me in shock. I couldn't believe it: I was being judged by a porn czar named Starr. A LITERAL PORN **STARR**.

But I shook it off. I took my vodka with a splash of bloody mix and put my headphones back in, this time cranking up some music to block out the haters. I had zero fucks to give. And I think that was inspired in part by Starr. If she could stream sex chats at thirty thousand feet without batting one of her Daisy Duck–level fake lashes, I could have a damn drink or two to get through this flight. In a world of judgment and people always looking over your shoulder or trying to get a peek at your screen . . .

Be the Starr!

But please don't force porn on other people on a plane. It's just rude, guys.

That's So-Noma

IF THERE'S ANYTHING that I've learned in my time on this planet, it's that there is **nothing** more sacred or more important than your female friendships. As you get older, your girlfriends become your rock, your therapist, your sole source of empathy when it comes to the female experience of dealing with today's world. And having someone who knows your history is important. Being able to say, "Oh my god, remember the time . . ." becomes less and less available as you get older and new people get cycled through your life. So it's necessary to hang on to the good ones. The ones who have known you through *bad* haircuts and *bad* relationships and *bad* versions of yourself and still consider you to be their *good* friend. And I've been lucky enough to have that in my high school bestie, Ashleigh.

Ashleigh, or Ashole, as she is so lovingly referred to in my phone, is like my sister. Metaphorically speaking, anyway. She's not like my *actual* sister, who is a raging tornado of brash hilarity. Ash is quite the opposite. She's funny and smart and definitely speaks her mind . . . but goddamnit if she isn't the sweetest woman alive.* I've seen her apologize to a doorframe after running into it. I've seen her apologize to a waiter for ordering something they were out of. And I've definitely seen her apologize to me after calling her out for apologizing too much.

Ashleigh is your quintessential Southern lady. She is great at her job, and her friends, and her marriage. Every outfit she wears looks like it was taken off a perfectly curated Pinterest board. She has a beautifully decorated Tudor home in Charlotte and a hilarious and sweet husband, and she does things like run marathons and host a soup club once a month at her house. Yes, you read that right. A *soup* club. They exchange Tupperwares of their brothy goodness so that you get a week stacked with various homemade soups to try.† The woman clearly has got her shit together. Meanwhile, I'm the human equivalent of Taz from *Looney Tunes*, who spins around the globe leaving a mess in her wake. But despite our yin-and-yang approaches to life, when she and I get together . . . IT'S ON.

One of our favorite things to do together when I come home to North Carolina is go wine tasting. For the past ten years, *tons* of small vineyards have begun popping up in my hometown area and the counties surrounding it. And thank the God of Grigio, because when I was growing up, Yadkin County was drier than my cooter after a guy tells me he's a Republican. If you wanted alcohol, you had to cross county lines. Convincing someone's older brother to buy you booze in high school is difficult enough, but add in him having to drive his Dodge Ram twenty minutes to the next county, and you've set yourself up on a hell of a mission.

---

* Besides my mother . . . I am legally bound to say that.
† The only time I eat soup is because I crave pho and ramen when I'm hungover, and even then it's usually accompanied with a Tsingtao.

So now going to these vineyards has become sort of an annual tradition for me when I visit my family. Each vineyard is adorably *down home*. While the tasting rooms in Napa look like they got dropped in from Tuscany, with marble countertops and stone fireplaces, the ones in North Carolina are more like Cracker Barrel gift shops. Traditional vineyards give you water crackers to cleanse your palate so the flavors don't get muddy between each taste. At RagApple Lassie in Boonville, North Carolina, they give you Cheez-Its. That's right. Fake cheese-flavored squares from the local Food Lion.

But these trips home aren't as frequent as I'd like. Luckily, Ash came up with the brilliant idea to plan a girls trip . . . to Sonoma!

It was July 2015, and I was in full preproduction mode for my movie *Dirty 30*, which was shooting a few months later. My brain was filled with everything from script changes to casting to location scouting. Sure, it was a small movie, but you wouldn't believe how many meetings you have over things like whether "we see the guy puke into the fountain or just hear it." I was halfway through sending a very stern e-mail to my director about how important it was to hire an extra who would let me take a body shot off them when an e-mail from Ash popped up in my in-box.

"Lady Vaca! Cheers, Bitches!"

In perfect form, Ash had put together an adorable Evite, complete with little wineglasses and glittery hearts.

"If you are getting this invite, I want to travel with you! In an effort to prevent a lengthy discussion about where and when we could all go, I picked for us . . . Sonoma! Let's go drink some wine and take in the Cali sun. I promise not to plan every hour of your day! ☺"

And right below that was a tentative plan of essentially every hour of the vacation. I loved it. For weeks, I had been knee-deep in minutiae related to the movie, and here came my knight in Anthropologie armor, ready to plan out a vacation where all I needed to do was show up. I was *in*. Drinking some crisp pinot among the vines with a bunch of North Carolina sorority sisters was just what I needed.

Not *my* sorority sisters, though. Ha! Can you imagine?! The closest I ever got to being a part of the Greek system at UNC was frequenting the Pita Pit so often that they started letting me throw on gloves and build my own pocket. This is not hyperbole, and I'd like to formally apologize to the Chapel Hill franchise for how much feta I overserved myself. Anyway, these were Ash's sorority gals. Luckily, I already knew them from her wedding and bachelorette party.*

These women are hilarious. They start 30 percent of their sentences with "bless her heart," which, in case you aren't from the South, is the equivalent of saying, "Listen to this shit . . ." For example:

They say, "Bless her heart, she's fallen on some hard times with the law."

Which means, "Listen to this shit: bitch got arrested for weed possession."

Or

They say, "Bless her heart, she's been through the wringer with her husband."

They mean, "Listen to this shit: Daryl can't keep his dick in his pants, so she's leaving his ass."

But don't be fooled just because they sound like Sally Field in *Steel Magnolias*—these girls know when to hang up their

---

* Which is described in a riveting chapter in my first book called "Frame the Cookie," in which I accidentally hired a sixty-five-year-old drug addict to teach us how to pole dance. Classic mistake!

monogrammed cardigans and get down and dirty. I knew this trip would start off with *class* but that one (or most of us) would end up showing our *ass*.

After a few months and a Lady Vaca e-mail chain longer than *War and Peace*, I headed up on a quick flight from LAX to SFO. When I say "quick," I mean quick: it's a forty-minute flight. There is nothing more ridiculous than watching the flight attendants roll up their cart to the front of the plane, serve three people their drinks, then wheel the cart back because the captain is about to descend.

I stood there at the girls' arrival gate, rocking what would be my signature look for this trip—a floppy hat and romper—wondering if I had time to pop over to Cat Cora's for that delicious cucumber martini. Then, like a country angel from above—or at least from the jet bridge—I heard Ash screaming, "Mame-a-ho!" Coming at me like a J.Crew billboard brought to life were Ashleigh; Lindsay, an old friend from high school I hadn't seen in years; and the four other gals from the bridal party.

And wouldn't you know it? Every damn one of them was decked out in a floppy hat and romper. Ash came in for the first hug, complete with the awkward "we are both wearing huge hats" dance.

A floppy hat didn't stop a strong hug from my girl Lindsay. Lindsay is the type of person who will dive straight into conversation with you as if when you said bye to her a decade earlier, you just hit Pause on a remote and then hit Play again. She doesn't skip a *beat*. Within thirty seconds, you're waist-deep in the type of local dirt usually only doled out at the salon.

"Mames, you aren't even gonna *believe* what's going on with my sister these days."

"Which sister?"

"Both of them." Before I could get sucked into the vortex of gossip, Ash swooped in, putting her arm around mine as we walked to baggage. "Mame-a-ho! I'm so happy you could come. I know your schedule is insane right now."

"Are you crazy? I wouldn't miss this. Where's Molly?" I asked, scanning the pack of girls. Molls and I were closest out of Ashleigh's friends. She always comes over when I visit Ashleigh in Charlotte and was the only person to puke out of a moving vehicle at Ash's bachelorette, so we were obviously kindred spirits.*

"Oh, I thought you knew . . . she's pregnant."

"Really?!" I asked, clutching Ash's hands.

"Yes. And bless her heart, she is so sad she's missing out on all the wine. Talk about timing, huh?" Ash said. "We'll have to send her selfies. Now, let's go get turnt."†

And turnt we got. And by that, I mean these girls were jet-lagged, and after a snail's crawl through San Francisco traffic to our adorable Sonoma inn, we *turnt* our sleepy selves in to our hotel beds. Ash, Lindsay, and I were splitting one room, and the other four gals split another. Not that I wouldn't have shared a room with girls I had only hung out with once before (I've shared rooms with people I've known for three drinks, he he he) but I just needed to be near my old-school girls. The girls I would ride around with looking for boys all while blasting Juvenile's "Back That Azz Up" from our shitty Honda speakers.

"Aww , you guys," I said, getting into bed with Ash. "When's the last time the three of us slept in one room together?"

"My god, probably 2001, at your house," Ash chimed in from

---

* What's the deal with me gravitating toward people who vom out of cars? Should I talk to someone about this?

† Side note: At this point, "turnt" was still very much an in and cool thing to say. Just throwing that out there in case you're reading this and thinking to yourself that Ash sounds like a grandma trying to sound hip.

below the duvet. "Except now we aren't sleeping on a pallet on your floor and your sister isn't trying to secretly get us high when you aren't watching."

It was true. While I was infamous in high school for maintaining a squeaky-clean track record of not smoking weed, my sister was infamous for getting people to try smoking weed for the first time. She was like the Mrs. Robinson of grape-flavored blunts.

I snuggled under those blankets, totally content. It was like old times. Just a few minutes later, I conked out, dreaming of all the wine we'd drink the next day.

The following morning, after slapping on some makeup and, of course, our rompers and hats, we met up with the rest of the girls at the lobby's continental breakfast. Everyone was carbo-loading like calories just magically didn't exist in Northern California—I'm talking toast, waffles, cereal, Danishes, all the perfect foundational elements for day drinking. However, I myself abstained, as I'm not much of a breakfast person. I prefer to drink coffee until I don't know whether I have the shakes or if an earthquake is happening.*

But skipping breakfast wasn't just out of habit. It was strategy. After all, I. CAN. DRINK. Not saying these women weren't capable of putting back a twelve-pack at a college tailgate, but drinking is essentially my profession. I *start* feeling it after a bottle of wine. Let it be known that I am not proud of this, nor do I think this is a good thing. Do you know how much money and time and calories I would save myself if I could get buzzed off a glass of pinot grigio like a normal woman of my height and weight? My stature might say "average-size female," but my tolerance is that of Fat Bastard from *Austin Powers*.

---

* Living in LA, this happens more often than you'd think.

Skipping the waffles would hopefully let me start feeling the wine on the same schedule as everyone else.

We piled into the limo and headed to the first vineyard, drinking mimosas on the way. It felt like we were all headed to a very classy prom, unlike the ones us Yadkin County gals had attended in a badly carpeted conference room at the Comfort Inn off exit 82.* But this time, we weren't headed to a hotel that shared a parking lot with a Cracker Barrel; we were headed to classy establishments, with barrels of wine and crackers to cleanse the palate.

We rolled into the first tasting room, excited for what the morning held. The room was gorgeous, with exposed wooden beams and lots of stone. Seeing as though it was all of ten A.M., and Ash had scheduled to have a private tasting with the sommelier, we were the only ones there.

"Today, we'll be diving into a variety of white and reds," said the mustachioed sommelier (we'll call him Som) as he poured everyone a dollop of cabernet. "You'll notice the first one we are tasting is very dry"—we all nodded—"with strong notes of black cherry and even a little tobacco."

"No thanks, I quit years ago!" I said while exaggeratingly sniffing my wine. The girls all laughed. I knew this was because they were already buzzed from the road mimosas, but I didn't care. A captive audience is a captive audience.

Som continued describing the wine, only pausing to swat

---

* True story: every year my high school would have a prom fashion show thrown by a local bridal boutique. The best singers from show choir would sing as the jocks and preps modeled. Moments before my solo of "My Heart Will Go On" from *Titanic* (hey, it was '98), the bridal store owner ran up to me, clutching something massive. "You have to put on the Heart of the Ocean," she said, lifting a giant replica of the necklace from the movie. I protested, but apparently she had it special ordered, so I was forced to wear it. My sister and her "bad kid" friends never let me live it down.

away a fly every few seconds. We watched him trying to keep his composure while talking about the subtle bouquets and tannins, but this fly was circling him like he was Pig Pen from *Peanuts*.

By the third wine, Som's face was redder than the pinot we were about to taste. "This damn fly! It has been pestering me for days."

"Looks like you literally . . . caught a buzz!" I said, buzzing like a fly to really send the pun home. Laughs all around. I was on FIRE. This was my Apollo audience, and based on Som's unenthused expression, he wanted to be the Sandman and straight-up shepherd's hook my ass offstage.

"I wish I could catch that buzz," Som said, while opening another bottle. "I tell you what: if one of you caches that fly, I'll give you a free bottle of any of the wines we're tasting," he said, with a little laugh in his voice until he realized what he had just done.

You gotta remember, this was a group of girls who grew up in the country. Not only do we love free shit, but everyone in that room had dated someone in high school who had hunted, if they themselves didn't hunt.* So, Som continued describing the wines, and we kept sipping and nodding, all while keeping the fly in our peripherals.

"Now for our first white is a steel-cast chardonnay that . . ." THWAP!

Everyone looked over to Ashleigh, whose hand was suction-cupped over her tasting glass. Underneath . . . was the fly. "You did it!" I exclaimed, as if she had just wrangled a wild tiger with her bare hands.

"I think I'll catch and release," she said, slowly standing up

---

* Myself excluded. The closest I've ever come to hunting is being rip-shit drunk and buying an animatronic mounted deer head off eBay.

and making her way to the door. With great flair, she released the beast as we all applauded.

"I will take a bottle of the pinot noir, kind sir," she said, curtsying and plopping back on the corner couch proudly. "Unless you were joking. I'm sorry, were you joking?" Classic Ashleigh. So nice that even though she trapped that fly like a boss, she wasn't going to make the man pay up.

"A deal's a deal. Now, as I was saying, this chardonnay is extra special because at first you'll taste the crisp honeysuckle flavors, but let it rest on your tongue for a moment, and notes of green bell pepper will start to emerge." We all sipped and oohed and aahed as if we could taste anything that this man was talking about. He was halfway through describing what stones we were supposed to taste on the back notes when, don't you know it, that fly was back at it.

The poor guy* was trying his best to block out the buzzing and continue on with the presentation as it hovered around us. As he started pouring our sixth and final wine, the buzzing stopped and the fly was out of sight. It was finally silent. That is until . . . I started giggling.

I couldn't help it. Something was lightly tickling my foot. I looked down, and the fly was perched right on my strappy sandal.

"Nobody move!" I said to the gals who were *definitely* not planning on moving anytime soon. "I got him." I looked up to Som, who froze so perfectly that if wine didn't work out, he could totally be one of those street performers who paint themselves gold.

"If I can get this fly out of here, do I get a free bottle of wine, too?" I asked, hope glimmering in my eyes.

"I guess . . ." he started to say. That was all I needed to hear.

---

* Or should I say "pour guy"? Bahahaha— Oh, no? Just leave it as is? Got it.

I rose to my feet with the precision and balance of a tightrope walker. And for the next three minutes, I took the world's tiniest steps, inch by inch, making my way to the door. This was harder than it sounds seeing as I was wheezing laughing. The combination of morning drinking, while admitting my feet were so gross that they were a goddamn Golden Corral buffet for that sucker, was too much to handle.

This is basically *Man on Wire* except *Bitch on Budget.*

I finally got to the doorframe, looked at the captivated group, and said—are you ready for this?—"Talk about SHOE FLY, don't bother me!" kung fu kicking the fly into the outside heat. Guys, when I say the joke killed, I mean it. I almost retired right there, but instead I graciously took my hard-earned bottle from Som, and we continued on our journey.

For the rest of the afternoon, we cruised around to other vineyards, doing our tastings, having a glass on their grounds, then drinking whatever we bought when we got back in the limo. It was top to bottom an afternoon of laughing and cutting up and telling various gorgeous women in their early twenties who worked at the vineyards that we were jealous of them and that they had luminous skin. It was the perfect day, but I could tell that Ash was a little distracted. She was smiling and joking, but when you've been someone's best friend for seventeen years, you just know. But I wasn't about to confront her about it in the back of this stretch limo in front of everyone. This wasn't *Vanderpump Rules*.

By the time we were dropped back at the inn, the whole gang seemed a little tired and a little cranky. I looked over to Lindsay, who was rubbing her eyes like a toddler, and knew we all needed to be put down for a nap.

"Let's all meet back up in the lobby at seven and go to dinner? Is that cool with everyone?" Ashleigh asked, the ever-consistent sweet mom of the group. We all nodded our sleepy heads and split off to our rooms for some hard-core napping, the kind of napping where you instantly start dreaming and when you wake up you freak out for a second that you slept until the next day. Luckily, I had set an alarm. Nothing like waking up at six P.M. already slightly hungover to know you did wine country right. Only thing to do now was power through and keep the party going.

I rallied the girls, and we sleepily fixed our makeup and put our hats back on to hide our bedhead. We headed to the lobby to meet everyone else before Lindsay was stopped in her tracks. "Holy hell, come look at this." Ash and I reversed it to meet her in front of a room with its door wide open. Inside was the rest of the crew, totally knocked out, one of the girls facedown like the dead man's float with her dress shimmied up so high, her ass was on display for anyone walking by to see. It was Hayley on the Cove Haven bed all over again.

"Aw, bless their hearts," Ashleigh said. "I feel bad waking them."

"Me, too," I said. "Let's let them sleep and go catch up just the three of us." They nodded as I crept inside to pull down the dress and cover the exposed booty. Then we turned off their light and gently shut the door.

We took a quick Uber ride to the main Sonoma square, stomachs rumbling. All the restaurants were packed, so we did what anyone would do: we put our name on the list at a Mexican place, then sat at the bar drinking margs and filling up on chips and salsa, to the point where we would eventually be too full when they finally called our name, also known as the most annoying thing you can do at a restaurant. We weren't two margs in before I looked over at Ash and saw she had tears welling up in her eyes. *Oh, please don't let her be having marriage problems. They aren't even a year in, and I refuse to stop showing people that pizza picture*, I thought to myself.

What's the pizza pic? Oh, only my FAVORITE pic of Ash of all time. Picture this: it's the end of her wedding night, and while the wedding party is bouncing back to the hotel on a party bus singing along to "Ignition (Remix)," as one does, I came up with the genius idea of going online and ordering from the local Little Caesars so that it would be delivered as soon as we arrived. I initially was going to keep this plan on the down low so everyone would marvel at my brilliance and be jealous of my piping-hot crazy bread, but if there's one thing I love more than stuffing my gullet full of food when I'm drunk, it's telling people when I have a great idea.

So, what was supposed to be me breezing through the lobby and grabbing my bounty like a marathon runner taking a cup of water without stopping became a wedding party pileup with everyone waiting for *their* orders. And while Ash and her hubs would've normally headed straight to the penthouse suite for wedding night bliss, Ash was distracted by the smell. She was more concerned with consuming pizza than consummating her marriage, much to the dismay of her hubs. She plopped her beautiful white gown down in a seat and refused to go upstairs until she got some. For a second I thought a hot slice of cheese was going to get the marriage annulled.

This is the face of a bride who just dieted for a year and can now eat whatever the fuck she wants, and the legs of a patient man who realizes he just agreed to put up with this shit forever.

I still laugh every time I see that pic. But there, in that Sonoma restaurant, seeing Ashleigh with tears welling in her eyes, I was not laughing. Finally, she broke down. "I'm so exhausted. Jeff and I have been trying everything and we just can't get pregnant. We're losing hope," she said, salty tears falling into salty chips. "I thought maybe if I planned a trip that was specifically for drinking, I would end up getting pregnant just out of irony."

My heart sunk. Here she seemed to be effortlessly running the show, when secretly, she was stressed as all get-out. Lindsay and I rubbed her back and listened to her unload everything she had been feeling the past year, her stopping every few minutes to apologize to us for crying. The fertility methods, the close calls, the laborious adoption applications process. How she had been trying to keep it together while watching all her other friends get pregnant so easily, not bringing it up so as to not rain on their parades. No wonder she was stressed.

Something struck me while I sat there on that barstool. For the first half of our friendship, it would have been our worst nightmare to see two lines on a pregnancy strip. Now, for her, it was opposite. Gone were the days when the word "pregnancy" was always followed up by "scare." Ashleigh was the kindest, most nurturing person I knew. Whether that was babies or taking care of a drunk Mamrie after a field party, motherhood suited her. And now the only scare was that it wasn't going to happen naturally, like she'd imagined.

In that moment, I finally felt what it meant to be in a real adult friendship. Back when we were teenagers, our biggest problems being our high school boyfriends not calling us when we clearly sent "911" to their pagers, or figuring whose older brother was going to buy us a handle of Popov for the weekend. Most of the time, I still feel like a teenager pretending to be an adult. Like the movie *Big*, except instead of saying to Zoltar, "I wish I were big," I say to

him, "I wish I were a dress size smaller."* But sitting in that restaurant, I was weighed down with the reality of growing up.

A few more margaritas and a lot of tears later, we trekked
back to the hotel to pass out. I said good night to Ash, told her I
loved her, and closed my eyes, agitated that I couldn't fix anything. It's not like when your friend gets dumped and you go,
"They didn't deserve you. You're going to find someone better!"
and then take them out on the town to get their mind off it and
hopefully get them to make out with a stranger on a seedy dance
floor. Nope. Can't go "That unfertilized egg didn't deserve you!
Now, go put your tongue in someone's mouth to the pulsing
beats of Pitbull!" All you can do is listen.

When we all met in the lobby the next morning, it was the
open-door crew that looked bright-eyed and bushy tailed. Meanwhile, the Boonville gals were wearing our floppy hats a little
lower as to shade our bloodshot eyes.

"Well, there y'all are!" one of them called to us, to-go cups of
coffee in hand. "Sorry we slept through dinner last night. We
must've just went down for a nap and never recovered."

"Y'all didn't recover, and *you* weren't covered at all," I said,
pouring myself the dregs of the remaining coffee, "Nice ass, by
the way, Heather."

"What did we miss?"

Ash and Lindsay and I all exchanged a quick look, but I spoke
first. "Oh, nothing. We just went for a super chill dinner. Came
back and were asleep before midnight." I grabbed Ash's hand and
gave it a little squeeze. "Is anyone else starving, by the way?"

---

* Side note: I recently Googled the kid from *Big*. Turns out, he didn't grow up to look
like Tom Hanks, but he did grow up HOT. Hot enough that he used to be engaged to
Kerry Washington! This is officially the most random celeb fact in this book. Feel free
to drop it at dinner parties or anywhere else where people are *hard up* for facts.

"Not us," Heather spoke up again between drags of her morning Parliament Light. "We ended up eating Mexican food." What the hell? Had they been at the restaurant and we were too busy crying and yammering that we hadn't seen them?

"Yeah, we woke up at midnight starving and called an Uber to take us through a Taco Bell drive-through." Look, you can take the girls out of the white trash, but they're still gonna stink.*

We spent our last day together dragging but staying on the planned itinerary, feeling like tiny fairies beside the giant trees of Muir Woods, and getting a waterfront lunch in Sausalito. Before heading to the airport and flying our separate ways home, I took Ash aside to let her know to reach out if she needed to talk, not to bury it all inside. She agreed—plus, as an upside, I knew she was coming to LA two months later for work, so I'd have the chance to cheer her up then.

Two months later and Ash was in Hollyweird. At that point, I was deep into production of *Dirty 30*, which was perfect—she was going to get to see me in action! Acting in scenes, sitting with headphones on in the producer's chair, demanding that craft service make more vegan Southwest eggrolls. Once we were wrapped for the night, Ash and I bolted to my friend Joselyn's book release party. I was so happy she was getting this full experience of seeing me do my LA thing. Plus, I could introduce her to some of my friends before inevitably cornering her to pick up where we had left off on the baby convo, this time without the haze of all-day day drinking.

We got to the party, and it was packed. After hugging Joselyn and taking a few pics in the adorable DIY photo booth, Ash

---

* I'm kidding, Heather et al! Y'all aren't white trash. You aren't even that redneck. Ashleigh and I went through a phase where we smoked Dorals. Now, *that's* neck.

and I moseyed up to the bar. It had been a long day on set, and Mama needed a stiff one.

"I think it's a vodka soda night for me. I need to wake up clearheaded. What are you having, Ash?" I looked back at my girl as a smile slowly spread on her face.

"I'll take one, too, but hold the vodka." At this point, the woman was *beaming*. "It's too early to tell people, but Jeff and I found out a couple of weeks ago. I'm pregnant." There it was! The happy reveal. I, of course, immediately started crying. We hugged for possibly too long in the middle of that party before breaking it up and socializing. I was so happy for her. It was possibly the first time I've ever been happy that a friend wasn't drinking with me at a party. It was a full-circle perfect ending. . . .

Until the next day, when Ash got food poisoning and had to stay in her hotel so she could privately shit her brains out. In the words of a future mom of the year, *Bless her heart.*

Long-Lasting Friendsips

I REMEMBER WHEN I first was introduced to my dear friend Wine. I'll be honest: she didn't give me the best first impression. I was ten years old and attending communion at my grandma's Episcopalian church in Panama City. Back in Boonville, where the county was still dry and people didn't eat bland food if they didn't have to, communion didn't have real wine and stale wafers; it was Welch's and Hawaiian potato bread. But not at Grand's church. I took a sip from the chalice thinking I was about to have a cold, crisp grape juice crushed by Jesus himself's feet and nearly spat it back in the minister's face. It was warm! And in my kid brain, I thought it must have gone bad. A handful of years later, and I would be back to the bottle, drinking pink Boone's Farm at a party. I thought *I* had gone bad . . . ass.

Luckily, as an adult, I realize that calling Boone's Farm wine is like calling Olive Garden authentic Italian.* I'm into the real stuff

---

* Totes kidding, Olive Garden exec who's reading this. I love your establishment and would gladly take a lifetime supply of free breadsticks.

now. The cabs and merlots and pinots and syrahs. Remember that song from the nineties, "Mambo No. 5," where Lou Bega lists all the girls he loves? The Monicas. The Ericas. The Ritas. Just change all those ladies' names to types of wine, and that is my anthem.

A lot of people get intimidated by wine because there are so many different options. I get it. Sometimes when I'm supposed to pick out where to go for dinner, I'll have thirty tabs opened on my phone comparing menus until I eventually say *fuck it* and eat a bag of baby carrots. But there's no reason to be intimidated by wine. Wine is your friend! And just like how you would want to hang out with certain friends in certain circumstances, I am going to give you a crash course on what wines to drink when.

Let's start with reds, because the phrase "let's start with whites" just sounds inherently racist.

CABERNET: This is your ride-or-die bitch. Super dependable. Cabs are often full-bodied and can have fruity and peppery notes. She's easy to get along with but can occasionally surprise you with a li'l kick, depending on the day. Go split a rack of ribs with this one, 'cause you're going to need a belly base coat for a long night. Cabs are so easy to drink with, you'll definitely be calling a cab home.

MERLOT: Merlot gets a lot of shit for being a basic bitch. But "basic" is just another word for "popular," and speaking as my high school self, there ain't nothing wrong with being popular! We are not living in the movie *Cruel Intentions*. Sometimes people are popular because they are just nice and get along with everyone. Same with merlot.

PINOT NOIR: This is your skinny bitch friend. Not a ton of depth with this one. It's like when you're going to hang with a friend you know isn't going to have a convo with you about religion or politics. While hanging out with them still can be fun, this is more of a "let's get lunch" friendship, not necessarily a dinner date. Especially 'cause you know she's not going to want to share any fatty appetizers.

SHIRAZ: Have you seen the movie *Rough Night*? Shiraz is basically Kate McKinnon's character. This is a spicy, earthy-as-hell wine that packs a punch. If it had a human job, it would be a doula. Like, super interesting to talk to for a while, but you don't want to be cornered by her for too long at a party. It's overwhelming.

CHIANTI/SANGIOVESE: These bitches are Italian and bold as fuck. I'm talking the type who won't sit with her back facing the door in case there's a hit on her. Best paired with Italian food, obvs, her flavors are loud and will usually wake me up with a solid headache the next morning.

AND NOW LET'S talk about some whites, shall we? These are the girls who are usually a touch lighter and sweeter. The types of gals you can cozy up to for a little daytime hair of the dog after a long night with your red friends.

CHARDONNAY: Ummm, who invited their aunt to this party? I kid! Chardonnay is delicious, but it often has an oaky, buttery vibe. It's decadent. It's eccentric. Just like grabbing drinks with an older family member, you've really got to be in the mood for it, and even when you are enjoying it, you probably want to limit it to a glass or two.

SAUVIGNON BLANC: With its tendency to be fruity and floral, consider this the flower crown of whites. A Coachella girl in a glass. While it's sweet and fun and great to hang with on a hot day, there isn't a lot of depth to sauv blancs. They kind of all blend in together and, personally, hanging out with them too much can give me a terrible headache.

PINOT GRIGIO: You honestly cannot go wrong with pinot grigio. She's the friend you can bring to any party, any social circle, and she's going to get along with everyone. Not because she's particularly interesting but because she's completely inoffensive. She's the girl your high school boyfriend ends up marrying, and when you meet her for the first time, she's fine, very pleasant, but nothing really sticks out . . . which makes sense because he was a dud, and him dumping you before college was the equivalent of Neo dodging those bullets in *The Matrix*. (A gif that I use every time my friend is being rejected by a dude, by the way.)

WHITE ZINFADEL: I'm not mad at white zin, but do I want to drink it? Hell no. The hue alone makes me immediately hungover. But I don't think it should have the bad rap that it does. Not any more than . . .

ROSÉ: I'm gonna get real here, and a lot of you might not agree with me. Rosé is basically white zinfandel with a classier name and a lot more adorable T-shirts made in honor of it. There are so many "Rosé All Day" tote bags but no "Zin for the Win" when I can't tell the damn difference between the two. Rosé is like that friend who has always been a little trashy and self-deprecating, but now she has a British boyfriend, so she's somehow "cultured." Like how Lindsay Lohan all of a sudden has a weird European accent now, when you *know* that bitch is from Long Island.

That said, hand me a glass of *sparkling* rosé, and I will immediately act like I'm on a yacht in Monte Carlo and forbid anyone to make eye contact with me.

AND JUST LIKE friendships, may I suggest trying all of these on for size? What you got along with in your twenties might not be your ideal pairing in your thirties. People evolve, and so do their tastes, and holy hell, if that is not a perfect segue into the next chapter—one that you might want to pour a glass of your favorite friend to have on standby—I don't know what is. . . .

Singled Out

WHETHER YOU KNOW me from the Internet, or from my first book, or from my mother convincing you to buy this thing at your last choir rehearsal,* you know that I am pretty private when it comes to my love life. Will I tell you at the drop of a dime the inner details of my last colonic? Of course I will. But have I ever mentioned who I'm dating on a public forum? Nope! Never. But I figured this is my second book; I should dig a little deeper. Which is also what I told the person administering my last colonic. Hey-yo!

Can you tell that I get so uncomfortable opening up this side of me that I feel the need to ease you in with terrible garbage humor? I mean it! This is all new for me. But, fuck it, I want to share my experiences, and I already cashed my book advance, so let's do this!

Ahem . . .

---

* Shout-out to the alto section of the Boonville United Methodist Church.

March of 2016 found me in a position that I had never been in before. . . . The flying reverse scorpion from page 87 of the *Kama Sutra*. Kidding! I wish. I was basically in the opposite position. I was single and couldn't have been further from physical contact with a male specimen.

You might be thinking, *But, Mamrie, we've all been through a breakup. Big whoop! Deal with it!* Now, before you get up on your high horse, let's get one thing out of the way: This was no ordinary breakup. This wasn't one of those "we fell in love, it was amazing for a couple of years, then he shattered my heart, and now I need to buy stock in Ben & Jerry's because I am solely keeping them in biz" type of situations. This was a major life event, because he and I had dated for more than ten years, and yet, there was no earth-shattering event that caused the breakup. We simply drifted apart, and it was devastating to finally realize that.

When I met my ex, I was about nine months out of college and living in New York. Having gone to a college where most of the women were blond, bouncy rich girls, I shockingly never had boyfriends. I was the girl you brought to your frat formal because I'd bring weed and have a shot-taking contest with the biggest bro, but I wasn't the girl you'd introduce to your parents on alumni weekend. It wasn't that I went on dates and they were bad. It was just after a few years of not being pursued, I kind of friend-zoned myself.

So when I met my ex, about a year into living in NYC, it was just the same. He had a girlfriend at the time, so a relationship was off the table, and we just became summer drinking buddies while our other friends had to keep responsible schedules. Perpetual friend-zone. A place I knew well. So when one night he told me he was breaking up with his girlfriend, I was thrown off. "I realized I have feelings for you," he told me in Bull McCabe's, a dark East Village bar where we would sit outside and drink beers all night as he smoked cigarettes and I blocked out the constant current of rats rolling by. I was in shock. Had I been suppressing a latent crush on my friend? Of course I had. But I didn't think anything would happen. I sat there sipping my Corona as he continued, "So, I'm going to break up with her tomorrow. It's not fair for me to have these feelings and be in it. Even if you don't feel the same—"

"I feel the same way!" I said. And that was it. I had a boyfriend. And for the next ten years, it was the smoothest of sailing. We had become friends first before any of the romantic stuff. Friendship led our relationship. I was accepted. And loved. And content.

I was also *grateful* to be off the meat market. With my personal life on lock, I didn't have that distraction. I dove headfirst into work with blinders on. I knew I could be completely selfish in the amount of effort it takes in this weird industry and still have someone being my cheerleader without being jaded about it.

Plus, dating seemed horrible! All the games. All the rules. My girlfriends would bitch to me over cocktails about their latest dating fiasco while I'd sit there nodding my head in solidarity before going home to my super stable partner. *Thank GOD I don't have to deal with that*, I'd think as they'd tell me about another teenage idiot trapped in a grown man's body. *Isn't it so great I got to hit fast-forward and skip all that bullshit. . . . Isn't it?*

The truth is, over time, I wasn't so sure. Don't get me wrong, our relationship was filled with the hardest of laughs and being our truest silly selves together, but after I turned thirty, the teeniest, tiniest little sliver in the back of my brain started to feel like I was somehow missing out on crucial life experiences by being in a committed relationship. I'd always heard people talking about how much they learned from every breakup, and I had never really had one as an adult. I started to become obsessed with that idea. Was not having experienced heartache in some way stunting my development as a full-fledged person?

In our ten-plus years together, I never had to deal with sadness. Our relationship was stable and supportive and fun and even-tempered, so much so that when I realized I might want to end it, it seemed unfathomable. IN WHAT WORLD would someone end a relationship where there are zero fights? Zero arguments? But therein lies the rub. Without those peaks and valleys, you can step back and see a flat line. We were best friends and great roommates and each other's cheerleaders, but we weren't in a true romantic relationship anymore.

We both knew it, even if we didn't want to admit it. There was an elephant in the room, an elephant who had been hanging out in our living room for a few years, chilling and eating all the snacks and not even apologizing for it. I knew that elephant was there, because the couch had gradually become my nightly bed and that elephant was on the floor snoring, keeping me up at night.

I tried to convince myself that everything was fine. Our relationship was fine. And maybe if I just made some positive changes for myself, it would have a domino effect on the relationship. Maybe if I felt more attractive, I'd be more inclined to get physical with my partner. So, I hightailed it to the gym. I lost a shitload of weight. I dyed my hair darker. I bought the dream car I always wanted. And in doing that, I saw myself starting to self-actualize into the person I would want to be if I was single. It was like when a dog goes into the woods alone because it knows it's going to die, only instead of heading into the wilderness, I started getting on the treadmill every day, pumping that incline to the highest degree like I was hiking away from my problems.

But no matter how good my ass was looking from all that steep walking, my head and heart were in the same place. I eventually stood still and confronted my feelings, which felt like an impossible task. He had done nothing but been loving and supportive and wonderful. So, how do you say you don't want it anymore? It's like ordering something at a restaurant, and when it comes out completely like you asked for, exactly how it sounded on the menu, you end up saying, "Nah, I think I'd rather just starve for a little bit. It looks great, though."

Sending that first hey, we need to talk tonight text set everything in motion. My heart was breaking, my stomach was aching, and I felt like I was living in an alternate universe. One in which I would no doubt be the bad guy, the villain who also feels unbelievable amounts of guilt. Maybe this was my fault completely. Maybe I was the one who leaned too much on the friendship, and he just followed my lead. Had I concentrated on my career too much? Maybe this was my Achilles' heel. My obsessive drive in work would always be my mistress, and I worried that eventually my partner would become tired of being a third wheel. Even if that wasn't the case, I still needed to know what it was like to be by myself. I drove home, hands shaking, wondering if I would have the balls to start the conversation.

When you are ending a relationship of that length, and without a true inciting incident or drama, there is no such thing as just ripping it off like a Band-Aid. It's a lot more drawn-out and painful than that. More like slowly peeling off the strips of duct tape you used in a lieu of a bra to keep your tits up in a deep, plunging dress.*

---

* I have zero shame in this being my favorite red-carpet beauty trick. Although it's a double-edged sword because despite the fact that your cleavage will draw the attention from plenty o' men, you are out of commission for the night because you can't get naked. You'll look like an old basement couch being held together with that tape.

The next two weeks were a slow burn of breakup conversations, of terrible moments crying together on our couch and then one of us saying something to lighten the mood.

"I'm going to get super ripped now. You know that, right?" he said to me at one point, making me laugh as I wiped away tears. "I mean it. I am going to be so in shape. I'm starting my own YouTube channel tomorrow." Him making me laugh in that moment made me love him more than ever, but deep down, it also told me I was making the right move. My love was now one of friendship and history and respect, but I needed more. Or to at least try for more.

But it was scary. To put it in perspective, I hadn't been single since I was fresh out of college. The last time I ever brought a new guy home, I was a naïve New York City newbie, living in an empty apartment in Prospect Heights, Brooklyn. My only possessions in my room were a suitcase full of clothes and an air mattress that had a hole in it, and for months, I was too broke to buy a new one, so I would just fold the flaccid plastic mattress in half to pad the hardwood floor a little more.

This was totally different. I wouldn't be out on the dating scene, drinking PBRs, and counting my ones to see if I could afford a cab home if the date went awry. I was a grown woman. This wasn't going to be *Girls*; this would be *Sex and the City* (though a couple of seasons in, when Carrie wasn't such a mess). Bring on the cosmos!

Because the breakup was my choice, I decided I would be the one to move out and find a new place. Being on my own was going to be a totally new experience for me. I had lived with my mom and siblings until college, then had roommates in my dorm, then roommates for a year in New York, and then I moved in with my ex. Finally, I was going to experience full freedom.

Knowing that if there were dishes in the sink, I couldn't be frustrated that someone else had left them or wait for someone else to clean them like a dirty sink standoff. Having a fridge full of things that I loved eating, without having to block out the mayonnaise or other ungodly white condiments.* What would my aesthetic be like? I had always decorated how I liked but with my partner's style in mind. Would I be super minimalist and modern now? Or would I go the opposite route and start scouring eBay for one of those lips couches from MTV's *Singled Out?* Fuck it, if I'm going for a big-lip couch, I might as well install my own champagne glass tub!

First things first, I had to actually *find* a place. I scoured Craigslist and found an adorable house for rent, and, with fingers crossed that it wouldn't be a murderer's den in real life, I made an appointment to see it. Craigslist can be hit-or-miss; when I lived in NYC, I'd go looking at apartments that looked like a penthouse suite in the photos but were as sketchy as a *Penthouse* magazine when I got there. So I knew it was a gamble. But by some grace of God(damn luck), this place looked exactly as it did online. It was perfect: a sunny one-bedroom in a walkable neighborhood that I loved. Plus, there was a yard that my dog, Beanz, could sunbathe in. And . . . there was a *hot tub.* It was a no-brainer. But just like any new ramen restaurant, when something is this good, there's inevitably a line for it.

"Hey, I know you're showing your house to lots of people," I said to the married landlords as the next folks waited in the front yard to be shown the place, their maniac toddler running and yapping like one of those windup dog toys that can do backflips.

---

* Yep. I hate mayo, sour cream, cream cheese, yogurt, ranch . . . basically anything white and creamy. Go ahead. Cue the "There goes your dating life" joke from *Clueless.*

"But wouldn't it be nice to rent it to a single, mature woman in her thirties who travels a lot? Instead of some starter family that has kids who will definitely try to trash the place? I mean, kids are nightmare!" I turned to the pregnant wife. "No offense." This was our actual interaction, and they *actually* chose me!

I moved in a few weeks later, walking up to the front door with a rolling suitcase full of clothes in one hand and a rolled-up air mattress that Joselyn had loaned me in the other. As I plopped down in my empty living room, I daydreamed about how I'd fill up the room with cool art and furniture. I couldn't stop smiling at the potential of what this life, and house, would look like a few months down the road.

The sun set, and I was about to have my first evening living by myself. I sat on the kitchen counter barstools sipping on a vodka soda, just relaxing in the moment. It was so peaceful. So quiet. So, so quiet. Jesus Christ, why was it so quiet?!

If there was ever a moment to cue "Hello, darkness my old friend . . ." it was then.

I started feeling anxious. It was total, immersive silence. I had previously lived in neighborhoods with lots of traffic, but this house was on a quaint residential street. My just-off-the-highway apartment in Brooklyn would make this place feel like a sensory-deprivation tank in comparison. I didn't even have a TV hooked up yet to distract myself.

But it wasn't just a noisy neighborhood that was missing—it was the noise inside, the noise that comes from living with another person. Someone to talk to, or make quips during *Shark Tank* to, or yell to bring you a towel when you got in the shower without one on standby. Another brain in the house to bounce an idea off of or someone who could band together with you to fight off an intruder. Even the simple concept of not having another opinion on what to cook for dinner, to not have an "I cook if you do the dishes" trade-off was mind-blowing. For the past ten years, there had been an alley-oop aspect to everything in my home life, and now I felt like I was tossing the ball toward the basket only for it to bounce right back down with a *thud*. I felt like I was having an awkward lull in conversation with myself. So while my anxiety just kept dialing up and up, I decided to crank something else that night.

Music!

Screw that "Sound of Silence" bullshit; I blasted some good ol' Sean Paul on my phone and danced in front of my new floor-length-mirror closet doors until I was drunk and dripping in sweat. If this visual seems kind of sad to you, don't worry. I had an audience. And by that, I mean I woke up Beanz, who had been sleeping under the throw blanket on the air mattress, to watch my moves. She was unimpressed, which is rude considering how hard I was working it. I was dancing at the level that while you're doing it, you can already predict how sore your thighs are going to be the next day.

Eventually, all the cocktails and aerobic ass shaking caught up with me, and I was ready to call it a night. My first sleep in my new place! I turned off the lights and slowly pushed Beanz over to one side. I tell ya, for being five pounds, the dog somehow hogs the bed. Doesn't matter if we are sharing a couch or a California king. It's like the jeans from *The Sisterhood of the Traveling Pants*—somehow, her body adapts and she takes up 75 percent of any sleeping space.

So, I got her bod to one side and snuggled in under the throw. *This isn't so bad*, I thought to myself as I stared up at my ceiling. *I am going to be just fine in this silence.* But it was at that exact moment that I heard the tiniest high-pitched noise. Like the lightest dog whistle, or when Pee-wee Herman would do his routine of slowly letting the air out of a balloon. And that's when I knew. Sonovabitch. This air mattress had a hole in it.

I shook my head in disbelief as I felt the mattress below me slowly starting to lose its firmness, like an overhandled peach. There I was, ten years since moving to New York. Ten years older. Ten years wiser. And yet I still found myself in an empty place, by myself, on a deflating air mattress. I couldn't tell if this was sad or not. It felt very full circle, but maybe full circle isn't a good thing since it means you end up where you started. Maybe these past ten years had just been a giant lap, and I was back at the starting line once again. My mind raced.

Is this just who I was when I was on my own? A girl who sleeps on deflated air mattresses? My ex would've never been in this position. He would've blown up the mattress and made sure it was okay way earlier in the day, not when he was too drunk to drive anywhere and get a new one. *Is this air mattress some sort of metaphor for not being able to take care of myself?* I thought as my body slowly descended to the hardwood floor. But rather than wallow in self-pity, I popped up off* the deflating raft and decided to take action. I wasn't the same naïve girl I had been back in Brooklyn. I was a woman now. An independent, successful woman! I didn't need someone to take care of me. What I needed was to solve this myself, to get my act together, and . . . to pay someone to deliver me some duct tape to patch up this damn hole!

Seriously, I went on a delivery service app and paid twenty dollars to have a three-dollar roll of duct tape delivered. "I swear this isn't for anything weird or sexual," I tried to tell Patrice, the

* Maybe I didn't pop up so much as awkwardly, slowly get to my feet like a sloth climbing out of quicksand.

very judgy-looking older lady who handed the tape from her car window. "Mmmm hmmm," she mumbled under her breath before speeding off.

But did I care? Hell no. Did the duct tape fix the hole completely? Of course not! I woke up a few hours later on a half-deflated air mattress with Beanz on top of me, scared I was going to roll over in my sleep and catapult her into the air like she was on one of those inflatable blobs people have off lake docks.

It didn't matter that my back was killing me. Or that I was already hungover and it was only five A.M. I was proud of myself. I had stuck out the silence. I wasn't that twenty-two-year-old in Brooklyn anymore, ignoring the discomfort of a broken bed. I was ready to fix my problems when I spotted them. Not just deal with discomfort because it seemed more comfortable than confronting it.

From the cradle of that plastic taco I was in, I got on my phone and ordered a real bedframe and a real mattress. My first home purchase. The only catch was that it was going to be a solid six weeks before they were delivered. But that was okay by me . . . because I had some traveling to do.

I Think I Cannes

DISCLAIMER: Feel free to take a moment to go online and download the sad-trombone sound effect to play in response to this chapter title. Not impressed? I almost named this one "Eiffel Crazy."

Every so often, I get asked to speak on a panel about the digital world or being a female writer or what have you. It's such a perk! I've done them so often that sometimes I feel like a parakeet who has only learned the words "authenticity" and "my brand." Other times everyone else on the panel is so eloquent and smart that I feel like a Beverly Hillbilly during their first interview. So, why do I do them? Easy: 'cause if I really get going, I can make even myself cringe, and cringing is great for your abs. Also because you can't spell "panel" without "plane." AKA, the panel is in a really cool spot and they cover your travel.

And no free trip has ever felt more glamorous than when I was asked to do a panel in—drumroll, please—CANNES! Yes, *that* Cannes.

The type of place that is so storied, so mythical, it sounds fake, like Ibiza or Bora Bora. Why was such a classy place letting a creature like me in? Ironically, because I had been a creature earlier that year! Several months prior, I had been lucky enough to be involved in a Web series called *Oscar's Hotel for Fantastical Creatures*. In it, I got to do something I've always dreamed about: become a Jim Henson creature!

As a girl who was obsessed with *Fraggle Rock* and *Labyrinth* and *The Muppets* growing up, it was an incredible experience. But as a girl who can occasionally get herself worked into a panic attack when she feels claustrophobic, being glued into a giant octopus costume for four-hour stretches at a time was not so amazing. Somehow, I made it. Here I am as Octochef!

I didn't operate this myself. To move the tentacles, there were four dudes underneath me. So, clearly it felt like home. ;)

At this point, it had been a couple of months since my breakup. For those first few, the grieving and guilt from ending it were omnipresent. Everything reminded me of it.

goes to bar... My ex and I used to go to this bar. I hope he's doing okay.
eats a taco... My ex loved him some tacos. I hope he's doing okay.
sees a bird... My ex loved bird-watching. I hope he's doing okay.

Not having a partner in crime was a new reality for me. Especially with texting! You don't realize how much you can text someone all day, like a stream of consciousness, until you don't. When I was out at night, I would feel something nagging at me, like I had forgotten to do something, until I would have to remember that no, you don't have to text anyone your whereabouts or what time you'll be home. When I started daydreaming about what I wanted for dinner, I had to remind myself that it was just my choice. There was no one to text and ask, "Whatcha hankerin' for tonight?" It was just me. And those first couple of months were tough. Where I would normally text a thought, I now just had the thought and swallowed it. But slowly, that feeling of free-falling began to feel normal. Empowering, even. I didn't feel alone so much as I felt independent. I was an untethered balloon, no longer tied to someone's wrist, and I was ready to fly, baby!

Specifically, first class to Cannes! Apparently, every year there is a huge convention called MIPCom in the South of France, or "MIP" for short. The production company that produced *Oscar's Hotel* was attending, and they asked me to join them. My excited brain was flooded with thoughts when they made me the offer. They came in as follows:

1) VIP TO MIP! THAT'S QUITE THE TRIP!
2) What the hell is a MIP?!
3) What do they want in exchange?

It turns out MIPCom was a place where people took their projects to be sold in international markets, and so the Jim Henson team was trying to sell the overseas rights to our show. All I was obligated to do during my time there was participate in a five-minute interview onstage in front of buyers, talking up the production company and project, and then I was done working. So, of course, my answer to them was an enthusiastic FUCK YEAH.

This was a dream come true and exactly what I needed at the moment. I had wanted to go to France since I read all the *Madeline* books as a little girl. (Hello?! An outgoing, outspoken redhead who's constantly getting into adventures? That bitch sounds familiar.) I dreamed about seeing the Eiffel Tower and spending my morning eating *pain au chocolat*, which sounded so much nicer than a "croissant with chocolate shoved in it." I wanted to wander the narrow streets drinking lattes, watching the sun set over the Seine, and then spend my evenings watching the dancers at Moulin Rouge. I knew I had to seize this opportunity, so I not only said yes to the trip but I asked them to fly me out of Paris so I could spend some time there. They agreed, so the plan was for me to be in Cannes for MIP for a few days, then take a train to Paris, where I would gallivant around and no doubt be mistaken for the grown-up version of Madeline by tourists.

As the weeks passed, my excitement built, which helped push any other feelings of sadness or weirdness onto the back burner.

I daydreamed about my adventures there, dining alfresco at one of those tiny cafés, observing the beautiful people around me sharing midday bottles of wine, munching on baguettes. I imagined myself skipping down the streets, wearing striped shirts and a little red scarf around my neck, saying, "Bonjour! Bonjour!" like the heroine of my own indie movie.

And deep down, I had to admit: I didn't just want to feel French on my trip . . . I wanted to *be* frenched.

While I had come out of my breakup assuming that I'd be a wild woman, months later, I still hadn't kissed anyone. If I was being honest, this urge to put my mouth on a new person scared me. What if my first first kiss in a decade was bad? I was pretty out of practice. But I had to start somewhere, I decided, and what better place to do that than Paris? My thoughts swirled. Hooking up with some handsome international businessman along the French Riviera wouldn't just be getting back on the horse; it would be straight-up sprinting like a USA gymnast, ricocheting off the catapult, and doing a 720-degree spin only to stick the landing on that diiiiick.* If I couldn't get kissed in a week in France, then I might as well join a convent and take a vow of celibacy.

I immediately went shopping for my France wardrobe (bye-bye, acid-washed jorts) and asked who else would be coming on the trip. First, there was Jarrett. Jarrett is a handsome, hilarious, sweet, and sensitive jujitsu-loving actor/creator. The kind of person who is as down to do a forty-minute bit in a fake British accent as he is to have a deep, hours-long conversation about how the brain processes love. We had been around each other in small doses and always enjoyed each other's company, but we'd never

---

* Just said "dick" 'cause it sounded better. I wasn't planning on fucking anyone. Or was I? Keep reading. You get no exclusives in this footnote.

hung out in a long stretch like this. Then there was Tony. Tony was Jarrett's creative partner and just a magical elf of a human. Not because he was small or anything; he was a normal-size man with bleached-blond hair and a big smile, but he had a Seuss-ish way with words that made him a delight to be around. Rounding out the crew was Cyrina. Now, I had never met Cyrina before, but we did have mutual friends in common, and once we had spoken for five minutes, it felt like I had known her forever. Cyrina is whip-smart and not afraid to make fun of herself, and she goes into a hilarious fake Bronx accent once she's had a few drinks. It was the perfect mishmash of different personalities who shared the same level of silliness. It was also the perfect mix of people I was comfortable with but not super close to, which was crucial. No one was going to try to do an hour-long interview with me about my breakup, which had been happening left and right with other friends. I mean, I get it. People are always curious as to why couples call it off, especially after so many years, but hot damn! With some friends, it felt like there was a single light-bulb swinging over my head as they interrogated me about the details, as if they were going to crack the case and find out that I cheated or something. I was over talking about it.

I landed in Cannes with a suitcase of outfits that said, "*Oui oui*, I'm French," and an inflated ego from flying first class. We were staying at the Carlton, where all the stars stay during the film festival. I don't know if I've ever felt more like Julia Roberts in *Pretty Woman* than when I rolled up in there. My room was *beautiful*. The ceilings were high, and the prices on the minibar were even higher. But they didn't have my credit card on file, so I sat on my grandiose bed and took those fifteen-euro cashews to the face. A few snacks later, and I heard the sound of a Whats-App message coming through on my phone. It was from Jarrett.

"Anybody down for a drink in the lobby bar? I could use a MIP or two."

And so began the constant punning up of the conventions' name as we sat in that fancy-ass lobby, drinking negronis. For example:

Man, this really is the MIP of a lifetime.

You guys, please don't drink too much and fall tonight. We don't need anyone to have a MIP slip.

I came to this convention before it was popular; one could say I'm a MIPster.

Are we actually in the South of France right now, or am I MIPpin' my balls off?

I just want to make sure we do this thing right. One might say I want to MIP it, MIP it good.

What a long, strange MIP it's been.

Cyrina, we already used the trip/MIP pun. Wake up, MIP Van Winkle.

Yeah, Mamrie, MIP her a new one!

There's something special about a group getting to know one another so far removed from their normal lives. It takes everyone out of their element, out of talking about the minutiae of their own lives, and instead just lets them focus on what's happening in the present. By the end of that first day, we had a million inside jokes and callbacks between us . . . mainly of MIP puns and how bad Cyrina was at them.

When it came time to actually go to the convention, the

laughing hit an all-time peak, thanks to some of the other projects there that were trying to be sold. Things like *Police Beauties
and Police Dogs* out of Japan. You know, just your classic show of
beautiful policewomen and their, in my opinion, equally beautiful dogs. But my overall favorite was a romantic film out of
China. I can't remember the title, but the log line will forever be
emblazoned in my brain and heart. Here goes . . . ahem . . .

> *Sometimes love is sweet like a salty rose,*
>
> *Sometimes it's sweet like candies.*
>
> *And sometimes it's so spicy that it makes your eyes watery.*

Nothing, and I mean nothing, makes me laugh harder than
bad translations. In my early Brooklyn days, I would scour dollar
stores to try to find the best birthday cards with nonsensical
translations. Things like "Birthday Happy Times Party Kitties!"
and "Hope Your Birthday Is Smile Trees and Sunshine Hugs."
But this poem? This was *art*. I immediately memorized it and
said it over and over again throughout the day.

The panel was as expected: a roomful of suits staring at us as we
gushed about how great it was to work with the production company. I'm pretty sure I only used the word "authenticity" twice! But
to be fair, I was only onstage for four minutes. Yes, these people
flew us out to be onstage for *four* minutes. Hollywood is insane.

That night I got so blackout drunk *(hi, recently single girl!)*
that I kept repeating my new favorite salty rose poem like a broken record at the bar we closed down.* I was in bad shape, guys.

---

* This was also when I asked the DJ to play A Tribe Called Quest, and when he told
me no, I flipped him off. Again, not sure why they let me come to this classy place.

Every five minutes I fell down like a five-minute-old deer. Flats or sneakers couldn't be a part of my classy French wardrobe, no no! I insisted on bringing the tallest heels to Cannes, which means my drunk ass was racking up new bruises left and right. Cyrina, bless her heart, tried to get me to just relinquish control and let her and Jarrett carry me home like the town drunk.

"Mamrie, just get in between us and put your arms on our shoulders," Cyrina said. "You can be the cream to our Oreo!"

Pretty sweet, don't ya think? Well, I didn't! According to Cyrina when she recounted this the next day, as soon as she dropped the Oreo analogy, I whipped around, looked her dead in the eyes, and said, "Stop being condescending to me." Somehow, we are still friends!

The next morning, my head felt like I had pulled a Mario Bros. and just spent the evening breaking bricks with my head. I was embarrassed, and not even quite sure of my actions from the night before, so I did what anyone would do: I blocked it out and pretended nothing weird happened, so as not to ruin the vibe of the trip.

"I can't believe we just have one more day here," Jarrett said as we waited for our round of double espressos in the lobby.

"I know!" Tony chimed in, chipper as fuck, because he's one of those rare creatures that doesn't have to drink to have a good time. "I don't want to go back yet."

"Then don't," I said with a smirk on my face. These were my kind of people. People who weren't calling out my drunk-ass shenanigans in the harsh daylight. And I knew they would be up for more adventures.

"Come to Paris with me. I'll bet they'll change your flight and then we can all get an Airbnb together. . . ." I didn't even have to look up from my coffee; I knew the guys were in. Sadly, Cyrina had to get back to LA and couldn't join us.

Twenty-four hours later and we were riding a train to Paris, hugging the coastline for the first few hours and then weaving our way through the French countryside. We couldn't get our seats together, but that was fine because my seatmate was a tiny old lady who was already asleep, her eyes shaded by Chanel sunglasses rimmed in pearls. As someone who once took an overnight Greyhound trip sitting beside a woman who used her stomach as a TV tray to eat a giant container of General Tso's chicken, I was happy as a clam. Specifically a geoduck clam, which basically looks like a MASSIVE penis, but you can save that Google image search until after this chapter.

Once our train arrived, we hopped in an Uber* to go check out our apartment. The car pulled up to a beautiful building with a metal gate, and after a few minutes of figuring out the lock, the three of us crammed into the teensy-tiny elevator heading up to the fifth floor. When I say "teensy," I mean it; this felt more like one of those chutes at a drive-through bank teller than a real 'vator. The apartment itself was massive and old and *gorgeous*, with its Louis-the-some-numerical-number-remake furniture and Juliet "balconies" at every window. I put that in quotation marks because it's a stretch calling those things balconies. I don't know how skinny Juliet was, but I could barely get half of myself out there.

"Anybody else want to just sit in cafés all day and drink rosé and eat *pommes frites*?" Jarrett asked.

"Oh, you mean some French fries and pink wine?" I asked in my thickest Yadkin County, North Carolina, accent. It almost felt blasphemous in such a beautiful space.

---

* Uber has changed the damn game when it comes to international travel. Now I don't think I'm constantly being super ripped off when I'm super ripped. This is not a paid footnote.

"Actually, I think I'm going to go explore the city. See le sights," Tony said in a thick French accent while lounging on a gaudy gold couch. Tony, God love him, is one of those people who immediately assumes the accent of wherever he is. I know this well. It's very common among actors or, more embarrassingly, my mom. A theater grad herself, and a wonderful actress, the second my mom hears a foreign accent, I can see her eyes go big and her lips start to move, practicing the dialect in her head. She can't help it. When I was in high school and she was working two jobs to keep us afloat (teaching high school English and theater by day and bartending at night), she told me that she would sometimes speak to her customers in a Scottish accent just because she was bored, and it always got her better tips.

While Tony set off to hit up le landmarks, Jarrett and I started walking through the neighborhoods to double down on that café culture. We couldn't believe our eyes. It was like we were walking through a set, like at any moment we could push on one of the baguette-and-bouquet-filled storefronts, only for it to fall over and reveal some stagehands on a smoke break.

We skipped through the streets, popping into tiny café after tiny café to have a little wine and watch the passersby. It started raining, which is normally a downer when you're exploring, but somehow it only made the city more charming. Whenever the rain would let up, we'd gallivant to another hole-in-the-wall, relishing in the insanely good wine and perfectly crisp *pommes frites*. It was the most picturesque, classy bar crawl imaginable. After a few burgundies, we became a teensy bit less self-aware and were no longer whispering but exclaiming, "That's so French!" whenever we saw something . . . well . . . super fucking French.

By our fifth café, we were both pretty lit. Conversations started to turn from light stuff to deep, real-life talk—everything from career choices to family to past relationships and, wouldn't you know it, the circumstances surrounding my breakup. Truth be told, I hadn't had a real conversation about the breakup with anyone except my super close girlfriends. It was the first time I was explaining the situation to someone who didn't know the history of our relationship.

As I sipped my five-dollar glass of Bordeaux that would've been twenty dollars back home, I started to really open up.

"The thing is, no one fucked up. There wasn't any drama. Sometimes life needs a little drama. We had just become passing ships," I said, tears starting to well up in my eyes. "I genuinely, truly, honestly just want him to be happy, and I don't think I was that person for him in the long run."

Luckily, before I could have a full-on breakdown over our baguette, a man smoking a cigarette while walking a French bulldog walked by. . . .

"THAT'S SO FRENCH!"

We screamed in unison, much to the chagrin of every couple there trying to get their romance on. "Do you think they just call French bulldogs 'bulldogs' since we are in France?" Jarrett asked. I was happy he had changed the subject. We settled our check and continued on our path down the moonlit streets, yelling, "That's so French!"

Were we being obnoxious Americans? Absolutely. Would we have maybe run through a brick wall, Kool-Aid Man–style, if we had seen a mime? Lord yes. But we were having a fun and magical night. One that I really needed.

I had kept myself so busy in my own Mamrie universe that it wasn't until that night when I realized how much I hadn't dealt with my breakup. This was obvious by how much the conversation bounced around to every topic like a pinball game but always ended up with me talking about it. To be honest, it was making me manic. One minute we'd be laughing fools, the next, I'd be taking deep breaths and pushing down the emotions.

By the time we got to the sixth or seventh café, and the subsequent number of glasses of wine, I couldn't keep it down anymore. The emotions boiled over. "I love him. I love him so much. And it kills me to know how much he's hurting right now," I said, while stuffing potatoes in my face. Jarrett listened, with an empathetic "Mmmhmm" here or there. "It's like this," I continued, grabbing the tablecloth underneath our bounty of carbs and booze. "It's like here was our life, and I just ripped it out from under him." I considered attempting the "ripping the tablecloth out" trick but luckily resisted. The couple beside us looked like they could get engaged at any moment, and they didn't need it ruined by some insane redheaded lady with a purple-wine mouth attempting to do a magic trick.

I pulled myself back together, taking a deep breath. "Enough of this cute shit. Let's settle up and go find a dive bar," I said, tossing the end of a baguette in my purse. I was back to skipping down the street with Jarrett. We ended up finding a rowdy little bar, tucked into a side street. Truth be told, in that part of Paris, there weren't any dive bars per se, but this place was the perfect mix of grungy and quaint.

We started talking to the locals, and by that, I mean I started flirting with old men. This is my favorite sport. Not in a "This old man thinks he's going to get laid" kind of way; that's not my end game. Just a little harmless banter to remind them of some firecracker of a lady they knew back in their youth who was too much for them to handle and who they've always regretted letting go. I consider it my way of giving back.

It got rowdy. And by that, I mean we were doing shots of gin.

Who does shots of gin?! At one point, after being my sassy self, a man of at least seventy-five said to me, "You scare me. I've never been scared of a woman before. . . . I like it."

Many, many drinks later, Jarrett and I poured onto the street, the last ones to leave the bar. It was perfect out. The streets were empty, save for a few other drunkards here and there getting late-night street food. We had no idea how to get back to our place since we had just wandered around all day without paying attention. After about an hour of looking, we finally found our apartment.

"This is so goddamn French," Jarrett said as we were once again squished into the tiniest elevator known to man. "It's also a lot less scary when you've had four gallons of alcohol."

To our surprise, Tony was still awake. For a man who doesn't drink, he can stay up with the best of them. He started talking to us, in a slight accent, about all the places he had explored that day. He even bought us little light-up Eiffel Tower key chains because he's thoughtful like that. He was halfway through telling us about an art exhibit that knocked his socks off when I went to go check my phone. I had left it in the apartment to really take a day to soak in Paris and not be constantly trying to figure out how to ask for the Wi-Fi password at each new stop.

I picked it up and saw I had a message in WhatsApp. I opened it up, and it was simply a pic of Beanz from my ex. And that, dear readers, is when I lost it.

All the emotions and guilt and sadness mixed together like the ingredients for a science fair volcano, and I erupted. Besides reacting to an actual death, I was bawling harder than I ever had before. It was the kind of crying where you can't catch your breath; the type where you're howling/hyperventilating/wiping snot from your face on repeat.

"Are you okay?" Jarrett and Tony stood in my doorway, looking concerned. I motioned them in and tried to get my breathing under control. But it was no use. I started WAILING.

Rather than tuck me in and go to sleep with earplugs in, you know what those two dudes did? They *listened* as I dove into what I was feeling. "I don't have anyone waiting for a good-night text anymore, or to go back and forth with about what I want for dinner," I ugly cried. "And I'm gonna be okay with that. But what if he's not? How the hell is he going to figure out what he wants for dinner?" I was a blubbering mess, barely making sense, but that didn't matter to Jarrett and Tony. They weren't going anywhere.

Jarrett rubbed my back as Tony rubbed my feet. This was not how I pictured being touched by a man in Paris! But it was just what I needed. We stayed up all night, eventually falling asleep as the sun peeked through the Juliet balconies of our flat.

The next morning, I woke up dehydrated and a little embarrassed. But that quickly went away. Not the dehydration. That was staying. Mama needed some Pedialyte up in this pied-à-terre. But the embarrassment dissolved as soon as I met the guys in the living room, sprawled out on that gaudy gold couch.

I was greeted with smiles and hugs and, goddamnit, I was so lucky to have been there in that moment with these two. I thought about what an incredibly important trip it had been. In fact, that rom-com poster that I loved so much and thought had made zero sense was almost a prediction for the entire trip.

Sometimes love is sweet like a salty rose,

In our case, it was definitely salty like fries and rosé.

Sometimes it's sweet like candies.

Lucky for me, I had those two sweeties with me to lean on.

And sometimes it's so spicy that it makes your eyes watery.

Seeing as that was the hardest I've ever cried, them eyes were watery, all right. This was not how I had pictured my Paris trip, crying on two guys instead of falling in love with some hunky French dude. Based on my emotional breakdown, I was *clearly* not even ready to have kissed someone on that trip. But that was okay.

Months later, Cyrina came over to film a video for my YouTube channel and I told her how I had finally ripped off the Band-Aid and gotten some action. "It was time. I hadn't kissed anyone since my ex," I said as I set up the tripod.

"Mamrie, what the hell are you talking about?" I looked up at her, confused. "Do you not remember that night at the bar where you flipped off the DJ?"

I looked at her, concerned, as she continued, "I literally had to pull you off some local. You were making out with him in front of everyone!"

I burst out laughing. "Why didn't you bring it up the next day?!"

"Eh, you had had a rough night. You deserved to have a random makeout in Cannes. So, Jarrett and I decided that our MIPs were sealed. . . ." Her eyes went wider than turtle eggs. "I did it! I finally did it!" she exclaimed with such innocent pride, you would've thought she was a five-year-old who'd just hit a home run in T-ball.

It only took a few months, but she had actually nailed a pun. I was proud of Cyrina but even prouder of myself. There I was thinking that I hadn't reached the goal I'd set for myself in France, but I had crushed it all along. Was it with a hot, mysterious businessman or some toothless degenerate who didn't speak a lick of English? Maybe it was the DJ! Some men are turned on by an extremely rude woman who flips them the bird. We may never ~~ask~~ know.

All I needed to know was that I'd done it! I had officially kissed someone else and didn't have to worry about if it was good or not, or if I was out of practice, because I couldn't remember a damn thing. I had ripped off the Band-Aid! Or, dare I say, the Band-Aid had been *MIPped off*? Pee hee hee.

Jarrett is the brunette. Tony is the blond. Yes, I was in Paris with men this handsome and still only laid lips on a weird local. Face, meet palm.

Moulin Rouge

YOU KNOW HOW when you get into binge-watching a show on Netflix, you hit Next Episode immediately as soon as it gets to the credit sequence? I did this when I watched *Breaking Bad* to the point where I found myself in the same sweatpants and no shower for days, feeling like *I* was the one doing meth. Well, consider this chapter one where you just hit Next Episode because just as soon as that night in Paris ended, I was on to another adventure!

The day after my meltdown, I decided to get some fresh air and give those boys a break from my estrogen parade. Everything was even prettier in daylight: cobblestone streets lined with tables of beautiful produce, storefront after storefront of bouquets and baked goods. At any point, I expected an animated Belle to swing out of a store, running her trap about the latest book she read. But instead, I was stopped in my tracks by another sight:

My friend Sarah, looking down at her phone and talking to herself, trying to figure out directions.

"Sarah?!" She looked up. It was so nice to see her familiar eyes and shocked face.

"What the fuck!" she said, almost dropping her phone.

"I can't believe out of a city of two and a half million people, I run into someone I know on day two. And not just someone, but you! What are you doing here?"

"It's Lorraine's birthday!" she exclaimed. I had met Lorraine back on a trip to Costa Rica for Sarah's fortieth. Okay, before I go any further, allow me to give you a little backstory on these friendships so you can see just how kismet and perfect it was to run into Sarah on this trip.

Sarah was the drummer in the band I was in for seven years back when I lived in Brooklyn. We were called Cudzoo & the Faggettes and were a ~~typical~~ party band. We wore matching outfits and performed choreography and did antics onstage like burst balloons full of glitter as we screamed, "Pussy farts!"* This level of classy spectacle also made its way over to our song names, such as:

"Oops . . . I Fucked Your Brothers"
"14K Fetus"
"Machine-Gun My Poon"
"Daddy Issues"

We even had a song called "French Braid" about moving to France because no one in America appreciated the classic hairdo and wearing it in France somehow made you irresistible. We would count in the song by counting down in French, except (since it was Cudzoo) instead of "un, deux, trois, quatre," it was "un, deux, twat, cock."

---

* One time our friend said that he came to one of our shows and found glitter in his asshole a week later. It was the nicest review of our band I'd ever heard.

This album cover was taken on my actual stoop in Brooklyn. The amount of times I sat on that stoop drunk and crying 'cause I couldn't find my keys before going to the bodega to borrow a screwdriver to break into my own home, would astound you.

Clearly we were never asked to play at a wedding. Anyway! Sarah was our little Animal from *The Muppets*, rocking out behind the drum kit. But not only that, she's a goddamn neuropsychologist who also looks like Lara Flynn Boyle circa *Twin Peaks*.

"Jess is here, too!" Sarah said.

I almost slapped myself across the face. "JESS IS HERE?!" Jess was another bandmate and one of my best friends. Nowadays, she's a makeup artist and hair guru and owns her own eyebrow bar in Louisville, Kentucky. Honestly, the woman can somehow take pencil-thin, frown-emoji brows and shape them into baby Brooke Shields brows.

I was bugging out that this was happening.

"Wait, who else is here—you, Jess?" I was still in shock.

"Well, it's me, Lorraine, Jess, and then a couple of more girls you met on the Costa Rica trip."

This was amazing. Sarah and Jess are like family to me, and while I had only hung out with the Costa Rica crew once before, it was one of those trips that within the first few hours of meeting one another, we were running around the jungle naked and wasted and chopping open coconuts with machetes to fill with rum. These girls were hell on wheeling suitcases, and a wild night out with them was exactly what I needed after the previous night's cry fest.

"I have to hang out with you girls tonight!! Do you have anything planned?" I just knew with these ladies' track record that they were going to be up to something good. Or, ideally, no good.

Cut to four hours later and I am sitting in a tiny two-hundred-year-old church listening to a cello concert. Yep, that's right. Seven women sitting in silence, as a Swedish man performed a solo cello concert to five sparsely filled wooden pews. It was beautiful. It was surreal. And I was surreal'y tired because a few glasses of Côtes du Rhône and slow classical music do not mix. I looked to my right and saw Sarah doing the ol' falling asleep then as soon as your head is down, you pop it back up routine. Bitch was doing it to the beat. I nudged Jess, who immediately pursed her lips to try to seal off a laugh. That's when what I call the Mamrie Mumbles started up. The Mamrie Mumbles are a classic move that happens when I want to laugh in a socially inappropriate setting, so I just laugh without opening my mouth. My lips may be closed, but you can still hear the laughing inside my mouth chamber, like how you walk past a club and can hear the faint pulse of a driving bass.

The other thing I do when I either laugh really hard or am try-ing *really* hard not to laugh is physically hurt others. I'm a big "grab someone's wrist as hard as I can while I throw my head back laughing" kind of gal, and if I'm trying not to laugh, you're gonna want to get as far away from me as possible. I will end up gripping your thigh or pinching your elbow—whatever it takes to try to put my energy away from laughing and into something else.

There I was, trying not to piss my pants laughing in this beau-tiful, quiet, historic church. Not much had changed since the days of being a little girl sitting in the pews of Boonville Meth-odist back in the day. I'd see an old lady start to bob her head to sleep during the sermon or a dad a few rows up coyly try to pick a wedgie when the congregation stood for a hymnal and I'd turn into a four-foot-two giggle fest. My mom would give me death stares from the choir, and now I was getting those same old-lady death stares from a cotton-headed senior a row over. I gripped Jess's elbow, and after what seemed like a lifetime of mumbles and eighty-four concertos later, homeboy stood up for a bow.

"That was incredible," Sarah said, passing the pad see ew around the table of a teensy Thai restaurant across from the church.

"It was gorgeous," Jess agreed.

"It was," I chimed in, mouth full of piping-hot spring rolls. I held up a finger to denote these things were cabbage lava and did one of those chews where you are simultaneously blowing on the food as you eat it. You know, the kind of wide-mouth chomps that makes you look like a dog actor that's been fed peanut butter so a C-list actor can dub their voice to your flapping dog gums.*

---

* Has anybody else been waiting for *Air Bud: Now That's Some Good Bud* to come out now that weed is being legalized in so many states? A golden retriever weed dealer would be CINEMATIC GOLD.

I swallowed and continued, "But let's be real. I started counting how many times Sarah checked her program. Final tally?
Thirty-eight. And, Jess, you straight slept through a whole song.
I wanted to Snapchat it, but I was scared it would play back with
volume."

We all laughed and admitted how bored we were. I mean, we
were talking about a group of women in which three of them
used to be in a band that would force audience members to bong
a beer out of a giant penis if it was their birthday.

They nodded in agreement. "Look, I know y'all have been
doing a ton of cultural stuff, and that is super cool, but how
would you feel about me planning what we do tomorrow night?
Lorraine, do you care if I take over your birthday trip that I
wasn't invited to?"

Lorraine nodded her head. "I'd love nothing more."

"I know exactly what we are going to do," I said, a grin cracking across my face. Because I knew that the next day, so help me
God, we were going to do something that had been a dream of
mine since I was knee-high to a grasshopper. We were going to
go to . . . Moulin Rouge!

That's right. Since I was a wee thang, going to the world-
famous home of the cancan has been on my bucket list. My obsession with burlesque started when I was ten years old, when
my stepmom, Anne, showed me the movie *Gypsy*. *Gypsy* is about
a girl who grew up to be the most famous burlesque dancer in
the world, Gypsy Rose Lee. Hell, I was so obsessed with it that
my junior year of high school, I convinced my theater teacher to
do it as the spring musical. I, of course, had to play the namesake.

It was a great show. We built adorable sets and taught the
country boys in our school, who would finally come out of the

closet years later, how to tap dance. We even got a real baby lamb from a local farm that my character is given for her birthday. Perfect and adorable, right? Well, it was, until I got to the part of the play on opening night where I had to pull down the straps of my red sequined dress to appear topless while doing a breathy version of "Let Me Entertain You" . . . and accidentally made eye contact with my eighty-three-year-old papaw in the process. More than a little awkward.

My love for *Gypsy* bit me in the ass later in life, too. There was a magical six-month period when Anne and I were both living in New York City. She was still in the TV producing business (she's now a reverend—talk about a job change!), and the show she was working on filmed out of the city. It was a great bonding time between the two of us. We would get nice dinners and have sleepovers, and every couple of weeks, my dad would fly up to spend time with us. It was a blast.

One particular weekend was like any other in Anne's Big Apple residency. I joined her and my dad for an early dinner and said my good-byes outside afterward. They were headed to her Upper East Side rental, and my ass was going down to the Lower East Side to meet my friends and boyfriend for a burlesque show at the Slipper Room.

"Burlesque?!" Anne exclaimed, clearly feeling those chardonnays. "David, we have to go." I panicked. What? I hadn't had a guy meet my parents since high school. I couldn't let them tag along and have this first meeting take place in a grungy bar. But before I could object, Anne whistled for a cab—which I didn't even know she could do—and I found myself sliding over to make room for my folks in the back seat. I immediately texted my boyfriend to give him a heads-up. It read:

WARNING: I am running like ten minutes late. Also, my
parents are with me. Also, for the next few hours, you
aren't a smoker.

Once we got there, they all said their hellos while Anne tried
to not look like a drug dog sniffing out the tobacco on my new
boyf, and then we took our seats. It took about ten seconds of the
performance to realize that this was not the type of burlesque
Anne was expecting.

Let me try to conjure up this visual for you: the woman onstage had her left arm hanging like normal and a fake right arm
made to look like it was tied to her chest. THEN! Her real right
arm, covered in black with her hand exposed at the end, looking
all severed and cut at the wrist, appeared. For the next three
minutes, which felt like a leap year's amount of time, she danced
as if the detached hand was crawling all over her to the tune of
"I Put a Spell on You." Boob grabbing and simulating diddling
her Skittle was also included. This was not "Let Me Entertain
You." This was "Let Me Enter-my Own Body." You know that
feeling when you're watching a movie with your parents and a
sex scene starts and it gets unbelievably painful?

You. Don't. Know. What. Real. Pain. Is.

Anyway! Back to classier times . . .

You're probably familiar with Moulin Rouge from the 2001
Baz Luhrmann film in which Ewan McGregor's character, a
poet, falls in love with a bombshell cabaret star, played by
Nicole Kidman. Nicole gives, in my opinion, one of the greatest
foreshadowed "I'm about to die" coughs in modern cinema, second only to Claire Danes in *Little Women*, who straight killed it.
The movie is hyper-vibrant and flashy, as if everything is
coated in fairy dust and someone raised the saturation on it,

Instagram-edit-style. As soon as I saw it, I wanted to crawl inside of it and live there.

Once I scored the tickets for us, I could barely contain my excitement. I knew megastars Nicole and Ewan weren't going to be onstage or dancing through the sky, and the theater probably didn't have all the rights to the David Bowie songs that the movie's soundtrack boasted, but I WAS GOING TO THE MOULIN ROUGE! I couldn't wait to taste the cold champagne that flowed so freely in the movie and sit back in my velvet banquette to be entertained by dolled-up women practically floating in heels and bejeweled high-cut thongs behind giant feather fans.

I met the girls for a glass of champagne near the theater, excited to reveal my big plan.

Sarah on the left. Jess on the right. Some weird-ass *Game of Thrones* chair made out of wine bottles that hadn't been dusted since 297 AD behind us.

"I've always wanted to go there!" Sarah squealed, raising her glass for a cheers. "How did you get tickets so last minute?"

"I pulled some strings . . . specifically my purse strings. We have to pay for tickets, *but* thanks to a little finagling, we get a couple of bottles of bubbly for free!" We all clinked our glasses in celebration.

"Ewan McGregor was so hot in *Moulin Rouge*," Jess said, with lust in her eyes that can only be brought on by having been married for a year. I had forgotten about ol' Ewan in that movie. Maybe there would be a hot dude at Moulin Rouge who I could fall in love with. My mind wandered, because I am a cartoon human with a constant running thought bubble.

Mommy, Daddy, how did you meet?

Well, darling, I was strolling through Moulin Rouge one crisp, spring Parisian night when I walked past a table of obnoxious American women. As if in slow motion, the redhead laughed, throwing her head back and raising a toast to her friends. There I was, surrounded by dozens of some of the most beautiful women in the world, and it's like time stopped. Your mother was the only one I could see.

We strutted into the Moulin Rouge feeling whimsical and ready to have the romance take hold. Everything was luxe: the red carpeting, the velvet curtains, the insane chandeliers. We sat at our adorable table with a portly Frenchman beside it, ready and willing to pour us champagne. After a cheers and some excited giggles, the lights went dim and that's when I saw him. No, not my version of Ewan. I saw . . . the gayest man alive.

Y'all, I know that might not be the PC'est thing to say, but hot damn, it was true! The man made Liberace look like a drill sergeant.* This man was in head-to-toe sparkles in front of all

---

* For you younger readers, he made Tyler Oakley look like Brock Lesnar of the WWE.

the other dancers with their lavish headpieces. He was committed to every move with his whole being; however, he was also about one beat too fast for the rest of the group. It was painful, like when you watch someone giving their all in karaoke, but they're just a few words ahead or behind in the song than they should be. But unlike in karaoke, where the crowd can sing along and get their tone-deaf asses back on beat, we just had to watch this man and his off-time dancing from afar. We were witnessing the least sexy spectacle of our lives. Lavish? Yes. Garish? Yes. But sexy? Not in the least.

Out of the sea of dancers in their rhinestones, a backup dancer emerged, lifting one of the sheer-suited females with ease. He looked like a tornado that had just plowed through a glitter factory. Finally, the song's pace slowed down, and the female dancer dismounted. This man found his spotlight and smiled proudly into the audience.

"Doesn't that guy look like a fat Bill Hader?" Sarah whispered. I squinted my eyes past the sparkly mesh, and HOLY SHIT, he was the spitting image of Bill Hader from *SNL*, if Bill Hader had just been dumped and gained forty pounds. This is the moment in the show where I never stopped laughing. Just when he'd disappear into the wings and I could squelch the Mamrie Mumbles, he'd bust back out with such fervor that I'd lose it again. It didn't help that my friends kept saying things like . . .

"Man, Stefon really let himself go. Maybe he got out of the club scene and this is rehab weight gain?"

"I wonder if Bill knows he was born a twin but the other one was adopted in France. What's Bill in French? Still Bill?"

"Really cool the studio let Bill get out of his Trainwreck *press tour to come live his true dream. Life's too short, ya know?"*

Moulin Rouge is not the place you are supposed to be belly

laughing; it's supposed to be a sultry and swanky experience. Laughing at the show was as if your partner was dirty talking during sex and you return the favor by guffawing in their face. I was squeezing Jess's thigh with a death grip. Luckily, the lights went dim, and Fat Hader exited the stage before I ripped her leg off and threw it on the table à la Aviva popping off her prosthetic on season 6 of *The Real Housewives of New York City*.

We all agreed that this felt like the Moulin Rouge B-squad. It's like how people expect the Hollywood Walk of Fame to be glamorous but then when they get there, it's actually filled with dudes in knockoff Wolverine costumes charging five dollars for a pic. This wasn't that big of a letdown, but it was definitely the dollar-store version of what I had imagined. And it was making me laugh *so* hard.

I took some deep breaths and a few sips of champagne and tried to get back to normal. A few minutes later, the lights went dim again and the music started back up. The orchestral music was swirling as a spotlight shone at an opening at the far-left corner of the stage, several feet off the ground. We waited eagerly, staring at that spotlight waiting for something majestic to emerge and then finally it did. . . . Slowly but surely came . . .

FAT BILL HADER SUSPENDED BY CABLES DRESSED AS AN ASTRONAUT.

I lost my shit. Fuck the mumbles. Fuck trying not to injure my friends with my flailing arms and leg squeezes. I was losing my goddamn mind, arms a-flailing. At one point, my hand hit something hard, and I looked back to see an annoyed Gerard the Waiter trying to open this beautiful French brut as this brute American was acting like she was at a Larry the Cable Guy show.

Fat Bill Hader continued to walk in slow motion as the overworked cables slowly tracked him to the center of the room. There, he met his lady astronaut, who had come out from the opposite side of the stage as they lip-synched a love song together. This was no Nicole Kidman and Ewan McGregor falling in love while singing "Heroes." And if this was space travel, "Paris, we have a problem." After what felt like days, they finally pulled FBH backstage, just as slowly as he came out. And just like an astronaut returning to Earth, I could finally breathe again.

The show continued to be a ridiculous parade of costumes and dance numbers, each outdoing the last in level of showmanship and not making a lick of damn sense. After it ended, we bundled up and walked back into the cold Parisian night.

We all stood there in front of that neon windmill, flabbergasted at what we'd just seen. The Moulin Rouge couldn't have been more different than what I had imagined it to be. . . . It was even better. While I loved the mystique surrounding the idea of it all, it was comforting to know that its fabled level of glamour wasn't really accurate. And as a redneck Gypsy who once stripped in front of her grandpa and had a baby lamb piss in her lap onstage, I felt right at home.

After a few minutes of recapping, we said our good-byes—a kiss on each cheek, of course, because we were in France. It was such a quick visit, but that was okay because three weeks later, I was back in Europe with Jess, for a trip we actually had planned to be on together. Oddly enough, we found ourselves at yet another sexy stage show, but this one was going to be a little different. . . .

Amster-dayum

AMSTERDAM. 4/20. DIXIE Chicks.

One of these things is not like the others. However, all three of these things added together equals the most epic girls' trip on the books. Or at least in this book. Let's start from the beginning. . . .

Okay, so I like cool music. I know I sound like someone who is rationalizing their taste after their friend finds a Smash Mouth concert ticket in their purse, but you gotta trust me on this. You're talking to someone who decided to go to a George Clinton concert on her twenty-first birthday. I can do David Bowie's *Aladdin Sane* face paint on myself with my eyes closed. I have shaken Neil Young's hand and not fainted as he told me he loved my name. While most of my musical tastes fall in the rock-and-roll category, there's always been a special place in my heart for country music. Lady singers, especially. I'm talking Patsy Cline, Loretta Lynn, Tammy Wynette,* and the queen, Dolly Parton. As far as I'm

---

* To give you an idea of how Southern my family is, there is a rumor that Tammy Wynette and I are very loosely related because we share some ancestor who fought in the Civil War together. Like, what kind of backwoods rumor is that?

concerned, once you have fleets of drag queens impersonating you, you've made it. I can only hope to be so lucky one day.

These women are the classics, the standards. In the steak-house of country music, they're the prime rib. But every so often, you just need some greasy drive-through, ya know? In other words, sometimes you just need to crank some Top 40 pop coun-try and scream-sing about a terrible ex-boyfriend or how you're drinking beer in a field somewhere. It's one of my unconven-tional methods of therapy. No disrespect to *actual* therapy, which is super useful and necessary for lots of people. Therapy is great! But this particular emotional release of singing/screaming at the top of my lungs is something that's been working for me since high school. Your lover do you wrong? Crank up Wynonna Judd's "No One Else on Earth." Leaving your home state to go follow your dreams on the other side of the country? Why, that's a perfect moment to dance to Jo Dee Messina's "Heads Carolina, Tails California." Get to California and feel like white trash in West Hollywood? Crank Gretchen Wilson's "Redneck Woman" to eleven and get pumped about where you came from. I *connect* with these songs.

Unlike my bust size, my love of country music developed early in life. This is thanks, in part, to the fact that I grew up in Boonville, North Carolina. Imagine your quintessential small town in America. Now, shrink that down to 10 percent and throw in a lot of cows. That's Boonville. To say I grew up in the sticks would be giving it too much credit. I grew up in the *twigs*. A place where lyrics about hooking up down by the river were relatable, seeing as the Fridays of my senior year were spent camping out on the banks of the Yadkin River with the quarter-back and a quart of MD 20/20. While the average person might scoff at a song about a woman slashing the tires of her cheating boyfriend's Dodge Ram, if you lived in Boonville, you not only related to this, you probably had a cousin on probation for that very charge! That's how country Boonville was. Pop country feels like home to me like jazz does to New Orleans.

My high school years were prime time for country-pop music. You had your Martina McBrides, your Faith Hills, your Sara Evanses. It was a golden age for stacked-bob hairdos and flared light-wash jeans. But of all the music that blasted through my shitty Honda Accord speakers during those high school years, the most frequently played had to be the Dixie Chicks.

The Dixie Chicks are comprised of three gals, two of them sisters, who all sing like angels and play their instruments like devils. Specifically, a devil that went down to Georgia because one of them rocks the fiddle like a BOSS. Right out the gate, you know that the Dixie Chicks are the shit because they have the word "dixie" in their name. "Dixie" refers to the historical nickname for the South, but in my heart it's in honor of Dixie Carter from *Designing Women*. Both Dixies, the group and Julia Sugarbaker, have more sass in their left titty on a typical Tuesday than most people carry in their whole body during a lifetime.

When the Chicks burst onto the scene (or should I say "hatched"?) with their breakthrough album, *Wide Open Spaces*, I was in love. *Who are these brassy blond songbirds who can not only carry some sick three-part harmonies but also play their own instruments?!* I can't tell you how many high school afternoons were spent cruising around the back roads of my little county with my friend Emily, windows down, singing our asses off to that album. I can close my eyes and be taken back to those moments: the humid country air whipping through our hair, the smell of honeysuckle in our noses, and the occasional fast-and-furious rolling-up of the windows because we were passing a chicken house and those reeked *so fucking bad.*

Our love of singing that album was not confined only to my Accord or Emily's Plymouth, either. Occasionally, when we were feeling ballsy, we'd sneak into the one bar within a twenty-mile radius of my house to sing "Wide Open Spaces" at karaoke night. Yep, just your average bar filled with drunk rednecks and two sixteen-year-olds in head-to-toe Abercrombie & Fitch, trying to break out some show choir harmonies. Two members of the Little Rascals standing on each other's shoulders in a long trench coat pretending to be one tall adult would have blended in better than we did.

Wide Open Spaces and *Fly* weren't just catchy albums. They also had massive critical acclaim, too, racking up Grammys left and right. I thought nothing could stop the Dixie Chicks from soaring . . . until *the Bush incident.* The Chicks were performing at a concert in London right around the time when America was invading Iraq. Never one to shield her opinions, Natalie told the crowd, "Just so you know, we're ashamed the president of the United States is from Texas." Big whoop, right?! I mean, as I write this, that misogynist Cheeto of a man (Trump) is our president and says such blasphemous vitriol that I feel like I'm tripping every time I turn on the news. Meanwhile, Natalie says one comment and people started throwing their *Fly* CDs into a bonfire. Isn't that unbelievable? And not just because the visual of a bunch of burning CDs is so archaic. But just like that, the Chicks went into hibernation.

Despite not having a new album in a decade, I'd still listen to all their classics on my fave Pandora station. One day, while Swiffering with "There's Your Trouble" blaring on my speakers,

I went to go "thumbs up" the tune and show that algorithm who was boss. I looked down, and there was a pesky little pop-up ad blocking the button. Now, normally I would "X" out that pop-up like it was a porn ad and I was sitting in a prayer circle, but this one stopped me. The Dixie Chicks were going on tour!

I dropped the WetJet and ran to my laptop to Google it. Sure enough, there were dates! My teenage heart soared! But they were all in Europe! SPLAT! My heart dropped to my half-cleaned floor. *There goes that dream*, I thought to myself.

Later, while ~~checking Twitter~~ working, I decided to look at the dates anyway. *Okay, most are in April. I technicallyyyy could go then. You got your Brussels, your Oslo, your—shitting me, they're playing Amsterdam on 4/20?!*

My former stoner self was squealing on the inside. Going to Amsterdam on the unofficial holiday for smoking weed is ridiculous enough, but throwing a Dixie Chicks concert on top of it? This was a once-in-a-lifetime opportunity. I had to go, and I knew the perfect travel crew for this adventure. Enter . . .

JESS & TESS, THE HOT MESS EXPRESS.

Now, y'all already met Jess in the previous chapter, but let me tell you about Tess. Tess is not only my PR guru, she's a Roman candle of a woman, blasting off fun wherever she's pointed. She can handle her scotch like she has the BMI of 1989 John Goodman, and she also does wacky extravagant stuff like getting a Bea Arthur mosaic put on the bottom of her pool just because she knew looking at it would make her happy.

Not thirty-six hours into each of them agreeing with a huge "DUH," Tess was already blowing up our group text about lodging.

"Girls, I have found the perfect place. You're gonna die."

I was nervous. Did she mean we were going "to die" because the place was so damn posh? Or were we going "to die" because she wanted to save some scrilla and had booked us in a skeezy-hostel-from-*Hostel* situation? It's always a game of roulette when you are traveling with someone for the first time. I clicked the link with squinted eyes and, sure enough, I DIED. My corpse finger mustered up the strength to click through the pics of a hundred-year-old potato boat that had been renovated into a two-bedroom houseboat in the seventies. That's right—a rusty-on-the-outside, beautifully-modern-on-the-inside, century-old boat docked smack-dab in the middle of one of the most beautiful canals in Amsterdam. We were going to have this glorious vessel for three whole nights, and it would still be cheaper than getting hotel rooms.

Cut to two months later as we three ladies stood on the dock of our rusty abode. We were nervous it might be like a bad on-line date, where our boat looked like eighties Corey Haim in his profile but present-day Corey Feldman IRL. We opened up the rusty hatch, walked down the stairs, and BOOM! It was glorious. Sighs of relief all around.

Being jetlagged as hell and dehydrated from our flight, we each drank a bunch of water and made ourselves stay up to adjust to the change in time. LOLZ. More like, we each drank a bottle of red and passed out for five hours. We didn't mean to nap so long, but when you are in the belly of an old boat on a canal, it feels like you're strapped to a giant's bosom in a baby sling, being rocked back and forth. Once we woke up, we had to make up for lost time, aka head to the Red Light District.

And pardon me as I reach into my pocket and pull out an-other KOHLRABI!

For those of you who do not know what the Red Light District is or are not familiar with TLC's *Crazy Sexy Cool* album, this is the neighborhood for sex stuff. Anything from innocent peepshows, to full sex shows, to legal prostitution can happen there.

Before we went, we needed some liquid courage. We found an unassuming bar just outside the district that was full of dudes (shocker). "I don't even know what to expect!" Jess said as she took down her third shot. "Do people actually have sex onstage?" Tess and I nodded, and Jess looked a little queasy. "I don't think I can watch that."

"We're going," I said, motioning the bartender for another round. "It's part of the *culture*. You gotta experience it!"

We made a pit stop at a café for a strawberry-flavored joint, because nothing says "tourists from America" like three giggly girls surrounded by a cloud of smoke that smells like a scratch-n-sniff sticker. When we got to the Red Light District, I immediately found which sex show to go to. "This one has a neon pink elephant wearing a tie! It's gotta be good!" I squealed. My reasoning had no logic to it, but the girls agreed.

I grabbed tickets from the box office and headed into Theatre Casa Rosso, passing framed posters of various acts we were about to see. Of course, I couldn't read the signs because I don't speak Dutch, but if they didn't say "Cumming Attractions," I think we've all lost here.

Now, what I'm about to describe next is not for the faint of heart. And it almost made this Hart faint. We walked in and immediately decided to distance ourselves from the stage by grabbing the front-row balcony so that no one was blocking our view, but we were at least a good fifty yards from the splash zone.* We

---

* Even I am aware of how gross that sounds. Could you imagine showing up to a sex show in a clear poncho like you were about to see Shamu jumping out of the water or Gallagher sledgehammering some watermelons? To be fair, there was a lot of breaching *and* seed spreading on that stage, so I guess it's apropos. Hey-yo!

were the only people on the balcony besides a group of American girls who were in the *very* last row of the whole theater. I looked back at them as we carefully made our way down the stairs, each one of them had their hands either over their eyes or in front of their mouths.

Onstage, a man and a woman were having sex on a rotating circular bed as a generic techno song blared. At least, I assumed it was two humans. The sex resembled two cyborgs rubbing sprockets. Totally robotic. It was like they were going down a checklist of positions. After a few minutes of us giggling like wild women, we became entranced. The second the song was over, the duo popped up and walked offstage. Then the next couple came out. Same thing. This move, that move, this move, song ends, byeeeeee. It was like they clocked in for work (or should I say *cocked* in? Hey-yo!) and then as soon as their shift ended, they said, "Peace, bitch, I'm off to happy hour." Next up, two girls came out and performed a double-sided dildo routine. It was like the last scene of *Requiem for a Dream* but if the performers were actually on Ambien, dreaming. We weren't the only ones who were clearly expecting a different show.

"This is so not what I thought it was gonna be, Tiffany," I heard one of the girls a few rows behind us say in a thick-as-alfredo-sauce, Long Island accent. "I didn't know, Renee!" Tiffany clucked back, sounding like Janice from *Friends*. I can only assume that Tiffany was the poor maid of honor, tasked with planning a bachelorette, who had talked it up like they were about to Thunder from Down Under. I couldn't blame them. Even I was beginning to regret the fifty-dollar entrance fee, too. So I turned to Jess and Tess and offered them an out.

"Guys, whaddayasay we boogie out of here and go flirt with some real-life Dutch boys? Or even just go get drunk on our bomb-ass boat?" I could tell they had the same idea, but before they could admit it, the lights went dark and a bass-heavy techno song started pulsating through the speakers. We all leaned in, trying to understand the lyrics, which were spoken by the most Euro voice imaginable, like a rejected member from the nineties group the Real McCoy.* After a few rounds of the repetitious voice, I finally caught on. I looked over at my girls to see if we were all doing the same thing: bopping our heads to the driving beat while trying to mouth along with the muffled words. Then all at once we had it. We sang in unison. . . .

"Dark orgasm. Dark orgasm. Yesss. Dark orgasm. Highly addictive!"

Those were the only lyrics. We were voguing in our seats, singing about this highly addictive, dark orgasm, dying laughing. The Long Island girls were dying, too, but only because I don't think any of them had breathed since they'd entered the theater. Meanwhile, we were in our own little world of singing and dancing, which was way more entertaining than anything that was happening onstage. That is, until we were snapped out of our dancing by a high-pitched "Oh my gawd!" from behind us. We looked back to the stage, and there she was: an Amazonian of a woman, clad in patent leather ass-less chaps, a belt of a bra, with a leather crop in hand. She force-strutted around the stage in a manner that can only be described as a Clydesdale in stripper heels meets a Xena: Warrior Princess cosplay costume.

She continued clunking around to her orgasm jam, cracking that whip. I hadn't seen a performance so dead-eyed since I'd watched Britney perform in Vegas in 2013.† It was an absolute

---

* Or more specifically and niche, the singer of Rammstein's "Du Hast."
† That adventure can be read all about in my first book. Available now wherever books are sold. ;)

train wreck, and we were *living* for it. When she finally finished, the three of us stood up and applauded, giving her the standing O we thought she deserved. I mean, someone needed to get an O on that stage in general, standing or otherwise!

Before we could sit back down in our seats, we saw Xena was asking for volunteers to come onstage. "I'm going!" Tess said, taking down the dregs of her double Johnnie Walker Red. We cheered as she trotted up the stairs, attempting to high-five the Long Island crew, who recoiled in disgust. "That's my bitch!" I yelled as I watched her hightail it to the stage, foregoing the lift from a stagehand and hoisting herself up.

Tess stood in line with the other victims, waiting to see what they were going to be made to do. Was she going to have to strip for tips while being whipped? Things were about to get bananas!

And oh, they did. Literally.

Creeping up behind Tess came a man wearing, I kid you not, a gorilla suit. A GORILLA SUIT. Let me remind you that Jess and I were two very high girls watching our smiley friend being unknowingly approached by a man in a primate costume on-stage at a sex show in Amsterdam. Just needed to remind you of the full scope of this scenario.

So, Gorilla Man makes himself known, and Tess is cracking up, pretending she's gonna grind on him, much to the delight of the Asian businessmen in the crowd. We watched Xena put the girls in a line and explain to them what was going to happen. She wasn't mic'ed, so we couldn't hear what she was saying, but I imagine it was just a series of grunts. Xena walked offstage and came back with a handful of bananas, giving one to Gorilla Man, who was now lounging like a centerfold on the floor.

"Go, Tess!" Jess and I yelled in unison, like we were cheering on our li'l pumpkin in an episode of *Toddlers & Tiaras*. Tess beamed from the stage, giving two thumbs-up to the balcony. We shot her four thumbs right back until we realized what was about to happen. The first volunteer was on her knees, taking bites of the banana as Gorilla Man positioned it like an erection on his crotch, her head bobbing up and down to get bites. It was a lot more appalling than a-peel-ing!

Tess locked eyes with us up in the balcony and just shook her head no. We shook our heads right back. Then—and this is why I love her—the bitch went rogue. While all the girls took their turns getting their daily dose of potassium while simulating BJs, Tess started dancing around the stage. Twerking, dropping it low, and, if my dance background serves me correctly, she even threw in a few Fosse moves. "Put that 'Dark Orgasm' jam back on!" she shouted as Xena tried to get her back in line. But Tess wasn't having it. She did a spin move away from Xena like she was a Harlem Globetrotter. Xena snapped and pointed for Tess to get in line, but Tess was not ready to make nice.

Meanwhile, Jess and I were *losing our minds*, cheering for our girl and trying to get the rest of the crowd on her side. We were like sex show warm-up comics pointing to an applause sign before a commercial break. The song ended, and mercifully, the gorilla left the stage. Tess curtsied for her stage moms, soaking it all in. She was too busy hamming it up to notice that the gorilla had reentered the stage, this time with a new accessory.

And that accessory . . . was a GIANT strap-on. And this was no ordinary giant strap-on!* No, no. That primate started working his equipment, and SPLASH! It was also a massive water gun, and the gorilla was shooting the audience and volunteers onstage with fake jizz. Tess burst out laughing and pointed toward the door. Jess

---

* We can go ahead and add that sentence to my "Things I Never Thought I'd Say" list.

and I started up those stairs so fast we fell down at the feet of the Long Islanders, who at this point were the living embodiment of the "hear no evil, speak no evil, see no evil" chimps.

Reunited, the three of us busted out of the theater doors, wheezing with laughter as we ran down the cobblestone street. "Did that really just happen?! Or should I say 'strappen'?!"* I asked Tess, who was high on power, among other things. She ran into the nearest falafel shop, said, "Give us some free fries," and *they did*, no exchange of currency needed. They were either terrified or in awe of Tess, and I'm guessing both. We walked through that district like we owned it. Girls in light-up window displays catcalled us as we continued shoving fries in our face and recounting the night.

ME: You just made a sex show your own personal dance recital!
TESS: I told that dominatrix that her dancing had no heart. She needs to put some passion into it! The Red Light District could be so much better with a few changes!

Leave it to Tess, PR extraordinaire, to focus on how the sex show needed to rebrand itself. When we hit our humble, floating abode, we knocked out.

The next day was spent recovering. Truth be told, we kind of blew our load on the first night, pun so goddamn intended. So we slept in to conserve our energy for the next night's show and spent the day sitting on the deck of SS *Tater Tot*, drinking red wine, blaring Dixie Chicks to get us pumped up, and smoking

---

* No, no, I shouldn't.

the delicious strawberry-flavored joints we'd bought at the café. Once those munchies kicked in, we rolled up so high to a Thai restaurant that when I asked the waiter if the food was coming out so quickly because they wanted to get rid of us, he said, "Absolutely." We went back to the boat and smoked another joint, reminiscing about the night before. "Oh my god," Jess said. "Can you imagine if the Dixie Chicks asked us what we like most about Amsterdam and we were like, 'Probably the ejaculating gorilla we saw at the sex show last night'?!"

"We are disgusting people," I said, shaking my head and opening our millionth bottle of wine. I belly laughed so hard in the belly of that boat that night, it actually scared me, and I had to climb outside to get some fresh air before passing out from exhaustion.

I woke up the next morning not knowing if I was nauseated from all the red wine, or laughing, or because I was just straight-up seasick. But no upset stomach was going to stop me that day. It was 4/20! Dixie Chickmas!

We headed to the show, literally skipping into the stadium. While we had bought our own tickets, my agents had hooked us up with a meet-and-greet after the show. So, not only were we going to hear these beautiful angels play, we were also going to get a hurried, awkward photo with them! If I could go back in time to show my teen self a pic with the Chicks, she would say, "Wow, I'm going to grow up to be awesome! Also, I am going to start moisturizing daily, 'cause those are wrinkles, girl."

We were going in with lofty expectations for the show, and the Chicks far exceeded them. Not only did they sound tighter than a Pentecostal on her wedding night, they were as ballsy as ever, even showing pics of Chris Brown and Trump during

"Goodbye Earl." We sang, we cried, we yee-haw'ed too hard every time they mentioned that it was 4/20.* After, they wrapped up their second encore, the time had come. It was time to meet the Chicks.

We headed backstage, ready to stand in line for our quick step-and-repeat pic. Turns out, however, this wasn't a cattle-call situation. There were only ten of us backstage, and they were going to take us back in small groups to meet and chat with the Chicks in a more intimate setting.

"Y'all are up." The sweet assistant motioned us over as she pushed open the heavy metal door. And there they were: Natalie, Martie, and Emily, a heavenly glow surrounding them. Natalie was finishing her conversation with a previous meet-and-greeter, Emily was making herself a drink, and Martie was trying to shove some much-deserved salad into her mouth. We stood in awe but were snapped out of it by just how damn nice they were! They kept asking us questions about ourselves and couldn't believe that we had traveled all the way to Amsterdam for their show. "Are you kidding?!" I said, realizing how strong our drinks had been during the show. "As soon as we found out y'all were touring, we knew we had to bring this sin wagon across the Atlantic!"

"Well, that deserves a cheers, and I for one need another drink!" Natalie said, then turned to me. "You're the drinks girl, right? Make me a drink!"

Holy fuck. I was about to make a drink for Natalie Maines, a woman whose voice pumped through my shitty Accord speakers for years, whose melodies echoed through the halls of my

---

* Come to find out, 4/20 is solely an American thing based on all the reserved, seated Dutch audience shooting us judgy looks.

freshman dorm until some nerd would inevitably tell me to turn it down. I scanned the ingredients at the bar like I was on an episode of *Chopped* and Ted Allen was about to start the clock.

"Girl, I just want some tequila with a bunch of lime juice in it," she said, clearly noticing the conflict happening in my head. Oh thank God! I didn't have to be creative. I squeezed those limes like my life depended on it, shook it with some silver tequila, and handed her a glass. "I call it a Maines Squeeze!" I said, beaming from my ability to make a pun despite my starstruck-ness. We *cheers*'ed, and as I lifted the glass to my mouth, I wondered if Natalie would prefer to get matching BFF necklaces or just go whole hog and spring for matching tattoos.

Right as the Don Julio was about to touch my lips, I heard Jess snicker from across the room. She was clearly dishing out some good story based on her exaggerated arm movements, but I couldn't make out what she was saying through her laughs. Then, clear as day, I heard Emily's voice say, "Wait a minute. It wasn't *real* jizz, was it?!"

I froze as I watched the Hot Mess Express shake their heads like a couple of bobbleheads in the back window of a car. How the hell were we going to become besties with the Dixie Chicks if they knew how crazy we were? For the first time ever I was jealous of Earl and his poisoned black-eyed peas. I scanned the room for open windows. I was ready to run. But before I could take that bottle of tequila and smash it over my head, Natalie grabbed my arm and pulled me over to the girls.

"Hold on a second here, start at the beginning. Y'all went to a sex club?!" Cut to one hour later and the Hot Mess Express and the Chicks were piling into an SUV headed straight to the Red Light District.

. . . I wish! Instead we chatted with them for a while longer, kept our cool, and then screamed our heads off on the dock of our boat as soon as we got out of our Uber. To celebrate, we went to the bar closest to our boat to play the jukebox. After all, some days you just gotta dance.

The next morning, we said bye to the boat and headed off to our separate flights. As I sat there on that tarmac listening to the Chicks on my headphones, I couldn't help but smile to myself. I pictured my teenage self in that bar back in North Carolina and how all the words I sang had come true. I had found wide-open spaces, and room to make big mistakes. I had seen new faces, and I knew the high stakes. . . . I just didn't realize how *high* they were gonna be.

Pure Cunt'ry

IF YOU ARE someone who gets offended by the word "cunt," then I am sorry . . . that you are so uptight, that is. Personally, I love the word, and I don't know why people hate it so much. In fact, when I was little, I used to say "C U next Tuesday" as just a regular way to tell people good-bye, having no idea what it meant. I just thought it was a saying! But apparently ten-year-old me was inadvertently calling people "cunts," complete with finger guns to really up the charm.

I've heard the argument made that being called a "pussy" isn't an insult because pussies are unbelievably strong and resilient and can be thanked for all life on Earth. Well, the same thing applies to "cunt." Take back the word, ladies! You gotta own it! I owned it on national TV less than a week before I wrote this chapter.

I was filming an episode of my favorite, and recently cancelled (RIP), show, *@midnight*, playing against Howie Mandel, when through a series of joke callbacks, he called me a cunt. I wish I could go back in time and tell younger me that not only would Maurice from *Little Monsters* one day call her a cunt, she'd be so confident that she would take a breath, smile into the audience, and say, "Ya damn right I am."

Anyway, this is a roundabout way of saying some of my favorite cunts* are in country music. A lot of people attribute the girl power movement to the Spice Girls hitting the scene back in the nineties, but country has been doing it for ages. And, while I loved singing in a British accent and figuring out which Spice Girl I wanted to be among my friends when we choreographed dances, I related more to songs about Southern girls growing up and figuring out their life.

But I'm sure some of you weren't lucky enough to grow up in the land of truck nuts and meth labs. Some of you grew up in classy places, with classy parents who probably cranked NPR and Bach while you sat in the back seat. Well, pop in your other monocle and have your butler pull up your iTunes, 'cause this here is a perfect starter pack for female empowerment with a drawl. May I recommend downloading all of them, then blaring them in your car as you drive through some back roads with your windows down? Or, ya know, just pour a whiskey and dance around your house. Here's your "C U Next Tuesday" playlist.†

"Wild One"—Faith Hill

This is such a great "fuck you, parents!" anthem. The song is about being told by your parents to stay in line and follow the rules, with your classic "don't listen to rock and roll" and "don't date the bad boy" type directives. Every time, she brushes them

---

* Remember, I mean this as "strong, resilient woman"!
† I didn't put any Dixie Chicks in there because obviously you just need to download their whole catalog and memorize every word.

off, like "hell no, I do what I want."* But it really won my heart when they tell her to brush her hair and she says, "Some kids don't." Bish is so rebellious that she won't brush her hair as a statement. As someone who has to lose rock, paper, scissors to herself to take a shower, I feel you, Faith.

"This One's for the Girls"—Martina McBride

Just like the Dixie Chicks's "Goodbye Earl," where they kill an abusive husband with poisoned black-eyed peas, Martina also has a killer song about murdering your husband out of self-defense called "Independence Day." But "This One's for the Girls" is a sweet one, giving little pep talks to ladies through various phases of their lives. It's the type of song that's so universal, it makes you feel like it's written specifically for you. You think, *Wait a sec! I also have been twenty-five, with a shitty apartment, and living off SpaghettiOs!* Yeah, naw duh. Everyone's been there. But it still makes you feel like you are in this special lady club.

"Heads Carolina, Tails California"—Jo Dee Messina

Okay, fine. Maybe this one personally speaks to me because it literally is about the place I grew up and the place I now live. But it's a bop! There are so many songs that romanticize the South, but in this one she's like, "Let's get the hell out of here." I love where I came from. It made me who I am. But do you see me hanging out at Dodge City every night, drinking Miller Lite

---

* But, like, in a still-respectful way because it's America's sweetheart Faith Hill, and homegirl isn't going to ruin her chance at a future Super Bowl halftime show by singing expletives.

and hoping I don't hit a deer on my way home? Nope! This country girl needed city life. And so did Jo Dee. In addition to crooning some great tunes, she's a fiery redhead, and again, her name is JO DEE. If that doesn't sound like a woman you want to roll into a dive bar and pool shark some dudes with, I don't know who is.

"She's in Love with the Boy"—Trisha Yearwood

This is the only one on the list that's about love, but I had to include it. It's your stereotypical song about a father not approving of his daughter's choice of boyfriend, so it's not reinventing the wheel. However, I love this one because the dad basically says that his daughter's beau is an idiot, and then the mom busts in to say, "My dad hated you when we met, too. Get over it." In real life, Trisha is married to dream man Garth Brooks, has a cooking show on the Food Network, and actually looks like a real woman. She doesn't try to be a rail, then go on TV and pretend to eat all the comfort food she cooks up. Not that anyone would do that. *cough Giada cough*

"Born to Fly"—Sara Evans

This is one of the more saccharine of the bunch, your classic anthem with the theme of "how do you keep your feet on the ground, when you know you were born to fly?" Typical, right? But it gets extra points because the first few lyrics are comprised of her literally talking to a scarecrow. Sara, we've all been lonely, and I understand that mental health help is expensive, but confiding in a man who is just your dad's old flannel shirt filled with straw is no substitute for therapy.

"Guys Do It All the Time"—Mindy McCready

This is one of those songs that make you want to stand up and scream, "Preach it, girl!" like you're a damn Wendy Williams audience member. It's basically a song about how hypocritical dudes are when women party. She comes home, her dude is mad, and she's like, "Oh, hell no." As a woman who can outdrink men four times my size, I appreciate her standing up for the boozehounds.

"Any Man of Mine"—Shania Twain

I think we can all admit that our favorite Canadian country crooner took it a little too far in "That Don't Impress Me Much." Honey, if you truly aren't impressed by a rocket scientist or guy who looks like Brad Pitt, well then your expectations might just be too damn high. But she gets off her high horse and makes her requests a little more relatable in this cowboy stomper. All she's asking for is for her man to lie when her dress is too tight, disagree when she's having a bad hair day, and say her burnt-ass cookin' is delicious. Some people think in a relationship that "honesty is the best policy," but I honestly think the best policy is "a little lie can keep it fly" . . . never said that in my life, but consider it trademarked!

AND NOW A couple of old-school cunt'ry classics to pop into your dive bar's jukebox for immediate street cred. . . .

"Harper Valley PTA"—Jeannie C. Riley

This song came out in '68, and I'm pretty sure it's the first song ever written about slut shaming. The subject of the song is given a note from her daughter's PTA saying she wears her skirts too short. Homegirl walks in there with her miniskirt and drops the mic, saying things like, "You're a drunk," "You got your secretary pregnant," "You keep asking me out and I say no." By the time she walks out of the meeting, she has spilled all the PTeaA. Don't come for Jeannie's wardrobe unless you ain't got any dirty laundry yourself.

"The Pill"—Loretta Lynn

Y'all, Loretta Lynn is just the badass of badasses. I mean, besides the old stuff, she made one of my favorite records of all time with Jack White (from the White Stripes) when she was seventy-two! But back *in* '75, she was pissing off conservatives, aka my current favorite pastime on Twitter. This song's basic message is that it's not fair that her husband gets to go out and have all this fun while she's just at home popping out babies, so she decides to start taking birth control. Considering Christian folks thought BC was a sin back then, this was a risky move. But Loretta got married to a dude known as Doolittle and had four children before she was even nineteen, so I'm pretty sure she had some real-life experience to draw from. She must be honored for such badass-ery.

AND, LAST BUT not least, of course, **ANYTHING DOLLY PAR-TON**. The woman is a goddess and hilarious and one of the greatest songwriters of all time. I mean, how can you not be in awe of someone who was born in a dirt-floor shack and now has a theme park named after her? One day I hope to gouge all of you with admission and overpriced turkey legs at Mame Town, but until then I will continue listening to "9 to 5" and "Why'd You Come in Here Lookin' Like That?" on repeat.

LOOK. AT THE end of the day, there's always going to be "cooler" music, more obscure or classic tunes that are more impressive to name-drop. But, I'm telling ya, when you fall in love with some pop country, you fall hard and you don't care who knows it. You will blare those tunes to the eye rolls of other friends and significant others. You will love it and not care what others say, like Trisha Yearwood's protagonist in "She's in Love with the Boy."

Go forth and get your female country on. I recommend cruising around with all your windows down, singing at the top of your lungs. Or singing these after a few glasses of wine at karaoke at your local watering hole. For myself, it's more powerful than therapy . . . but like a real therapist. Not a scarecrow, Sara.

Sliding into My DMs

PEOPLE SAY THAT we are living in the golden age of television. More and more channels are pumping out artful and cinematic series with boundary-pushing content. "Prestige" TV, if you will. But sometimes you don't want highbrow art. Sometimes you don't need a Michelin-star meal with foie gras cotton candy; you crave a Hot Pocket. Or even a gas station meal. And the gas station meal of the small screen has got to be reality TV.

Personally, I'm a sucker for the type of show whose reunion episode ends with crying, screaming, and "To Be Continued" flashing across the screen as a stretcher is being rolled out. The shows you can only watch in total solitude, and even then, you can tell your dog is judging you as you're reacting to it. For me, at the top of this watch list is none other than *Dance Moms*.

IT. IS. THE. BEST.

For those of you not familiar with this garbage fire of a show, it centers around a dance teacher, Abby Lee Miller, and her dance company of young stars. Every week, the girls learn a new routine to take on the road to various competitions, which happen in exotic locales like a community college's performing arts center in Akron, Ohio.

Business Opportunity Sidebar

Thinking of starting your own dance competition? I've got you covered. First you need a name, so choose one word from each of these lists:

Power	Star	Competition
Elite	Showbiz	Showcase
Platinum	Dance	of America
Encore	Talent	Championship

Now, put that name on a large banner,* grab yourself some trophies and a sexually ambiguous male host to hand them out, and VOILÀ! You've got yourself a money-making dance machine.

While putting children and tweens under intense amounts of public scrutiny is a perfect recipe for meltdowns, the girls on this show handle the pressure with grace, even as their stage moms have epic shit fits every episode. How much drama can a low-stakes dance competition with suburban moms really produce? Oh, it gets WILD. Every episode includes a backstabbing,

---

* Ideally with the silhouette of a leaping ballerina. Be sure not to use the iconic fire dancer from the Dave Matthews Band *Stand Up* album. You can find this by a simple Google search or tattooed on the body of anyone I avoided in college.

screaming spectacle with mothers raising hell because their daughter "deserved a solo." Add that to the fact that they clearly always have a few glasses of pinot grigio at Panera Bread on their lunch breaks, and BOOM. It's a recipe for disaster, and the chef controlling all of it is Abby Lee Miller.

Abby is a tornado of teased bangs straight outta Pittsburgh: she's brash, she's terrifying, she's manipulative, and she's fun as fuck to watch. Just when you think her conniving has hit a new low, she takes out a shovel and goes lower. I've watched her scream at mothers and pit young girls against each other, I've seen her choreograph countless dances about death for ten-year-olds, and I've eagerly read every article related to her bankruptcy fraud charges. This story is about the time Abby Lee Miller kept *me* out of jail. But before we get to that, let's take it back to trace the roots of why dance competitions are so close to my heart.

From the time I was four years old through high school, you could find me at my local dance studio, tapping and turning and complaining that my feet were bleeding when I eventually went on pointe. Dance classes taught me discipline, teamwork, and (most important) that I had an insatiable hunger for the spotlight. I may as well have been a moth in a tutu considering how badly I wanted to flutter around in the warmth of that light. Dancing was my first foray into being in front of an audience.*

Here are some top highlights of my years on the scene:

1) Kindergarten recital: On the first shuffle-ball-change of "Jailhouse Rock," I kicked my tiny tap shoe into the audience.

---

* Dance is also why I have zero modesty and am fine dropping trou in front of any other female. Girls throw off their leotards quicker than a New Yorker tosses a mattress during a bedbug outbreak.

2) Junior year: I am Michael Jackson in the big company number to "Thriller" and am worshipped by the younger girls who are super scared of the dance.

3) Five years after graduating and on the studio's twenty-fifth anniversary, I am asked to revive said "Thriller" role and come home to North Carolina thirty pounds heavier after quitting smoking. The little girls are still scared of the dance, but mainly because my out-of-shape ass almost coughs up a lung in the wings.

My sister and I were notorious for losing pieces of our costume. This usually ended with me freaking out at the studio on picture day and then us hanging up a sheet in the living room and doing our own DIY photo shoot.

Like the *Dance Mom* girls, I performed as part of a troupe, but, luckily for me, Dance with Mitzi was run by the kindest and sweetest lady alive. Mitzi ended her classes early on Wednesdays so she could walk across the street and lead the Boonville Methodist choir, and she once described adding more sequins to a costume to distract the judges from our sloppy routine by saying, "Let's throw some glitter on this chicken shit and pretend it's a rhinestone!" Years later, when she came and saw me do a live comedy show in Charlotte and I broke out a split onstage, she stood up, did the Arsenio Hall Dog Pound arm, and screamed, "You go, girl!"

The point is, Mitzi is pretty much the opposite of Abby. Yet as much as Abby was brutal on-screen, I was convinced her ruthlessness had to be an act, that there was some amount of "putting it on" for the camera. No woman would tell a crying child that they need to suck it up and only cry if their "arm is hanging off or somebody died," right?*

Well, let me tell you, I was about to find out. A few years ago, my friend Grace Helbig was hosting her own show on the E! network and had been kind enough to ask me to be a guest on it several times. But one day she gave me the opportunity of a lifetime. "Mames, you have to come on next week," she said with a quickened breath. "Because my guest is . . . Abby Lee Miller."

The concept for the segment was that Grace and I would interview Abby and then perform a quick, ridiculous dance for her. She would then decide who out of the two of us would make it onto the ALDC (Abby Lee Dance Company) elite team.

On the day of the taping, Grace and I were insanely nervous. What if she yelled at us? Or didn't understand our humor?

---

* This is an actual quote that Abby has said on the show.

Before we could imagine all of our worst-case scenarios, homegirl came in barefoot and braless like she'd just escaped a house fire. When the producers told her that her dressing room was down a flight of stairs, Abby wasn't having it. She changed right then and there in the set kitchen, whipping off her caftan faster than a Golden Girl on spring break. In fact, she was in the middle of putting a shirt back on when Grace and I approached her to introduce ourselves. Grace, being the host, led the conversation.

"Hi, Abby! We are big fans and—"

"Which earrings should I wear?" Abby said, cutting off Grace mid-gush. She was holding both a massive silver star and a massive dangly rhinestone earring over each lobe.

"Definitely the star. 'Cause you are one!" I responded, grossed out by myself. "Hi, I'm Mamrie."

Saying the woman gave zero fucks is an understatement. But there was no time to attempt another intro. Before we knew it, we were mic'ed up and sitting on a tiny couch, Abby firmly planted in between us.

"You need to raise the camera," she said, directing the professional cameramen whose living is based on knowing how to shoot a camera. "See, if they shoot you from a higher angle, your face looks thinner," she said as Grace and I acted impressed, as if we don't each take four hundred selfies a day and haven't been editing our own faces for years.

We ~~kissed her ass~~ made small talk as best we could while the crew continued setting up. I have no clue what actually came out of our mouths but clearly Abby could tell we were fan-girling, and so she blessed us with some DM dirt, going off about certain moms and dancers. She was one second away from telling us what she really thinks of Kendall's music when she stopped dead in her tracks.

"Is that a two-way mirror?!" At first, we didn't respond. "Is that a two-way mirror?!" Abby asked with heightened alarm, pointing at a mirror above the fireplace.

"No, just a regular mirror," Grace assured her as we cut eyes to each other. For a woman who talks a lot of shit, she sure was paranoid. Her eyes looked crazier than they do when Nia falls out of a turn or when Kendall is a beat behind in *every* trio she's ever done.* "Are you sure that's not a two-way mirror that the producers watch from behind?" I half-expected her to get up and pound her fists on the glass like an enraged convict being questioned on *Law & Order.*

"No," Grace said, her brown eyes as big as Cinnabons. "I'm pretty sure behind that is just a wall and then behind *that* is a hallway."

"Good, because I do *not* need the producers hearing what I say."

Grace and I shot each other another look. Here this woman was bossing around the crew like she was Scorsese but didn't realize that we were mic'ed and everything we said was being directly pumped into the headphones of every producer and agent sitting around the monitor?

The *actual* director called, "Action!" and Grace immediately snapped into host mode. She conducted the interview like a pro, very Diane Sawyer meets Pee-wee Herman.† Meanwhile, I AM NERVOUS. Grace and I had choreographed a thirty-second routine to an (obviously) royalty-free song, just like they do on *Dance Moms.*

---

* My apologies for those of you who don't watch the show for all these niche references, and you're welcome for those of you who do.
† Which is not only my ultimate compliment but also my ultimate threesome.

Here Abby watches as we perform a dance with
wooden emoji heads that I'm pretty sure we titled
"Cat Shit." You could almost hear her eyes roll in their
tan sockets.

Oh, what? I didn't mention my favorite thing about the show, which is how all the dances they perform have to be done to royalty-free music because the budget is so low? IT IS THE BEST. For instance, they did a commemorative dance in honor of Prince's passing, but since they obviously couldn't get the rights to "Purple Rain," they danced to a sound-alike entitled, no lie, "Purple Pride" by Evan Olson. This was no Prince. More like Pauper.*

We finished our routine and waited to hear who she thought would win. Y'all, after years of showing up to the dance studio

---

* Hell yeah, I *did* just drop a Mark Twain reference. I am smarter than I give myself credit for. . . . I can't lie. I had to Google who wrote that. Thought it was Dickens, TBH.

for hours every week, torturing my feet in those pointe shoes, forgoing weekend keggers to attend dance competitions . . . all that hard work become worth it when I heard Abby say those three magical words: "Mamrie is decent." It was like a son pining for his father's affection finally getting an "I love you" from Dad's deathbed. I was satisfied.

A few months later, I was home between some of my international jaunts. Not much had changed except that I was off the air mattress and in a real bed now. My mornings were spent nursing red wine hangovers and taking out the dried contact lenses* that I fell asleep in after my usual late-night dance party in front of

---

* True fact: I'm so blind that regular glasses are too thin for me. The one year I did wear glasses, I found out that one of my sketch teammates at Upright Citizen's Brigade thought I'd been doing a bit all year. He thought they were PROP glasses.

Beanz. This particular morning was especially tough because I had to go to a promo shoot.

In a few weeks, I was set to host the Shorty Awards in New York City. If you've never heard of them, congrats! You are the majority. The Shorty Awards are basically the Oscars of social media, and I was going to be their Billy Crystal. We were shooting a funny intro to the show, which combined my two favorite things—*Dance Moms* and dogs—the concept behind the video being that I am the Abby Lee Miller of pups, turning average pets into Insta celebs.

In the spirit of everyone's favorite Pittsburgh dance czar, I had my makeup laid on thick and my hair teased to the heavens. Seriously, there was enough hair spray lacquered on my head to deflect a bullet. I spent the next few hours corralling commoner dogs and yelling at their owners for their lack of Instagram presence and unimaginative captions. Guys, y'all have not lived until you've looked a tiny French bulldog in the face and made fun of him for not being able to breed naturally. It felt SO evil. I felt SO Abby.

Once the shoot was over and I was done individually apologizing to each of the pups, I headed to my ex's to drop off Beanz and pick up the last of my stuff from the house. It was quite the haul—the back seat alone had five garbage bags of clothes, not to mention trinkets, books, toiletries, the whole shebang. And don't get me started on that trunk, which was packed full of random shit I was saving for future videos.

While I was driving, I couldn't help but notice people were checking me out. Every light I stopped at, people in the crosswalks were giving me the eyes. I was serving young, skinny Abby Lee realness. It didn't hurt that I was also in a major bodysuit phase and rocking a white turtleneck à la Claudia Schiffer during the Fashion Cafe days. I looked good and I knew it, nodding as passersby checked me out. I wasn't even considering the fact that they could have been staring because they wondered why this woman, who was clearly a homeless hoarder living out of her car, would splurge on professional hair and makeup.

I was en route to Joselyn's to decompress over some wine when at the busiest intersection, in the hippest neighborhood in LA, I heard it. The *woop* of a cop car.

I looked in my rearview, and, sure enough, there was a cop with his blue lights behind me.* I immediately broke into a cold sweat. Did I have a gun in my car? Did I have condom filled with heroin up my ass? No matter that I don't even own a gun and there's no way I could fit that up my butt, but these are the things that run through my head when I'm around any type of law enforcement.

All the people I thought were checking me out before were *really* checking me out as two LAPD officers surrounded my car, one at each front-seat window. I was simultaneously mortified and terrified. I rolled down both windows and looked to the officer on my left.

"Ma'am, are you aware that your registration is six months expired?"

FUCK. I had totally forgotten. My registration had expired in October, then I filmed a movie, went to Australia, traveled for a month, then broke up with my boyfriend, then traveled more. I hadn't been driving consistently in six months. Also! I had never gotten my own car registered. To me, that was one of those boring tasks that my boyfriend took care of and I just assumed

---

* One time in high school, I was the DD for friends who were on Ecstasy and we got pulled over. I literally had to make them stop raving in their seats to the cop lights before the officer came to our window.

happened on its own, like the garbage being taken out, or the romance remaining intact despite not putting any effort in.

"I'm so sorry, Officer," I said, fighting back real tears. "I haven't really been in the country the last few months, and it completely skipped my mind."

"Let me see your license."

Let it be known that I am one of those idiot people who refuses to carry a wallet. I stick my ID and cards in the back pocket of whatever pants I'm wearing. It's a great way to avoid carrying a purse and also a fun way to induce a panic attack every time you think you've lost your ID . . . which is weekly-ish for me.

I began frantically looking through my things. "I know it's in here somewhere, I just—" I looked back at the driver's-side officer, who was having none of it. "Sorry, I'm just a little unorganized because I'm going through a major breakup and my stuff is everywhere and—"

"Ma'am, do you have your license or not?" he asked sternly. I swallowed hard and turned to him with eyes sadder than a geriatric basset hound. "I—I—I don't think I have it." I could feel a lump start to form in my throat like I'd swallowed a softball. I did not want to cry. Hordes of hipsters were walking by, and I felt pathetic.

"I'll be right back," he said, walking to the cop car. I looked in my mirror, wiping away the tears that had fallen.

"You're gonna be fine," I heard, just then noticing the other cop was still there. I had forgotten about him completely but was relieved to see his friendly eyes and Erik Estrada smile. I smiled back. "Sorry, I feel like a mess. I'm just— I'm going through a breakup, and my boyfriend usually took care of these things, and I moved out so my stuff is everywhere, and this isn't normally how I look and—"

"Hold on a second," he said, cutting me off. "Look in your rearview." I looked in the reflection, expecting to see Bad Cop coming back with handcuffs or a German shepherd. The only thing that could be more embarrassing than getting drug searched in the middle of Sunset Boulevard was them making me open my trunk to reveal . . .

1) Girl Talk board game
2) Dream Phone board game
3) Mall Madness board game
4) Novelty-size martini *and* margarita glass
5) Blender
6) Box of copies of my first book
7) Piñata that looked like a giant eyeball
8) Family-size bottle of Advil spilled everywhere
9) Fake E.T. hand
10) Replica of Michael Jackson's jacket from "Beat It"

(You think I might be exaggerating, but this was exactly what I had back there. Popping my trunk would've been a Pandora's box of questions and, no doubt, jealousy, because hot damn, those are some enviable board games.)

"What? What am I looking for?" I asked him.

"No, look at you in the mirror. You're telling me that gorgeous woman is single?"

I leaned back in my seat. Was this cop actually hitting on me? "You aren't going to be single for long. You're friggin' gorgeous," he continued. OMG. CHiPs had a thing for the teased hair and Abby Lee makeup! He was *digging* this look. "Let me see what I can do with my partner here. He's a real tight-ass." Apparently he wasn't the only tight-ass, I thought, as I watched him walk back to the car.

I tossed my hair in the mirror. Was I into this? This was the kind of scenario you only see in movies, specifically of the porn variety. After what felt like forever, CHiPs was back. "Okay, beautiful, here's the deal. You've got to get your registration up to date. Normally your car would be impounded for this.* Also, I told my partner that you found your license, or else that would be a five-hundred-dollar ticket. So, just write down some numbers and you'll just have a fifteen-dollar ticket." He handed me a form.

"Wait." I was confused. "I just write down a fake license number?" He nodded. "If it's not my real number, will this ticket even count?" He smiled. Damn, he really did look like Erik Estrada.

I wrote down some numbers frantically and handed it back to him. He handed me another paper. "What's this?" I asked. It was just a blank paper. "Oh, that's for you to write down your phone number." My jaw dropped. Guys. In retrospect, I am aware how much of an abuse of power this was. Like, what, I refuse to write down my number and then he gives me a real ticket or impounds my car? I couldn't say no. But I also didn't want to. He was real cute, and I was real sad and lonely.

"I'm Marco, by the way," he said, holding out his hand. I resisted the urge to tell Marco that I liked his polo and kept it cool. "Mamrie," I said, shaking his hand and handing him my number. Our beginning of a porn moment was interrupted when Bad Cop appeared at my driver's side. "Miss Hart, here's your warning," he said, handing me the fifteen-dollar ticket. "Please go get your registration sorted out. Then take care of this ticket."

"I will, Officer. I swear I'm not normally like this." Bad Cop walked off as Marco leaned in. "I'll call you," he said, then walked away.

---

* *Yeah, you'd like to impound this,* I thought but, thank god, I didn't say out loud.

I was stunned. Was it wrong of me to have gone along with Marco's obvious power move just to get out of a ticket? Was I a bad feminist? Was it wrong of me to have allowed my giant teased hair and heavy nineties makeup to subvert the law? Furthermore, if this look garnered such attention, why wasn't I dressing like this all the time?!

I decided to table my head full of questions for a moment, mainly because there were several cars laying on their horns, and instead just tried to sit with the emotion of gratitude.

If I had been done up like my normal self, I think I would've lost my car that day. But instead I drove off with a fake ticket and a new cop boyfriend. So, in conclusion, I have to give credit to Abby Lee. While I knock her style on the regular, it really goes over well for a certain audience.

This was literally seconds after the whole ordeal.
I don't even think they had pulled away yet, but I was
feeling invincible!

Unfortunately, that audience is full of SHIT. Turns out, Marco never called and the ticket *did* count. However, I didn't know that because I hadn't had my mail forwarded yet. I found out only when I was on vacation in Hawaii while writing this book and I got a voice mail from a collections agency saying my license had been revoked for failing to pay the ticket for six months and not showing up in court.

Luckily, even though I had to pay a fucking ridiculous fine, I wasn't taken to jail. Abby, on the other hand, is currently serving 366 days behind bars for that bankruptcy fraud charge, which is the only reason I had the balls to tell that story from Grace's show.

Give 'em hell in there, Abby! Also, please don't come for me when you get out. I have a gun and a butt full of heroin, and I'm not afraid to use them.

Pros and Cons

IT WAS A few months into singledom, and wouldn't you know it? I got invited to do another convention. YES. Another one. Even I knew it was excessive. At any point I expected my friends to perform a Convention Intervention, reading me their letters about how much they love me and need me to stop talking about myself on panels. But I didn't care! I was still very much into keeping myself distracted and my house was still 90 percent empty, so when San Jose asked me to come to their first-ever Comic Con, I quickly accepted.

They had decided to have a panel about YouTube, which felt like a weird one in the world of cosplays and nerd culture. Would I walk in and feel like a dweeb entering a football locker room? Or a quarterback walking into a game of Dungeons & Dragons? I had no clue! All I knew was that they were flying me there and putting me up for two nights, and I never say no to an opportunity to drink from a minibar in a hotel bed.

When I got to my hotel in San Jose, I was told I couldn't

check in to my room yet. Shocker. Part of me thinks that telling a customer that their room is being cleaned but should be ready in an hour is all a plot to drum up more business for the lobby bar. And guess what? I fall for it every damn time. The concierge hadn't even set down his walkie-talkie that he was using to "page housekeeping for an ETA" before I had saddled up to the bar. It was your classic hotel bar, one that hadn't figured out its identity yet. The type of bar where the top half of the menu is edamame and cucumber martinis but the table tent is advertising $3 Jager shots and a buffalo wing special.

It was there, Sake-to-me-tini in hand, that I discovered my new favorite activity: sitting by the window of a bar near the convention center during Comic Con. Honestly, it's like sitting front-row center to a parade. Some might argue it wouldn't be entertaining if you, like me, know only about 1 percent of the characters that people are dressed up as, but that's what made it so much fun! It was basically like being planted in front of a brand-new universe, or what I imagine Tokyo is like. Just a never-ending carousel of one insane look after the next.

For about three hours, I sat there, drinking up this alien spectacle. Turns out there are only a certain number of niche characters from *Sailor Moon* and *Silent Hill* you can watch walk past before you get desensitized. So, with my belly feeling like a boozy boba tea (a couple of martinis and a handful of edamame thrown in), I decided to venture out into day one of this convention.

People were buzzing everywhere, all moving together toward the convention center in intricate costumes. It was so packed that you had to time yourself to join the foot traffic, like someone waiting to find the right moment to hop into the swinging ropes of double Dutch.

I kept my head down so as to not be recognized before realizing that no one gave a shit. Nary a single double take. *Oh right*, I thought. *This isn't an Internet convention where everyone knows everyone on YouTube. Literally no one here knows who you are.* It was the first time I had been able to walk around a Con without being stopped by anyone. It was like I was wearing Harry Potter's invisibility cloak! (Which is about as nerdy a reference as you'll get from me.) Normally at a convention, I'd have to go through back doors and service elevators, hopping into town cars and being dropped off at service entrances to avoid the madness. But that wasn't the case here. I could bob and weave among the attendees totally unnoticed because who the fuck cares about a medium-tier YouTuber when there is a reunion of the cast of *Back to the Future* happening?!

After swimming upstream with the masses for a while, avoiding sharp and potentially dangerous costumes became tiresome for Two-Martini Mamrie, and I dipped out, taking solace on a creature-free sidewalk a few blocks away. I stopped dead in my tracks as a group of young girls with slicked-back buns, sequined outfits, and faces loaded with makeup ran past me to cross the street. *Those aren't comic book characters*, I thought to myself, a smile spreading across my face. *Those are* . . . and then I looked up to see a theater across the street from me, shining like a beacon in the sun. A banner was draped across the front, proclaiming, "Starpower Dance Competition March 18–20!" Was this a mirage?

I had no choice. I *had* to go in. I don't think I even moved my legs; I just levitated and floated into the performance hall the way you see abductees being lifted into a UFO.

I didn't get two steps into the lobby before I was hit with that familiar scent of stale venue + hair spray + new leather ballet slippers. It was pure nostril nostalgia. Or Nostralgia (trademark pending). In a sea of sci-fi, I had sniffed out my people!

The lobby was packed with girls bustling about practicing routines, merch tables selling pink tutus and purple boas, and parents scrambling to buy their kids whatever tiny duffel bag they wanted so as to not upset their angels on the day of the show. I pushed through the lobby and continued to the carpeted hallway. Nervous groups of girls practiced their routines in sped-up 8-counts, marking the steps. I saw one girl bossing around her teammates, clearly from nerves, to go over it one more time. Aww, the memories! I was that girl, the Nervous Nelly who would want to go over the routine nine hundred times before going out.

I peeled myself away from staring at strangers' children and pushed through the double doors to the theater. It was dead silent until a loud voice boomed through the speakers. "Contestant 257, we have Abigail with 'Baby Love.'" A light clapping trickled through the audience, and then the lights came up with a girl in head-to-toe sequins in a perfect starting pose ready to impress those judges. I looked around, knowing exactly what I'd see: a few dozen parents scattered throughout the crowd, not paying attention until their kid hit the stage. *Yes*, I thought to myself. I had found my mecca on the illustrious solo day.

I (very easily) found a seat away from any of the parents so they would not be tipped off that a rando woman had stumbled in from Comic Con. I looked around at the crowd, locking eyes for a second with a mom with a severe bob and an even more severe stare. Anxiety coursed through me until I realized I had nothing to worry about. For all they knew, I was just a nonsocial mom whose daughter was performing that day and who just happened to smell faintly of vodka. *How dare they judge me? They don't know how hard it is to raise my little Maggie all by myself,* I thought. *Lord knows her deadbeat father doesn't do anything but watch* CSI: Miami *and drink Bud heavy!* Yes, this inner monologue might've been the paranoid ramblings of a buzzed woman, but at least I had my alibi prepared if confronted by a parent.

For the next hour, I sat in that dark theater in complete bliss. I didn't want to forget one detail, but I also couldn't videotape it, seeing as that would be creepy,* but I did, however, take some notes on my phone to remember the spectacle, Siri acting as my stenographer as I quietly dictated to her without having to take my eyes off the action. Hell, if the parents in the audience didn't at least buy that I was a mom, maybe they thought I was some weird talent scout, looking for the next Maddie Ziegler.

Notes

- We are clearly on solo day today. There's a tiny, chubby girl with massive blond curls doing a dance to that fifties song "Stupid Cupid." Very confusing song. She says she's carrying his books at school but describes his lips as wine. Is this about underage drinking?
- Holy shit. This next solo has a prop, and it's a giant high heel. I repeat. A giant high heel has been wheeled out to the stage. She's doing a dance called "Call Me Princess."
- Get the fuck out of here. I just looked down at my phone for one second and there's a DIFFERENT high heel on-stage. This number is called "It's All About Me." This one is leopard print. Both pigtails are clip-ins.

---

* Also because I coyly Snapchatted ten seconds of one of the dances, and as soon as it ended, a voice came on the PA system reminding everyone that no videotaping was permitted at this competition.

- The next soloist is named Chloe, and, just in case the judges forget her name, a giant mirror with "Chloe" painted down the side has been rolled onto the stage. Sassy. Is this the prop category? Why are there so many props? The trophies should be handed to the dads for making these things/wheeling them onstage.
- Three Chinese cuties doing a dance called "The Lotus Fairies" to some plucked Chinese harp. While all these other girls are sassy and vain, this is just a straight-up traditional dance. It's so pure!
- BAHAHAHA. When the lotuses bowed, another song accidentally started. It's Nicki Minaj's "Anaconda," and those poor sweet girls are still slowly walking offstage, smiling at the judges, while the lyrics "Boy toy named Troy used to live in Detroit / Big dope dealer money" played them off.

I couldn't handle it anymore. I was the only one laughing, and I was straight-up *wheezing*. I busted back through those double doors and got the hell out of there, Severe Bob shooting me a *look* as I ran out. I took my invisible self back through the crowd before finally tucking into bed with my tiny Tito's and sodas.

The next day I headed to the chaotic convention center and met my fellow panelists, one of them being Alx James (pronounced "Alex"). I shook his hand, and before I could ask him if his mother was allergic to vowels, I got the question that no one wants to hear: "You don't remember me, do you?" he said with deadened eyes. I was mortified. "We've met before . . . at Scott and Mitch's house." Still nothing. "I was about forty pounds heavier, had a beard, and since then I've gotten a nose job?"

Motherfucker, what? You can't blame someone for not recogniz-
ing you when you've had a makeover like you were on the short-
lived reality show *The Swan*! While his calling me out was
ridiculous, I appreciated his lack of fucks given and decided I
liked this Alx guy, so as soon as the panel was over, I asked him
if he wanted to grab lunch. He agreed despite having recently
taken up smoking to help curb his appetite.

We sat there, ~~drinking~~ eating our lunch and getting to know
each other. We talked about YouTube over apps and our mutual
love of dogs over entrées, before realizing our biggest common-
ality over ~~another round~~ dessert: we both were utterly obsessed
with *Dance Moms*.

"Wait, you love *Dance Moms*, too?!" He nodded. "I watch it
religiously. It is my religion. I want a crucifix necklace with
Abby on the cross."

"I know," he said, pushing his food around his plate. "And
can you believe that Maddie is leaving after this season? Sia better keep that wig on to protect her identity because Abby is
gonna get out of jail and come for her."*

"This is going to sound weird," I said, as his eyes lit up like
he'd just been gifted a fresh carton of Marlboro Lights.

"I like weird. I *love* weird. What is it?" he asked.

"Would you have any interest in going back to the hotel, making to-go cocktails, then attending day two of the San Jose Starpower Dance Competition?" If you looked hard enough, you
could almost see the wrinkles in his forehead spelling out DUH
in cursive.† "Check, please!" he said, motioning to the waiter. We

---

* If you understood any of what that meant, congrats, we can be friends.
† This is obviously hyperbole. Of course Alx James doesn't have forehead wrinkles.

ran back to the hotel and through the throngs of costumed crowds, once again rocking that invisibility cloak of anonymity because no one gave a shit about these YouTube dorks.

Within a half hour, we made it into that dark auditorium, coffee cups full of vodka soda. We were in *heaven*. We clapped hard for the girls who gave a standout effort. Quietly critiqued them when they could've done better. Tried not to audibly gasp when one girl clearly fell out of a triple pirouette and just did a double. After about an hour, the lights came on. "There will be a ten-minute break for our judges, and when we return, we will start our jazz trios."

"Trios!" we said in unison with the joy of a child hearing the ice-cream truck. "You know one of them is going to fuck it up and bring down the points."

"Oh, I know. Just keep a duet. No one needs a Kendall thrown on top to mess up the rhythms of the fouettés!"

"Speaking of, you know some of the *Dance Mom* girls follow me on social media."

"Really?!" I asked, trying to squeeze one last sip out of that to-go cup.

"Yeah, they love YouTube. I bet they follow you, too." I looked around the room to notice a few girls staring, some whispering into each other's ears.

All of a sudden, it felt like that moment in *Toy Story* when Buzz Lightyear gets stuck in the claw machine at Pizza Planet and all the aliens turn their eyes to him. Or in the 1991 movie *Sleeping with the Enemy*, when Julia Roberts realizes her husband is indeed the enemy. Everything came into focus.

"We've been spotted," I said. It was like our invisibility cloaks had just been ripped off and we were standing there fully exposed. I grabbed his hand. "Don't make any sudden movements,"

I said. We slowly stood up and backed out of that auditorium as if we were face-to-face with a pack of mountain lions. Once we made it past the sign-in desk, we busted into a full-on sprint back to the hotel.

We slipped into our crowded lobby elevator just as it was clos-ing, pushed up against a couple of people in full special-effects makeup and masks and ridiculously huge fake weapons, a ninja, and a nightmare-esque Harajuku nurse. We were safe. I mean, safe enough considering I was currently standing beside a guy in a metal mask holding a flail above me. Just a casual, medieval ball covered in spikes dangling over my head. NBD.

"That was close," Alx said, trying to catch his breath.

"I know! Could you imagine?" The rest of the elevator re-mained silent, but I didn't care if they could hear us. We had our invisibility cloaks back on. "Like, what if someone asked us what we were doing there? Oh, ya know. Just being two sketchy adults watching other peoples' children dance in spandex with coffee cups full of vodka."

The doors opened to the third floor, and Alx stepped out. "So fun hanging," he said before the door closed. "Let me know when you want to go spy on children again. And next time, don't act like we're meeting for the first time, bitch!" The doors closed, and I was left alone with the Comic Con'ers. The only thing more quintessentially awkward than being in an elevator with strangers as Muzak faintly plays is being in one that's completely silent.

DING! The doors opened, and I stepped off by myself, happy to be away from the mayhem of it all.

"Excuse me, Mamrie?"

I turned around, expecting to find that I'd dropped my room key, but—wait a sec—how did they know my name? Then ol'

Spikey Ball asked from behind his sheet metal mask, "Can we take a picture? I'm a big fan. I won't tell anyone about the kids."

In that moment, in an elevator full of what looked like the first round of rejects from a Gwar audition, I knew I was the biggest freak of all. A convention pro who's anything but conventional.

Backstreet's Whack, All Right!

THERE'S NOTHING BETTER in life than a good documentary. I love a rock doc, a bio doc, an underdog doc. A doc about docks, doctors, Doc Holliday, you name it! I will find any excuse to go to a film festival and spend the days watching documentaries. Film festivals are my happy place. You watch movies all day, go to a delicious dinner, schmooze at a party with an open bar, wake up hungover only to grab a massive coffee (with Baileys), sit your ass back in a dark theater all day long, get dinner, and then go back out to parties to do it all again. It's like the plot of *Groundhog Day* but with more swag lounges and less Andie MacDowells (depending on the festival).

But sometimes I want to get my documentary on in a more relaxed setting. As in, I'm going to have to watch one at home without a Q&A with the director like a damn peasant. That's where my friend and fellow documentary enthusiast Joselyn comes in.

Every few weeks, Jos and I will text each other to see what veggies we have lying around in the fridge and then figure out what we can cook up together. We call these "inventory meals." It helps clean out the fridge, and Lord knows, I'm a fan of anything that resembles a cooking competition. Here's an example of this menu building challenge:

JOS: Woman, I got quinoa, a couple of sweet potatoes, a shit ton of cilantro and citrus, and an onion. Whatchu got?
ME: Siiiiick. I've got a can of black beans, some baked tofu, radishes, and tomatoes. Let's make cilantro lime quinoa, Mexican veggie and tofu bowls, and I'll quick-pickle the radishes for some added crunch and acidity on top.
JOS: Fuck yes. See you at 7.

This is adult female friendship in a nutshell. We cook and drink and settle in front of the TV with a bowl of yumminess, a big glass of sparkling rosé, and a doc on deck. This particular evening, we were extra excited about the night's viewing. The subject of the doc wasn't a pressing social issue or the life of some niche artist—nay. This documentary was about none other than . . . the BACKSTREET BOYS.

Let me just say out of the gate that back in high school, I liked my boy bands the same way I like my and my girlfriends' menstrual cycles . . . *NSYNC. Sure, Timberlake's ramen noodle curls looked like he was one bouillon packet short of a college dorm room feast, but that didn't matter to my fifteen-year-old self. And don't get me started on that "Bye, Bye, Bye" video.* But, guys, *Backstreet Boys: Show 'Em What You're Made Of* is a game changer. In one hour and forty-one minutes, I went from

---

* Seriously, that little smile he gives when he jumps off the ledge and lands on his feet like some sexy cat fully made sophomore me tingle in my boy-cut undies.

like to *love* with these dudes. Their band name did not hold up, because they were boys no more! They put the MEN in docu-MENtary. Especially Kevin.

"Oh my god, he's like the band dad! I love him!" Joselyn said between forkfuls of tofu.

"You can tell how much they really care for each other," I said, refilling our glasses. "I just want them to be happy! Especially Kevin!"

When the final credit passed the screen, we were cheering. I was officially in love with the Backstreet Boys, ten years too late. It's like when I fell in love with Paul Newman in fifth grade after watching *What a Way to Go!* before realizing he was an old man by then. Crushing. To this day it's still hard for me to walk through the salad dressing aisle without old feelings resurfacing.

I rolled home from Joselyn's that night with a Tupperware of leftovers and an airtight crush on the BSB. I laid in bed ~~farting~~ reading a very thick, smart-person book, but I couldn't get the doc out of my mind. I needed to know *more* about my newfound crushes. So, I took to my laptop to give the guys a quick Google. Maybe there would be pics of them getting together for a fun weekend or doing something adorable like having a picnic complete with three-legged races. *I bet AJ would make a joke about how he doesn't need a partner because he already has a third leg . . . as in his dong*, I thought, delighted in this completely made-up scenario I was creating for my own pleasure. I clicked on that Google search, and what popped up changed me forever.

"Backstreet Boys Mediterranean Cruise 2016!" What in Kevvy Kev's name was this?! I researched further. Apparently for five years running, the Boys had done a special cruise through the Caribbean with their superfans, each night putting on different performances and theme parties. This year, however, they were taking their maiden voyage across the Atlantic, for a trip leaving from Barcelona and docking in Cannes and Italy, before returning to the City of Lisps.

I immediately called Joselyn to share this news, which, if you are friends with me, you know means serious business. If I was being kidnapped by a drug cartel and had a moment to call the cops, I'd probably just text 911 "Ack! Totes being kidnapped! SOS ASAP! TTYL!" out of convenience. She answered.

"Jos, you're not going to believe this, but in two months the Backstreet Boys are doing a cru—"

"I'M ALREADY PRICING OUT FLIGHTS!" she yelled, cutting me off.

"It says here that there's a party with the Boys every night on the main deck. Holy shit! We could party with Kevvy Kev!" I screamed.

"And on the last night, they give an acoustic concert in the main hall. BSB unplugged!" she shrieked, with the sound of her laptop keys tapping feverishly in the background.

It was settled. In T-minus two months, we would be on a giant boat with two thousand BSB megafans, setting sail from Barcelona. Sure, we were going to have fun, but we were also going on a mission. Come hell or high water, Joselyn and I were going to meet and get a picture with Kevin.

Before I knew it, I had landed in Barcelona. It felt extremely surreal as I stood in the aisle waiting to deplane. What kind of idiots travel halfway around the globe to go on a cruise with a boy band?! Before I could further ponder whether this was a huge, and costly, mistake, I was snapped out of it by a thick Pennsylvania accent. "Howie is gonna remember you! Quit being an idiot, Chrissy!" I looked back and saw exactly what kind of other idiots would travel for this cruise. Behind me stood a mother/daughter duo, both rocking matching Steelers hoodies and speaking at a volume usually saved for Heinz Field.* The poor guy who'd been sitting beside them was staring at the exit like a dog with cheese on its nose, just waiting for the signal to go for it.

I made it through customs, got my bags, and found the nearest coffee shop to fuel up and wait for Jos. I hadn't had one sip of my latte before the two Steelers grabbed a table beside me. The daughter, who I guessed was in her late twenties, was still yammering about whether Howie would remember her from the past four cruises they'd been on as the mom *literally plucked her chin hairs.* I'm not talking about a quick "oh no, my pesky chin hair is back, better pluck it real fast." I mean a full thirty-minute session of chin-hair plucking in the middle of a café in front of dozens of people. If this was any indication of the type of ship people we were going to be on with, it was going to be a *long* five days.

After trying to block out Mama Steelers collecting enough chin hairs to fashion herself a Howie D voodoo doll, I couldn't have been happier to spot Joselyn coming out of customs. I grabbed her and changed her direction, shielding her from the horror that I had just witnessed. One of us needed to be unscathed.

That night, we popped from one tiny tapas bar to the next. In one particularly adorable one, with our table covered in cocktails and *papas bravas,* we started to mentally prepare for the cruise. Up until this point, it had been a whirlwind idea that seemed ridiculous. But we were here, damnit, and fewer than twelve hours from boarding this ship show.

---

* Obviously I had to Google the name of the stadium that the Steelers play in. Also, spoiler alert, it's not shaped like a giant ketchup bottle.

"I have no idea what to expect," Joselyn said, taking a long swallow of her negroni.

"Well, based on the folks on my flight, it's gonna be a doozy. Oh! I know. We should check the hashtag on Instagram. It's gotta be #BackstreetCruise or #BSBCruise2016. Something like that."

We asked the bartender for the Wi-Fi* password and tried to connect. It was slower than a snail on quaaludes, but eventually we were on! And OMG, was it a goddamn gold mine. People had been using the hashtag for *months* in anticipation of the cruise. We were straight-up poseurs compared to these die-hard fans.

We went in hard on those tags. I'm talking a deep dive of Instagram history. There were fans who had been on every BSB cruise since its inception. Fans who were meeting other fans that they had befriended from across the globe. Fans who were coming halfway across the globe solo! We picked out three favorites and gave them nicknames. . . .

1) **KEVIN'S ANGEL:** This woman was sporting a perfect tat of our beloved Kevin's face on her left biceps and none other than Buffy the Vampire Slayer's main squeeze, Angel, aka David Boreanaz, on her other arm.

2) **NICK'S CHICK:** This curly blond cutie couldn't be more obsessed with the baby of BSB. She had photos from upward of thirty meet-and-greets on her profile, spanning back through multiple Nick hairdos.† This one threw us off, because the girl looked like a beauty

---

* Besides "Where is your bathroom?" asking for a Wi-Fi password is the only other phrase I can say in more than five languages.
† Remember when white boys would twist their hair and throw some product in it for a one-night dreadlock look? The late nineties were truly the Depression era of hairdos.

queen: tan, fit, bright smile. But despite being able to get probably any guy she wanted, this hottie couldn't be harder for Carter.

3) **MISS'TERIOUS:** This fan didn't show favoritism toward any one of the guys in her IG feed. She did, however, demonstrate a *huge* love of face-altering phone apps. I'm not talking about the ones that smooth out your crow's-feet or plump up your lips a little. I mean the ones that give you full fake eyes and hair a la *Toddlers and Tiaras*. Every single photo used these filters, so it was virtually impossible to know what she actually looked like, besides having a distinctive labret piercing. To give you an idea of how doctored her photos were, here I am after using the app.

I'm sure you think I'm exaggerating about how bad the photoshopping was, but it was this level awful. Obvs I changed the labret for a lip piercing so as not to cop her style.

We boarded the cruise the next day ready for the adventure ahead. As we made our way down the narrow halls to our room, the scene felt familiar. Pairs of girls were standing outside their doors, decorating them with printed-out photos, construction paper, streamers, the whole Michaels craft store mother lode.

"Oh my god," I said to Joselyn as I stopped in front of a door covered in a world map with a tiny glued-on airplane showing a flight path from Florida. "This is just like the first week of college, when girls rush sororities." All down the hallway, girls were bustling about, decorating, singing, talking. This was a Backstreet Boys Sorority Semester at Sea.

After dropping our stuff off in our matchbox-size room, we headed straight to the bar, passing the pool deck along the way. Now, here is where the whole idea of a cruise is messed up. When you think "cruise," you probably think of tropical weather, neon bikini–clad girls dancing to "Rump Shaker," all the top visuals from MTV's *The Grind*. This was not going to happen here. It was fucking *freezing*. I don't know why I didn't put together that maybe the Mediterranean wouldn't be the warmest place in May. I just assumed you go on a cruise and it's tanning time. Not here. If you went out in a swimsuit for more than twenty minutes, you would look like you were doing some Laura Palmer cosplay.

But the strong gusts of wind and constant misting of rain and ocean water were no reason to not drink like we were on spring break. We headed to the bar in the ship's Mexican restaurant. "Ohhh, this jalapeño margarita sounds good," I said, passing the table tent menu to Joselyn. "Make that two of them," she said to the unamused bartender. I turned to Jos, but before I could dive into my idea for how to find Kevin, I was stricken with shock at our bartender's technique for making margaritas.

Guys, as a former bartender myself, there are few things as

horrifying as when you see someone pick up one of those dehydrated bottles of sour mix. Use fresh juice, for godssakes! Do you see a parrot on my shoulder? These aren't the pirate days, but I still don't want scurvy.* But I tried to block it out, to not be a bartending snob. That is until homeboy dropped the drinks in front of us. I looked at that glass like I was just given my *Fear Factor* challenge when I realized that these "spicy margaritas" were made with . . . PICKLED jalapeños.

insert Wilhelm scream here

The only time a pickled jalapeño should be in a drink is when you eat your taco directly over it and that shit falls in. Jos could see I was horrified, but at least we were horrified together. "Cheers to Kevvy Kev and possibly the weirdest five days of our lives," she said before we clinked our glasses and took a mouthful of vinegar. "How are they?" the bartender asked monotonously. "Amazing!" I said with a face that can only be described as those YouTube videos where a baby tries a lemon for the first time. Nothing like a margarita that tastes like sour syrup and quesadilla! We took them to the face, then had a few (safe) vodka sodas before hearing the music start up on the pool deck.

Each night brought a different theme party, the first one being "Bon Voyage." Supposedly people dressed up for the parties, but we were doubtful. "Here's for tonight," Joselyn said, handing me a sailor hat. "I also brought feather boas for 'Casino Royale' night, tiny Oscars for 'A Night at the Cinema,' and lace gloves and masks for 'Fifty Shades of Backstreet,' the closing party." Good Lord, Jos was a peach. She knows that I love a good theme, but I had been too distracted to pack correctly, what with my life

---

* Do you know what a pirate's ideal body type on a wench is? S'curvy! Bye, guys, that's my time on Earth! *straps on jet pack and jumps off planet*

Yes, those are BSB hats and sweatshirts. And as you
can see by Joselyn's face, we were an equal mix of
excited, terrified, motion sick, and drunk.

imploding and my living out of my car/suitcase and constantly
traveling and whatnot.

"Do you think people will really dress up?" I said, downing
the last of my drink. "I hate when people half-ass a theme party."
When we walked out to the pool deck, my question was answered. Everyone was in costume . . . barely. And by that I mean,
holy slutty Halloween, Batman! The deck was filled with booty
shorts–poppin', tits-up sexy sailors. It was as if booking the cruise
came with a 50 percent off coupon to "that section" of Party City,
and Joselyn and I were the only two who didn't get the memo.
These girls were going *hard* to get the Boys' attention.

We started to make our way through the sea of seawomen
but were stopped in our tracks as soon as we heard the first

measure of that first BSB single, "We've Got It Goin' On," come out from the damp speaker. Those sailors screamed and rushed the tiny stage so fast, you would've thought it was a mutiny. One by one the Boys appeared onstage, each rocking a crisp ship captain's uniform, with Kevin bringing up the rear. "Kevvy Kev!" Jos and I screamed in unison, clutching each other out of excitement but also because the wind was smacking us around.

Onstage, Howie grabbed the mic and started speaking to the crowd. I think they welcomed everyone to the ship, but I couldn't really hear above the screaming. These women were losing their minds, and voices, like this was 2001 and they had just been invited up from Times Square to the *TRL* studio. Joselyn and I stood there, waiting for the Boys to bust into song, or a synchronized dance routine, anything. But nope.

After Howie was done with his speech, the boys just kind of danced around the stage aimlessly, mouthing along to whatever pop song was playing over the speakers. They'd take turns walking to the edge of the stage and taking selfies with fans before breaking away to continue lip-synching along to Usher's "Yeah!" or whatever other decade-old pop song was being blasted. This went on for a half hour, the entirety of which Joselyn and I spent being very confused by what we were seeing. It was like a low-energy *Lip-Synch Battle* between five noncompetitive people. Or, thanks to their excessive use of lackadaisical groin thrusts, the third shift of a non-Union *Magic Mike* tour. Didn't matter, though. The women were bringing the energy of a bachelorette party, fawning over every tired move and face-palming others out of the way for their chance at a selfie.

"A photo with Kevvy Kev isn't going to be as easy as we thought," Joselyn said as she watched a woman attempt a crowd surf to get to the front of the stage.

"I have faith," I said. "But it's not gonna be tonight. Maybe later in the cruise, when everyone has already gotten selfies with them. Right now, they are hungry for their first kill."

We decided to head back to our room, passing through the decorated door gallery on the way. "Look who it is!" Joselyn hissed as she stood frozen in front of a door covered in photos. My eyes started darting everywhere. It felt like that scene in *A Beautiful Mind* when Jennifer Connelly discovers Russell Crowe's secret wall of newspaper clippings and schizophrenic scribbles.

There before us was the door of none other than Nick's Chick. All of the meet-and-greet photos from the hashtag were taped up, along with cut-out hearts. This girl had photos dating back to the days when AJ would unironically wear a fuzzy leopard-print cowboy hat and Howie had shoulder-length hair with a middle part. But we'd seen those photos; that's not what had us standing there, mouths agape. On either side of the door were posters that she had custom made. These were full on 24" x 36" posters complete with clouds and hearts surrounding them. Must've cost a fortune at Kinko's.

"We *have* to find Kevin's Angel and Miss'terious," I said, still in shock. "We're clearly not gonna get close to Kevin, so this is our new mission." We crawled into our tiny beds and drifted off as the boat charged toward Cannes, France, the first stop on the trip.*

When we arrived, the city was madness because we just so happened to dock during the film festival. Rather than be part of the paparazzi madness, Joselyn and I splurged on a guided tour of a hundred-year-old perfume factory outside the city. We

---

* Now, mind you, this was my second time going to Cannes that year. As someone whose previous beach experiences include almost being arrested at Myrtle Beach for flashing her tits out the back of a '97 Wrangler, clearly I had arrived. ☺

loaded onto a charter bus full of other cruise-goers and started winding up the mountains. It was *majestic*. Once there, we were ushered through an old factory as a woman with the most exquisite French accent showed us how they would press hundreds and hundreds of jasmine flowers into animal fat to extract the scent. The whole process was fascinating; particularly how hot the dudes were who manned the soap-cutting station. They'd be models back in the States, but here they were just humble factory workers who always smelled good? JESUS.

Of course, no touristy tour is complete without them trying to gouge you at the gift shop at the end. But this gift shop wasn't cheesy T-shirts and key chains—it was a full-on QVC-level demonstration of all the different scents that we could buy. Imagine a group of twenty women, most clad in Backstreet paraphernalia, passing around strips of paper to sniff, nodding their heads and deciding on their favorite. It was quite a scene. As I turned to my left to grab a swatch of their signature jasmine scent, I was met face-first with Kevin's face!

Not the real one, mind you. A tattoo of Kevin's face. I looked up to meet the smile of a woman who was at least six-three, rocking overalls, a sleeveless tank top, and a crew cut. *Could this be Kevin's Angel?* I thought to myself. Only one way to find out. I coyly moved to her other side and, sure enough, the other biceps had David Boreanaz circa *Buffy* plastered across it. I glanced over to Joselyn, whose face resembled mine during the jalapeño debacle. God bless her, Jos is so sensitive to smells that this was her hell. Her Smell Hell. She finally looked in my direction as I mouthed, *It's Kevin's Angel.*

"What?" Joselyn said loudly. I shushed her, which caused our tattooed conquest to look down at me. I smiled at her like a Fraggle caught by a Gorg. She smiled back and then continued listening to our tour guide, who was now offering package deals. I motioned Joselyn to come over and pointed at the tat. Her grin spread, and she silently lifted her hand for a high five. Two down, one to go.

Back on the ship, it was the "Casino Royale" themed party, so we draped our shoulders in our Party City feather boas, only to be met with a cruise ship full of women in floor-length ball gowns. After about thirty minutes of freezing out on the deck and watching the guys be twelve-people-deep for selfies in their Bond-style tuxes, we called it a night. The dream of meeting the Boys was becoming more and more futile. In the world of Bond, we were feeling like the two zeros in 007.*

The next day, we docked in Italy. Joselyn and I decided to forgo a planned trip with a bunch of people trying to sell us stuff and ventured out on our own instead. We knew that Pisa was only an hour's train ride away, so we figured we'd head there for lunch. Easy enough, right? WRONG. The town we docked in had no Ubers or cabs, so we walked three miles to the train station. By the time we made it to take the iconic picture in front of the leaning tower, I was such a hangry bitch that I almost just knocked the tower over with the sheer force of my mind. But we got that pic!

It had taken so long to get there that by the time we snapped a few photos and made fun of everyone else doing the exact same thing (it was somehow dumber when they did it), we only had time to grab a quick lunch before heading back. GUYS. I am not exaggerating when I say we ate the most delicious pasta of our lives during this quick trip. I knew the pasta would probably

---

* Fun fact! My first screen name, in sixth grade, was "Ballet007," because I was obsessed with dance—as you know—but I also wanted an edge. Like, I was somehow going to do barre work and then go order a martini at a bar. What a weirdo.

You can almost see me screaming, "Did you get the fucking shot?!" through my clamped-teeth smile.

be better because we were in Italy, and maybe it was a combination of the surroundings and the fact that we had been eating cruise ship food for three days, but this bucatini with fried sage in a creamy sauce that I'm assuming was made of reduced angel tears was one of the best meals I've ever had.

It was wrong to leave something we had just found that gave us such pleasure. It was like finding the one person who could make you reach orgasm, and then they jump off a cliff. I wanted to move to Italy just to be with this pasta. I wanted to become the first woman on Earth to marry a plate of food. But, alas, we still had one box left unchecked in our mission. We needed to find Miss'terious. Sure, we had only seen pictures of her with her face modified, but that wasn't going to stop us. So I *definitely* picked up and licked the plate with zero shame, and we headed back to the boat. I left a Pisa my heart in Italy that day.

That evening's party brought us a "Night at the Cinema." But rather than waste a free hand that could be better used to double fist, we left our fake Oscars in the room and headed to the deck in our normal clothes. Everyone else had really brought their A game that night. There were Marilyn Monroes, Chucky and his Bride, Beetlejuice, Superwoman. It looked like a convention for knockoff characters from Times Square—if everyone was there to make their ex jealous. And, yes, I do mean even that Chucky Doll costume was a li'l bit slutty.

We slammed a few drinks out of the gate to warm us up, or as I prefer to term it, we put on our "liquor ponchos." The Boys came out and did their lip-synching-and-selfie routine again as Jos and I stood there, observing a Minion bent over and backed up on a fellow Minion like they were re-creating Rihanna's "Work" video.

"You know what's a bummer?" I said to Joselyn as I watched a Shrek and a Donkey grind.

"That we'll never get to eat that pasta again?"

"Yes, to that. But also that it's been so goddamn cold that we haven't gotten in the pool once." I looked over to the empty pool and hot tub.

"Fuck it, let's get in the jacuzzzz!" Jos squealed. "I don't care what any of these people think. Let's suit up!"

And we were off! We ran down the decorated halls to our room, high-fiving Nick's Chick's poster on the wall, put on our bikinis, threw our dresses on top, and beelined it to the hot tub. By the time we got to the edge, I was amped on adrenaline, screaming, "Cannonbaaaaall!" as I started my approach. But the shadow of something made me stop myself from launching in at the last second.

"Oh, hello," I said to a figure in the hot tub. Upon closer look, it was the silhouette of a woman dressed as Ariel from *The Little Mermaid*, her face hidden in the darkness. "Sorry, we didn't see that anyone was in here."

"That's okay," she said quietly, emerging into the night. She had really gone all out. Mermaid tail, shell bra, red wig.

I stared at her. Something about her was so familiar. Then it hit me. I started imagining her normal eyes replaced with massive baby-doll ones and her regular mouth with huge fake lips. Her labret piercing switched with . . . HOLY SHIT. It was Miss'terious! Joselyn and I realized this at the same exact moment as evidenced by us grabbing each other's hands like Thelma and Louise before they drive over the cliff.

We slowly backed away as she retreated to her shadows. "Have a great night, Miss'terious," I said before we took off. As soon as we reached our rooms, we cracked open a bottle of red to toast. Screw that deck party; we were just fine whooping it up in our sardine can.

The next morning, the sun peeked through the blinds as the ship continued through the windy seas. It was our last full day and night on the cruise, and there was no port stop, just another full twenty-four hours on this island of BSB-yatches. We decided to skip out on such riveting activities as taking a cooking class with Brian and his wife (brilliantly named "Cooking with the Littrells"*), instead choosing to get a little day-drunk at the

---

* Did they not even try to be creative when naming these classes? This was Littrell'y the worst name they could've chosen. Ba da ching!

bar and then take a nap. We had the acoustic performance to look forward to that night, but we were prepared to sleep through everything else.

When we got back to our room, we were adequately tipsy and ready to conk out. Before I could swan dive into my bed, though, I noticed that our phone was blinking. "That's weird; we have a voice mail," I said, pushing the button and holding my breath. *What a nightmare it would be if there was an emergency back home and we were stuck at sea*, I thought to myself. I started flipping through a Rolodex of possible disaster scenarios, then hit Play to put myself out of my misery.

"Hi, this is [insert name here], calling for Marmie Hart." Honestly, after thirty-something years of having my name mispronounced, this didn't even elicit an eye roll. "Hi, Marmie. This is kind of random, but I work with the Backstreet Boys, and Kevin's bodyguard, Keith, is also his best friend since childhood. Anyway, Keith's daughter saw that you are on this cruise and is a big fan. We were wondering if you could meet with him to sign an autograph? Call me back when you have a sec!"

I hung up the phone slowly and looked at Joselyn, shaking my head. "Oh my god, what?! Is everything okay?!" I sat on the edge of my tiny bed. I could hear her own disaster Rolodex flipping at lightning speed. "Mamrie?! What is it?!"

I took a deep breath, raised my head to meet her eyes, and smiled. "We're one step closer to Kevvy Kev."

Within five minutes of chatting with the lady who left the voice mail, Jos and I were walking to the piano bar to meet this Keith so I could help a dad grab some street cred for his, no doubt, angsty teen with great taste in YouTube content.

"You're Mamrie?" he asked, with a bit of disbelief in his voice.

I think he was expecting another Miss'terious or Kevin's Angel, not two normally dressed chicks who had an air of being over it.

"You know it," I said before grabbing his phone to record a video for his daughter, letting her know how cool her dad was.

"I can't thank you enough. She's gonna freak out. Hey, you should come to the after-party tonight."

Jos and I shot each other a look. "To be honest, Keith, we haven't loved the parties. It's kind of a shit show." I couldn't help but be truthful to his sweet, good ol' boy Kentucky face.

"Oh, I know. The fans can get a little . . . let's just say 'intense.'" We chatted for a bit, and he got my number so he could text me his daughter's reaction. Joselyn and I said good-bye and headed back to the room, disappointed. We had gotten one degree closer to Kevin, but no cigar.

Laying on our tiny beds that afternoon, we decided we'd go to the show and then call it an early night. We needed to be fresh for Madrid. The show itself was totally excellent and worth putting up with the screaming throng of women around us. Truly, you haven't lived until you have watched the Backstreet Boys sit on stools, singing acoustic versions of "I Want It That Way" and "Backstreet's Back." Was it cheesy? Yes. But like a finely aged parmigiano reggiano lightly dusted over the best GODDAMN PASTA YOU'VE EVER EATEN.

After their fifth encore, we pushed ourselves through the throngs of formal dresses* and went back to our room, ready to call it a night.

All of a sudden, my phone dinged like a text was coming

---

* Yes, more formal gowns. It was like one last-ditch effort to have their fave BSB look into the crowd and go, "You, yes, you in your blue tulle floor-length that was previously a bridesmaid dress and you want to get one more wear out of it. You. I love you."

through. "That's crazy," I said, picking up my phone. "Nothing has come through since we left Italy. Watch this be AT&T to tell me I've got roaming charges from the sea the whole time."

Girl, where you at? Come hang! I want you to meet
Kevin!—Keith

I dropped my phone and looked at Joselyn. "Mamrie, I swear to God, that face! Unless someone died this time, that face is not okay," she said.

"Oh, you's about to die," I said, handing her my phone. She read the text to herself, locked eyes with me, and then we both crashed through the door at high speed, getting stuck like we were Lucy and Ethel.

We ran through the boat. Everyone had gotten out their rhinestone prom attire to get decked out for the final theme: "50 Shades of Backstreet." For those of you over thirty, it looked like a lost segment from the show *Real Sex* that used to be on HBO in the nineties. It wasn't the type of crew you were used to seeing decked out with a leather crop; it was more like walking in on your fifth grade social studies teacher in a sex dungeon. We pushed our way through the pleather and up to the front lounge of the boat to find Keith.

Guys, I'm not going to go into all the details of the night because they are both surreal and super blurry. But let's just say that within thirty minutes, Joselyn and I were sitting in a private room with Keith and KEVVY KEV, drinking a bottle of Pappy Van Winkle and laughing our asses off. Kevin was wearing lace across his eyes for the night's theme, and I believe I told him it looked like he had "ratchet panties" on his face. At one point, I looked over and Joselyn was telling him all about how we came

I think my face says it all. Let it be known that Jos and I both have ZERO recollection of what we talked to him about for several hours.

on the cruise because we loved him in the doc. It was weird, and perfect, and ~~sadly~~ totally innocent because he is a married man.

We somehow made it back to our room and passed out happy for what felt like about five minutes before someone was banging on our door. "No thank you," Joselyn mumbled, thinking it was housekeeping. But they wouldn't stop knocking. I looked at the clock on my phone. It was seven thirty A.M. Mind you, we hadn't even gone to sleep till five thirty. I only knew this from checking my Snapchat.*

I dragged myself to the door only to discover a very

---

* Isn't it fun how back in the day when you blacked out you would get random flashes of memory throughout the day to jolt your regrets? With today's technology, you no longer have to be hit in the face with these memories; just look at one of your social media timelines for immediate cringing!

stern-looking captain—I'm talking full-on *An Officer and a Gentleman* white suit. "You gotta be out! This boat is leaving!"

"We'll be out in five," I croaked.

Joselyn and I were zombies. The blasting of the cruise ship's horn felt like a personal attack on our irresponsibility of oversleeping *and* our hangovers. But it didn't matter. We zipped up our ramshackle suitcases, pulled up the handles, and high-fived without saying a word.

We came. We saw. We Kevvy Kev'd. Ratchet panties and all.

Pity Party

BY THE TIME summer officially started, I was exhausted. Between Paris and Amsterdam and the cruise, I had spent more time abroad than I had in my new house. Not that I was complaining! This globe-trotting was exactly what I had needed to distract me from life. It had felt good to get out of LA, away from memories and responsibilities, and just let loose. That spring had been one giant spring cleaning to deal with the breakup. And, wouldn't ya know it, it worked! Everything from losing my shit in Paris to being stoned and crying to the Dixie Chicks singing "Landslide" while being the cream to my friends' Oreo had gotten everything out of my system. It was like I had been a sponge, filled with guilt and sadness and just plain grieving. Those trips wrung out that sponge, and now I was ready to enjoy my clean brain . . . not to mention absorb some new love along the way.

Part of me believed that once word of my newly single status got out, there would be a proverbial running of the bulls, with me in a red cocktail dress hauling ass from an onslaught of men.

I was equally terrified that there would be radio silence, that I would go, "Hey, everybody! Guess who's single?!" into an abyss, check my watch, and then after five minutes, a male voice would finally echo back, "No one cares!"

My friends assured me that my dating skills would come back like second nature. I am here to tell you that sadly it was not as easy as they claimed. While I was cozy in my relationship, all of these "advancements" in dating had happened. I felt like I had been thawed out after being cryogenically frozen for a decade, or like I was Kimmy Schmidt emerging from the bomb shelter, saying weirdo dated phrases like "talk to the hand." Texting, DMs, sexy Snapchats? None of this had existed when I was last single. I met my ex in 2006. Back then, if someone said "dating app," they were probably referencing the mozzarella sticks they got at Chili's during their last date. Texting was just a way to communicate where you were going to meet, and that was the end of it—none of this flirting via text and waiting to text back for a certain amount of (extremely anxiety-producing) time. The word "emoji" didn't even exist, and *forget* about sending a sassy, over-the-shoulder butt shot. The quality on flip phones was so bad, your ass would've been in 8-bit.

Despite my apprehension, I was determined to polar-bear plunge back into the scene and finally go on a date—my *first* first date since 2006. I started asking my friends to hook me up with someone, figuring that a friend-of-a-friend approach would be a safe way to get back into it. Their response was inevitably, "What's your type?"

"Hmmm," I would say, tapping my chin. "I would say my ideal type is like a Courier New or Times New Roman." Once they finished rolling their eyes (turns out not a lot of people are fans of font jokes), they would still be waiting for an answer that I didn't have. My previous boyfriends from high school on were all very blond, blue-eyed, almost Nordic-looking dudes. But I wouldn't say that was my "type." Maybe I wanted to date a dark-haired, bearded guy. Or a guy covered in tats. Or a Spanish guy. Or an Indian guy. I was ready for my dating life to be an Epcot of possibilities.

While I didn't have physical requirements on lock for my future beau, I did have a specific list of personality traits I was looking for. I told my friends to hook me up with any of their hot, successful, funny, ambitious, kind (did I mention funny?) friends. Tall order, right? Oh, I forgot tall. Add that in there, too. And it was tough! I remember sitting with Joselyn, racking our brains over a bottle of sparkling rosé, about who I could date. Every name mentioned was someone who was either married, had a serious girlfriend, or just came out. Then I remembered a guy I had done a show with a year or so earlier. He was handsome and funny but definitely married.

"Not anymore," Joselyn said between sips. "Homeboy is divorced."

"I am just going to throw it into the universe," I said, holding up my pink bubbles in the candlelit oyster bar. "Universe, I would like to go on a date with [so-and-so]." I felt ready. I felt bold. I felt like we should open another bottle of rosé, and, damnit, we did.

The next morning, I had to get some coffee in my bloodstream to make up for the rosé-a-thon. I hopped in that hot new car of mine and popped over to my local coffee shop. Windows down and latte in hand, I drove back to my house, eager for the day ahead. And just as I rolled up to a stop sign, there across from me was the dude in his car.

I had manifested him. Literal **MAN**ifestation.

We both proceeded through the stop sign, rolling past each

other slowly with our windows down, definitely checking each other out. But it was too fast to say hi.

I immediately sent him a DM on Twitter (the modern-day Civil War letter romance) and basically said, "We just made eye contact, but it was too fast to say hi, so hi." This was the first time I had ever slid into someone's DMs. I was anxious. Normally the only place I do some sliding is at water parks and Cha-Cha/Electric Slides at weddings. I put down my phone, immediately picking it back up to reread my message twenty times to make sure it wasn't dumb, when DING! He responded. "That was you? Looking good!" I was in. Three days later, and we were meeting for dinner.

I was freaking out from nerves, as evidenced by the sheer amount of bodysuits I tried on, overanalyzing each crotch-hugging look in the mirror before trying on the next. *What if it's not a date in his brain?* I thought. *What if he's just being nice, and here I am showing up with date-level cleavage? What if we run out of things to talk about in the first five minutes and it's just awkward silence over our entrées? What if he tries to kiss me? OHMYGOD, what if he* doesn't *try to kiss me?*

I was filled with more "what"s than the beginning of Macklemore's "Thrift Shop," but all that anxiety dissipated when I got there. It was easy to talk to him, and he seemed like the nervous one. The date ended up being off-the-rails fun. *FUCK*, I thought to myself. *Here I am on my first first date in more than ten years and I already like this guy. Is this too much? Should I pump the brakes?* I proceeded to do what anyone going through inner turmoil does: I questioned my decision and then rationalized it.

BRAIN: You should be playing the field.
HEART: I hate sports!

BRAIN: You gotta sow your wild oats.

HEART: I have zero interest in farming.

Our dinner date turned into dominating the jukebox at my favorite dive, making out at my house, and then saying good-bye early the next morning because we both had flights to catch. We were both going to be gone for a week and a half, and I was curious to see if that meant any communication. I didn't know what the rules were on this type of thing, but I didn't have to wonder for too long, because he texted me midday. We continued texting a few times a day, just casual, cute "what are you up to?" stuff. Four days after our first date, he asked when I was coming back.

Me: I'm headed to NC tomorrow to meet my new niece, but I'll be back Monday.

Him: You're kidding me. I'm going to NC tomorrow for four days. We should meet up.

Are you fucking serious, universe? First, I manifest the dude I'd met once to pull up to the same stop sign as me; now we were going to be hanging out in my home state? I released the emergency brake in my brain. This was an Indiana Jones–style boulder coming down the hill, and there was no stopping it.

For the sake of word count, I'll speed up the next two months. We hung out a few times a week, going to concerts, overnights at the beach, and comedy festivals, and every night ended with dancing. We were having a *blast*. One night, he asked me if I was his girlfriend. I was terrified at the idea of being someone's person again, but looking at him in a seedy bar in Santa Monica after another perfect night, I said, "Of course." It was fast. And it was magical.

And it was over before I knew it.

At one point around the two-and-a-half-month mark, we couldn't see each other for ten days because of travel schedules. But still, because we were a modern couple, we FaceTimed every night.* He sent me love songs to listen to. I would send him cute selfies that looked effortless but I probably took sixty pics for every one sent to make sure I looked hot. And then, when we were finally in each other's presence again, he sat up and turned to me and exhaled. I knew what was coming from that one breath. I literally said, "Holy shit, you aren't doing this to me" off a single exhale. And I was right. It took all of five minutes for him to tell me he "just had a little voice in [his] head saying it isn't right" as I paced and shook my hands like the Crazy Eights improv exercise. I was shocked. I didn't need details. I didn't need to hear how great I was. That I was the kindest, funniest person he's ever dated. I needed to get the fuck out of his apartment because he didn't want to be with me, and I didn't want more words to replay and overanalyze in my head later.

I walked out of his building in complete shock. I felt like I'd just been in a car crash. One that you don't see coming; you're just punched in the face by airbags. The type where you walk away from the wreckage fine, but you can't believe everything is totaled. You don't know whether to bawl your eyes out, or scream at the top of your lungs, or just laugh because it's all so surreal.

AND THERE THEY WERE.

Those *feelings*. Those things that I felt I was missing out on in my twenties emerged, and damn. Suddenly, rejection and heartache and being alone didn't sound that glamorous.

When I got home, I broke out one of those wineglasses that

---

* Look at me, living in the future!

fits a whole bottle, filled it to the brim, and took down the whole thing before passing out from ugly-crying exhaustion. The next morning, I woke up with the kind of hangover that happens when your body is suffering from equal parts dehydration from drinking and crying. In a rare moment of morning motivation, I decided to take my friend Sarah up on her offer to go to Pilates to distract myself. The struggle was already real from the wine I'd drank the night before, but the combination of a two-minute plank and Robyn's "Dancing on My Own" blasting through the speakers broke me, and I started crying in my plank position. Normally I was humiliated in plank pose because I could barely hold it for thirty seconds, now I was trying to hold in my abs *and* my tears? I couldn't do it.

I walked over to Sarah, who was still in perfect form, and crouched down. "I gotta get out of here. Will you take care of my mat for me?" I whispered.

"Of course, babe, I'll text you after," she said. That bitch wasn't even winded.

Back home, I didn't know what to do with myself. So, naturally, I checked his social media. Ladies, gentlemen, whoever is getting fucked over by someone . . . for the love of Beyoncé, do NOT check that person's social media. Why? Because while your new pillowcase is tie-dyed from mascara tears, that mo-fo will be posting a new haircut selfie with a smirk. A damn smirk!

I tried to play music to distract myself, but with every skip of the Pandora station, I was smacked in the face with some sort of tie-in tune.* It got desperate, y'all. And by that I mean, I listened to Fetty Wap. I don't even *like* Fetty Wap. But there I was, sadly

---

* I swear to God, our go-to band was Guns N' Roses, and I heard "Sweet Child o' Mine" on the radio six times the next day. SIX.

dancing in front of Beanz to "Trap Queen." Even Fetty's monotonous singing made me think of this dude.

"And I get high with my baby"

I mean, technically we never smoked weed together, but we did love to drink, so that applies!

"I just left the mall, I'm getting fly with my baby"

He loved to shop! We went vintage T-shirt shopping on our third date and did, indeed, look fly!

That's when I realized I needed to turn things around. I couldn't sit alone in my house, feeling sorry for myself. No, I was going to do what I do best: invite a bunch of people over to get drunk and have fun as a means of distraction. If I was going to have a pity party for myself, I might as well make it a pity *rager*.

I grabbed my phone and texted all my fun friends—ones from my New York days, my college days, and some YouTube buddies. Party at my house tonight. I'll have booze and tacos. 8pm.

QUICK TIP: Don't invite people to a party way out in advance. The best time to invite people to a party is the day you are throwing it. Everyone who shows up had nothing else to do and were stoked to get that text. There are so many times we get an invite two weeks early and it sounds fun, but when the day rolls around and you get that Evite reminder e-mail, you ain't feeling it. When you throw a same-day party, everyone there wants to be there and is ready to whoop it up.

I stocked my fridge with beer, covered the counter in liquor and mixers, went to the local taco place and got a full taco bar spread and one hundred taquitos, and tried to keep the dude out of my head until eight P.M. rolled around. Sure enough, when the clock struck ocho, I was decked out in a red Wrangler bodysuit, welcoming folks as they started to trickle in. An hour later, my house was *packed*. People were seriously throwing down. Everyone around me was knocking back shots and hula-hooping in my living room. At one point, someone was filming slow-mo videos of tortilla chips being poured over their head.

As the night went on, I caught up with old friends, I laughed, I bitched about the breakup. My friend Molls brought me a card that read "Fuck anyone who isn't obsessed with you." I pitied and I partied and I cried and I laid on my bed laughing hysterically with a belly full of tacos surrounded by my buds. I felt more emotions coursing through my bodysuited bod than I'd felt in years.

I didn't need to block out the sadness that was so new to me. I needed to sit in it, take it in. This wasn't a movie I was watching; this was *my life*. I couldn't fast-forward. I needed these lows to feel the highs. I just hadn't in so long.

Everyone cleared out around three A.M., and I crawled into bed with Beanz at my side. *This year is crazy*, I thought to myself. But this was my test. I hadn't been bucked off the horse with my long relationship; I had done a safe dismount like an Olympian finishing her dressage performance. *This. This* was being bucked off. And goddamnit, I wasn't gonna stay down.

I threw the comforter off my bed, much to Beanz's dismay, cranked Ginuwine's "Pony" up on my speakers, and got that Wrangler up for one more dance. While this image would have seemed sad a few months earlier, now it felt empowering. "Fuck anyone who isn't obsessed with you," I said into my reflection as I whipped an imaginary lasso above my head. This horse was back on its track.

Get Online, Fellas!

REMEMBER THAT AMAZING horse analogy at the end of my previous chapter? Well, I might've been ready to hop on a (hung like a) horse, but the stables were empty. Trust me, I was looking! I had even acquired a wing woman in my hunt for dudes, my also newly single friend Veronica.

Veronica, or Vero, and I had known each other from my sketch comedy days, back when we were on a team together at the Upright Citizens Brigade. We hadn't been regularly in touch since we had both moved to LA three years earlier, but we were able to sniff out each other's singleness pretty quickly. Her, by seeing I had dropped weight, got a spray tan, and was constantly partying in my Instagram, me because she was posting just a few too many lyrics from Rihanna's *Anti* album. No shame in our game.

Vero and I became attached at the hip, prowling like two jaguars in the night, praying for prey. But no luck. People always say there's plenty of fish in the sea, but I kept casting my net and pulling up spare tires and litter. Things were not looking good for single Mamrie. If you had run into me on the street, my smile and demeanor would say "carefree and grounded," but my brain was a constant loop of 2 Live Crew's "Me So Horny." I ain't even gonna lie. Part of the reason I turned this book in late is because I was so distracted by trying to ~~get laid~~ meet a guy that I couldn't focus on writing.

After a few months of doing all your traditional stuff, like going to bars and attending every party we were invited to where the host promised there might be at least one cute, single dude, I found myself on a girls' trip to Hawaii with some of my faves.

"You've got to join Bumble," my friend Renee told me over morning mai tais.

"I don't think I can online date," I said, motioning the bartender for another round. "It feels so impersonal with all the swiping. I feel like people get desensitized."

"It's a numbers game, Mamrie. You gotta go out there and date randoms! See what it's like to go out with someone just once, or just three times, or date a few people at the same time," she continued. I put the drink's tiny umbrella behind my ear, contemplating. Maybe it was the combination of rum drinks coursing through my body without any food in it, but for the first time ever, I was considering it. Going out to meet people the old-fashioned way sure as hell hadn't been working for me— what did I have to lose?

So I bit the bullet and went into the App Store and downloaded Raya. If you haven't heard of Raya, it's basically a dating app that you have to get approved to be on. No one knows what the exact algorithm to get on it is or who the hell decides it. I like to think it's some cloaked council standing around a fire pit, holding each applicant's head shots up one by one and tossing the rejects into the flames. But, in truth, it's probably just some straight-outta-college intern who checks to see if you have a decent face/number of Instagram followers. I know this sounds corny as hell, but joining it was more of a hurdle of safety than anything else. I needed to be able to cyber-stalk these people to make sure they didn't cyber-stalk me. Imagine this . . .

You go out with a dude from a dating site and really hit it off, maybe even end the date with a kiss. Then when he drops you at your doorway, you run inside and immediately check his Instagram. *Cool, he goes to lots of concerts*, you think. *Oh, and his friends seem fun and are attractive. That's a good sign.* You scroll and scroll until OMFG! Down in the archives there's a picture of him standing beside you at a YouTube convention meet-and-greet. There he is, wearing a shirt with your catchphrase on it. I know this sounds insane, but it could happen! I had to take precautions. (And even if I wasn't an Internet person, I think some light social media stalking before a date is a good safety precaution for any woman.)

Within twenty-four hours, I was accepted to Raya. I let the app sit on my phone for the rest of the trip, profile totally blank, and didn't open it once. I'd occasionally hit it when trying to get to my Instagram and then would hurry to close it as if I had accidentally FaceTimed my parents. Sure, I had downloaded it, but I hadn't crossed the official threshold of being a person who "online dated." For the time being, it was my little secret.

But a few weeks later, when the glow of my attempt at a tan had faded and the five pounds I had gained from mai tais had become an official resident on my belly, I sat at my kitchen counter looking at the Raya icon on my phone as my girlfriends gabbed around me.

I sipped mezcals on the rocks as they regaled me with their

latest dating adventures. Five drinks in and I dropped the act. "You guys, I joined Raya." The sound that came next can only be described as an a capella group of pig squeals. My phone was immediately swatted out of my hand as they started talking over one another about what should and shouldn't be in my profile. First, they had to find the right photo. With their help, I picked one with a full smile to show my adorable gap, one with my dog, one being silly, one being sultry, and one professional photo that I had to creatively crop so it didn't have a cheesy Getty Images watermark.

Next up was music. You see, this specific app had your photo slideshow play along to a thirty-second clip of any song you wanted. This was a *big* decision. Do you go cool and put up a deep cut, like a Portuguese Bowie cover, à la *The Life Aquatic* soundtrack? Or do you just cut to the chase and throw up "My Neck, My Back" by poet laureate Khia?

Within twenty minutes, I decided that the true essence of my personality could be summed up in the first thirty seconds of "Mr. Brownstone" by Guns N' Roses. Nothing says "click the heart on this cool-ass bitch" like the instrumental intro to a song about heroin addicts. But it was SO right, for several reasons. First and foremost because I FUCKING LOVE GUNS N' ROSES. They are the epitome of eighties Sunset Strip no-fucks-given rock, a time I have always idolized. I remember being five when *Appetite for Destruction* came out and wishing I could be a hot groupie from their videos. I might've even worked the trunk of a sapling in our backyard like a pole, but there is no photographic evidence, praise Jesus.

The other reason I chose this song was because it was special to me at that exact moment. The best date I had with ol' Pity Party dude was when we went to see Guns N' Roses. Both of us were huge fans, but neither of us had seen them live, because, let's face it, without Axl and Slash, it's not Guns N' Roses.

Seeing the *authentic* GNR was freakin' *magical*. We had floor seats, and when they hit the stage, Pity Party started bawling his eyes out. But not in a "what a pussy" way. In a "holy shit, I am so happy I am getting to witness this" way. It was sweet.

By the second half of the show, the shock of actually seeing them live had waned and we were just straight-up rocking out. But during the final riffs of "Sweet Child o' Mine" in the second encore, the man could not stop crying. Everyone was filing out, so we joined the crowd, but twenty yards toward the exit, and there went the waterworks again. He sat down in the nearest seat, and I gently rubbed his back, knowing that he just needed to get it all out.

At one point, an employee who was trying to usher people out approached us. "Ma'am, I'm gonna need you to move toward the—"

"Look, we are breaking up after four years. Can you please just give us a minute?!" I snapped back. His face dropped, eyes as big as whoopie pies. "Take your time," he said, and continued herding the human cattle out of the stadium. I had nailed it. Pity Party was clearly impressed with my quick thinking. Or at least I had thought he was, because meanwhile, he was internally pulling a Shania Twain. . . .

"So you can convincingly portray dumping me after several years just so I can cry about a favorite childhood band for a few extra minutes? That don't impress me much!"

Anyway, as you can see, I adore Guns N' Roses and secretly hate that my magical night was tarnished with the subsequent garbage that went down. So! I used that song as an internal anthem to show myself that I was *over it*. No two-month rebound was going to ruin one of my favorite bands. I was taking that shit back.

Once the girls left, it was time to start checking out what Raya had to offer. Seeing as this was an *exclusive* app, I was hoping for like-minded people—writers, producers, creatives. I took a deep breath and a big sip of mezcal, and after loading for what seemed like an eternity, there it was. My first offering. And it was . . . drumroll, please . . . John Mayer. BAHAHAHA. I nearly threw my phone across the room in disgust. I immediately hit X instead of ♥.

It didn't take twenty swipes before I realized something. If you've ever watched *The Bachelor*, you will see how the producers strategically label the contestants' professions to either make them look great or like complete idiots. After scrolling through the app, I noticed that it was basically a rotation of only a few professions. Surely, some of these guys had to be inflating their résumés. Like, not every guy can be a . . .

1) Photographer

We get it. You can afford a camera that can take a great photo. That alone does not a photographer make. Throwing an Instagram filter on a photo of a potted succulent doesn't make you a pro, people!

Now, these guys weren't all poseurs; there were some actual editorial photographers on there. But even they didn't interest me. Most of their profiles contained *waaay* too many artsy black-and-white photos of nearly naked chicks. I understand that you're trying to build your portfolio, but I can't have a boyfriend who spends his afternoons with up-and-coming Russian models posing topless on a Malibu beach and expect him to be turned on when he comes home to find me in sweatpants, eating falafel with my hands.

2) Writer/Filmmaker

As someone who's written a couple of movies and, hopefully, TWO bestselling books, all I have to say is . . . in the words of Whitney Houston, "Show me the receipts." In LA, "writer" can sometimes be interchangeable with "unemployed person who is great at staring intently at a Final Draft document on their laptop at Starbucks, but when no one is watching, they toggle over to Tumblr." In most cases, it didn't seem worth the risk.

3) Pro Surfer

I mean, come on, how many people actually make a living being sponsored by Billabong? Even if these guys weren't full of shit, a pro surfer was a no-go for me. Surfers wake up at, like, four A.M.! I'm also not about that life of lying in bed next to someone who makes me want to suck in my stomach every time I'm the little spoon. A good body is great. But a great body is a pain in the ass.

Despite my doubts, I had to admit that a lot of these dudes were cute, so I hit some hearts. And that is where the message stage of online dating came in. Here's what I've learned about this experience: people either come at you WAY too hard, or they send a message and once you've responded, they disappear into thin air, as if they never had any intention of making a connection or having a conversation or, GOD FORBID, a face-to-face interaction. There were a lot of these dead ends at first, but after a few days, I got into my groove and had some real conversations happening.

Being on Raya became an all-consuming process. A free five minutes before going out with a friend? I was on the app. Said friend gets up to go to the bathroom? I was on the app. Said friend is busy going hard on our "shared" app? I was on that damn app. I've never been a person who downloads games to their phone. In fact, the last time I was super into a handheld digital game was way back when I had a Game Boy. And now, I was playing a literal Game of Boys. I loved it!

At the recommendations of my friends, I was messaging with a few dudes at once. Might as well keep my options open, right? One of the more promising ones was a pro basketball player. Sure, he was on a team on the other side of the country, and b-ball players are notorious for being players off the court, but our messaging felt like an ego boost. He was really sweet, even letting me know that my latest video was funny or my Instagram post was pretty. His team was going to play the Lakers soon after we started talking, and he said he wanted to see me. But when the time came, he ghosted.

A few weeks later, I went out with a normal-seeming hot lawyer, and by the end of the night, we went back to my place for one more drink and (hopefully) multiple smooches. We cracked open nightcap beers and started playing each other our favorite songs, taking turns playing DJ. Now, I've always considered myself to have pretty great taste in music, so this is a fun flirt tactic for me. As I played him the Talking Heads, the Clash, all the top "The" bands, he nodded along like he loved them. We were totally vibing—that is, until he took over the tunes and started blasting the only three-letter acronym less attractive than HPV. . . . And that is, EDM.

Song after song—at least I think they were different songs, but who can be sure because they *all* sounded the same—he tried to convince me that this act was great. They were not. There's a reason why people take so much Molly at EDM concerts. But he was into them, and I was into how excited he was. Then he played me his favorite song of all time. Guys, I kid you not when I say I sat there at my kitchen counter in total silence for the next four minutes as he played a *Michael Bublé ballad.* His eyes were closed, he would occasionally do a light air drum, and he was completely serious. You could practically hear my vagina dry up like salt on a slug.

Another guy was a total hobbit. No, that is not me being an asshole and saying this guy was short and/or ugly. He played an actual hobbit in the Lord of the Rings movies! We immediately had a playful repertoire and said that when he was back in town we would go out for drinks. I told him about my newfound love for mezcal, and lo and behold, he loved it, too! A couple of weeks of casual chatting ensued, and then I get a (*clearly*) drunk text from him, giving me graphic details of how he wanted to drink mezcal off my body. It was TOO much. We hadn't so much as hugged in person, and I was already learning about how he wanted to turn my body into an open bar. I retreated faster than an army realizing all their guns had been replaced with hot dogs.

Discouraged, I took some time off from the app while I was traveling abroad for shows. When our plane's wheels hit the tarmac at LAX, I turned on my phone to see what I had missed. It was all the usual. A bunch of texts. Too many e-mails from my agents. But then a ding! I had gotten a message on Raya. I opened it, hoping it wasn't a picture of the hobbit holding up a haul from the liquor store.

"I want to meet your dog!" read the message from a cute boy

with a sweet face. Dudes, the only thing hotter than you holding a dog* is you caring about a woman's dog. I messaged back immediately, "You have great taste." From there, we playfully messaged back and forth for a few weeks until BAM, we actually made plans to meet up.

And we did! And then we did again! And then again! My dating curse had been broken. But that wasn't the hard part. The hard part was learning how to not get attached out of the gate. To learn how to date, not just have a boyfriend.

There's an amazing Cher quote from an interview with Jane Pauley back in 1996 where she is asked why she has referred to the men in her life as "dessert." She says, "I adore dessert. I love men. I think men are the coolest. But you don't really need them to live." I happened upon that old interview right around this time, and it changed my perspective.

Think of men like dessert, huh? Let them be sweet, an indulgence, but not completely essential for enjoying the meal of life. It was everything I was really feeling in that moment, the exact sentiment Veronica and I had been trying to live out, but leave it to the goddess Cher to put it into the perfect analogy. She and I vowed to keep our priorities straight: we needed to be there for our girlfriends, stay laser-focused on our careers, and let guy stuff just be the icing on the cake. After all, too much dessert and you can get really weighed down and feel (and look) like shit.

And now I was ready! The world was my proverbial buffet of various male delicacies, and I had a stack of clean plates.

---

* One of the classic pics included in dudes' profiles. They probably don't even own a dog; they just know that a) women flock to that shit, and b) it is a visual confirmation that they are not a sociopath.

Just the (Unsolicited) Tips

As EVIDENCED BY the previous chapter, I'm no expert at dating. The only dating I'm good at is myself, with all of these outdated references!

Laughs *Sighs* *Blocks out fear of mortality*

When it comes to dating, I'm basically a fetus, as the kids would say.* Hell, barely a fetus. Just a twinkle in a daddy's eye. But just because I don't know much about a subject has never stopped me from giving unsolicited advice about it. So, here they are, some random gems about dating that I've picked up from my foray into singledom thus far.

1. Eat Dinner

Sometimes you say you're going to go out for a quick drink on the early side with your date. Surely, you will eat a meal after you're

---

* Ideally a fourteen-karat one, like in Cudzoo's debut song. Did I mention the first time we performed it, we dropped teensie dolls that we had spray-painted gold out from our crotches via string and then swung them around like a flapper girl twirling a boa? So very PC.

done! Plus, you don't want to roll in with a burrito baby while rocking those high-waisted jeans that make your ass look like a tasty teardrop, right? WRONG. You must eat to preserve your integrity. 'Cause if it's going well, one drink will become two, two drinks will become six, and then you're either too drunk on your first date or you end up playing *CSI: You* in the morning. I'm talking the Crazy Snack Investigation unit, which happens when you walk into your kitchen and go from crumbs to cans to shit spilled on the floor and then have to determine what exactly you destroyed when you came home drunk and hungry.

One time I came back from an "only drinks!" date, and the next morning I realized I had eaten a bag of dark chocolate espresso beans but must not have wanted to stay up all night from the caffeine, so I had just sucked off the chocolate and spit out the beans directly into my garbage disposal. Another time I woke up with little cuts on my swollen fingers because I'd eaten cold boiled peanuts straight out of a tin can . . . in bed. EAT DINNER, YOU GUYS.

2. Go Out with People You Have No Mutual Friends With

I know, I know. There's something wonderful about dating friends or outliers of your social circle. It's like a built-in background check. You can get the skinny on their dating/job/mental health history before you ever go out, and there are a lot less introductions you have to navigate at parties. But RESIST! If it doesn't work out, you will be so thankful that you don't have to run into them at parties. I specifically casually date dudes on the other side of LA (which may as well be the other side of the planet) so I don't have to run into them ever again. It also saves your friends from having to choose sides when you break up. Bonus!

3. Rebound Basketballs, Not Basket Cases

There is a fine line between exhilarating and erratic, and sometimes when you're blinded by "like, love, or lust," it's hard to see the difference. I've seen it happen time and again. Someone gets out of a stable relationship and is automatically attracted to someone a little wild. A change in energy. But trust me, take a step back and take a hard look at your situation before engaging. Is this person exciting or erratic? Because sure, right now it may be thrilling. You were down in the dumps, treading water, and now this person has your adrenaline pumping, like you're riding a massive wave. But, honey, that wave can't maintain. You're going to eventually get to shore and have to deal with real life. You don't need an undertow of crazy constantly dragging you back in. Choose calmer waters.

4. Get a Hot Tub

This is a costly tip, but I'm tellin' ya, if you have the means necessary, get a damn Jacuzzi and watch your social life blossom before your eyes. Your house automatically becomes the late-night party spot, and you get to check out what guys look like in their bathing suits. Honestly, having my hot tub that first summer of being single was like having guy soup in my backyard, changing daily like a Dude du Jour.

5. Always Groom

Good Lord. I get it, it's annoying. I would sometimes be like, *If I don't shave my legs, I definitely won't hook up*. WRONG. Hair is not a chastity belt.

You will get drunk, and your inhibitions will lower, and the next thing you know, your date will be busting through that bush like Westley chopping through the fire swamp in *The Princess Bride*.* Seriously, it's as if I only got laid when I decided to forego shaving for a week. The three times I have gone through the terror of a Brazilian in preparation for a night with a guy, plans have changed and we haven't hung out. I'll put it to you this way: if your legs feel like a cactus, you're probably gonna catch a prick.

6. Disregard My Previous Tip

If grooming's not your thing, or if not grooming brings you good luck, stay on course. He should be so lucky to touch your bod, even if it does feel like a bag of splinters!

7. Don't Intimi-Date

This is not what it sounds like. I don't mean you should shrink yourself so that the man can feel secure in his manhood, or the woman in her womanhood, or whatever Robin in his Robin hood.† Quite the opposite! I mean, don't intimi . . . date people who are intimidated by you.

When you're getting to know someone, it's nice to talk about things you are working on or are proud of, whether that thing is as big as a project of yours being funded or as simple as you starting to incorporate more leafy greens into your diet. Whatever it is, lay it all out there. If your date refers to you as "intimidating"

---

* Ideally, he is also, like Westley, doing so while saying "as you wish."
† Don't for one second sit there holding this book and not admit that the animated Robin Hood from the Disney classic cartoon wasn't hot. He was a literal fox, and Kevin Costner and Russell Crowe didn't capture that same magnetism in the role. . . . Oh! And Cary Elwes in *Men in Tights*. Damn, two Elwes refs in one chapter?

instead of just being supportive and interested in what you're saying, this is a red flag. Picture that gif of Whoopi Goldberg in *Ghost* saying, "You in danger, girl." Being told you are intimidating might feel like flattery in the moment, but down the road, those things your date was "impressed" by on your first date can fester into things your now-partner resents.

That's right. . . . You can't spell "IMPRESSED" without "PRIDE MESS."*

What's even worse is that sometimes, in this situation, you then begin to shrink or downplay your achievements so as to not make this other person feel bad. Don't fall for it! Don't be with someone you intimidate; be with someone who rises to your level. Or who makes you want to step up your game to rise to theirs. You worked really hard to carve your life into the thing it is, so be with someone who stands back and admires your work, not someone who grabs an emotional chisel and chips away at it.

So, in conclusion, WHOA! I got a lot deeper in this chapter than I thought I would. I didn't even make one "just the tip" joke.

The point is, I don't have all the answers. These are just things that work for me. They might not work for me a year from now. I could be rocking a full bush, have developed an irrational fear of hot tubs, and only be attracted to manic dudes who are completely daunted by any of my successes. Things change. People change. But one thing's for sure. . . .

ALWAYS EAT DINNER. Don't be a fool.

---

* Special shout-out to my number one homie . . . an online anagram generator.

Get a Clue!

I, Mamrie Hart, am a sucker for a game night. Ever since I was an itty bitty, I have loved board games: Girl Talk, Dream Phone, Mall Madness. Basically anything that was priming me to be a materialistic, boy-crazy, bitchy high schooler. But there was one game whose box wasn't hot pink that captured my heart, and that was Guess Who? Guess Who? kicked every other unisex eighties board game's ass! I mean, look at the other hits of that era.

OPERATION? I'm sorry, but if that weirdo with the bowl cut is dumb enough to swallow butterflies, a wrench, and a bucket . . . it might be time for evolution to just go ahead and take him out.

MONOPOLY? A "get out of jail free" card? There's no such thing. We can't be teaching our youth that actions have no consequences and that you should treat your life like a simple roll of the dice!

LIFE? Don't even get me started. In what world would I spend my time playing a game that includes having to buy car insurance?

So yes, Guess Who? was where it was at. It was essentially a game of elimination where both players would secretly choose a character and then ask questions to try to find out who the other chose. Questions like "Are they wearing glasses?" or "Is she a blonde?"* could help you ID a character. I got so good at it that I could ask if you had a hat or glasses, take one look at my opponent's face, and know that it was Bernard.† But even for a hardcore deductive reasoning kid like me, after a while, the ol G'Dub grew stale. I needed stakes! I needed intrigue! And then I saw the movie *Clue*.

If you're not familiar, *Clue* is a classic murder-mystery comedy from the eighties starring Tim Curry, my favorite curry besides massaman. Fun fact! When *Clue* was released in theaters, there were three different endings, and audiences didn't know which one they were going to get. What a unique and extremely expensive way to detract from spoilers!

I saw that movie when I was eight and was *hooked*. Normally murder-related things scared me, but this wasn't murder; this was theater! I vowed that as soon as I was old enough, I would have myself a murder-mystery party like the one in *Clue*. Nothing sounded more fun to me than wearing a floor-length gown, clutching my throat and screaming, "My pearls! Someone stole my pearls!" or blowing everyone's mind when I knew that it was indeed Colonel Mustard in the library with the candlestick.

---

* Nowadays, it would be a lot more "Would I ever have sex with him?" or "Does she look like that barista from the Coffee Bean who has Resting Judgey Face?"
† To this day I still compare people to Guess Who? characters. Just last week I went on a blind date with a guy who looked like a Frans in his profile pic but a Bill IRL.

Though I threw a lot of parties in my college days, I never got the murder-mystery theme off the ground. I did go to college in the South, so people were less into "whodunnit?" and more concerned with "who-done-got-a-fresh-keg?" Murder-mystery parties seemed ridiculous and cheesy to most people, which, lucky for me, was the exact recipe to make something cool in hipster, late-aughts Brooklyn! So, before I knew it, my friends were throwing murder-mystery parties themselves. For those unfamiliar, this is how they work. . . .

A few days before the party, the host e-mails you the character you're supposed to be playing, so you can dress appropriately as well as develop a little backstory for him or her. Once the party kicks off, someone will "die" in the first five minutes, and over the course of the night, the host will reveal a series of clues that leads to everyone interrogating one another while still in character. It's a fun way to get friends to come out of their shells and also see which ones have taken an Improv 101 class at UCB.

For one of these particular parties, I had RSVP'd late, and the host, my friend Alessia, had already doled out all the characters for her luau-themed evening. Rather than miss out on the affair, I volunteered to be the person who gets killed in the first five minutes—this person being a sleazy, mustachioed mobster. Perfect! I was going to rock a suit, draw on a 'stache with eyeliner, and slick back my hair with a quart of gel. I was ready for it.

Alessia's place was in Queens, and I lived in Brooklyn. But what might look like a simple three-mile straight shot north on paper was an hour-and-a-half subway ride into Manhattan, then back into Queens, or what us rednecks would call "Going around your ass to get to your elbow."

However! I am a professional actress; I wasn't going to show up at her house in my street clothes and then get changed there!

I needed to roll up in character so as to not risk losing the illusion for my fellow attendees.*

Surely a woman dressed as a mob boss in a ruffled shirt isn't going to turn heads on the goddamn NYC metro system, I thought. I've seen a man naked from the waist down, wearing shoes made out of duct tape, take a shit in the middle of a subway car while singing "Memories" from *Cats*, and still some passengers stayed just to not have to lose their seat.

My plan was thwarted, however, when the train broke down and I had to stand on a crowded platform for an hour waiting for another train. Here I am, being verrry natural at the Queens Plaza stop.

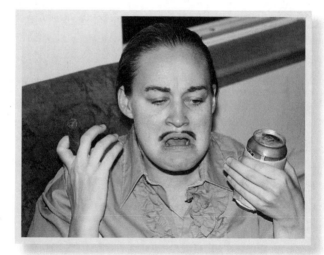

While I ~~got blasted~~ had a blast at these parties, they always felt like such open-and-closed cases. The killer would be found

---

* I barely learn my lines when I go to an audition, but I am straight-up Daniel Day-Lewis when it comes to a costume party.

before you'd gotten your share of hummus. In case you haven't
noticed, I like to go full-tilt in my quests for fun. Put simply, I
needed a full weekend experience dedicated to using my detective skills. But life happens and schedules fill with responsibilities. Free time needs to be delegated to gross things, like visiting
family.

So, when planning adventures for this book came up five
years later, I was beyond prepared and had already been eyeing a
spot. There was a murder-mystery weekend on Jekyll Island, a
little vacation spot off the coast of southern Georgia. The Jekyll
Island Club rang a bell for some reason, and then I remembered
where I'd seen this historic masterpiece: on the Bravo channel's
magnum opus, *Southern Charm*.

In Bravo's top-notch roster of *Top Chef* and *The Real Housewives of City-Where-Everyone-Screams-Constantly, Southern Charm*
was the turd in their crown jewels. In the first three seasons
alone, there were multiple pregnancies, a train wreck of a state
senate campaign, and an evil matriarch who rang a bell when
she wanted a martini. It's basically a telenovela but with a lot
more bourbon and Lilly Pulitzer luggage. But despite these
types of reality shows always being packed to the gills with dramatic thrills, they're always crazier when their characters are on
vacation. This was especially true when the Charleston gang
headed south for a weekend trip to Jekyll Island. Could it be that
this place was named after Jekyll and Hyde and made people's
personalities change? Would I become mad with power? Or
paranoid after a few clues? Or leave the island knocked up by a
potential state senator with a *definite* cocaine problem?

I knew I needed to have an excellent partner in solving crime
for this trip, so I invited my old pal Maegan. Maegan, based on
my side-eye observations of her at those NYC parties, was a

finessed interrogator, never breaking from character for a second. A veritable Meryl Streep of her craft. She was the perfect choice.

Before we knew it, we were driving over a bridge and onto the little island. It was *gorgeous*. Spanish moss hung from massive Southern oak trees. The buildings were perfectly maintained, all white columns and wooden shutters. We rolled up slowly, to avoid hitting the people riding by on their golf carts and beach cruiser bikes. It was just like the *Southern Charm* episode! Surely someone would throw a mint julep in my face in no time.

We checked into the hotel and received our itinerary. Essentially, the murder mystery would be active during all the meals of the weekend. We would meet for cocktails and dinner that night, all three meals the next day, and a closing breakfast on Sunday where the truth would be revealed. The rest of the time was ours to chill out and/or obsess about our theories. We popped into our *definitely haunted* room and got ready for the opening dinner.

Walking over to the cocktail hour, I was already nervous, and not just because I'd convinced myself that the ghost of a Civil War soldier had watched me get dressed. Maegan and I booked this trip on such a whim that we didn't really know what to expect.

"Are y'all here for one of the weddings?" the bartender asked us as we sat at the old mahogany horseshoe-shaped bar. "Oh no," I replied between sips of my martini. "We're here for the murder mystery."

"Really? Hmm," he said, his eyes scrunching up before turning back to his register. Maegan and I exchanged a "WTF was that?!" look, but before we could ask the bartender if these things were lame or if he was just being judgmental, he had pulled his till out of the register and was being swapped out for a fresh bartender.

As soon as we entered the mystery ballroom, we understood his "hmm." We looked out over a sea of men in polo shirts and pleated khakis and women in their finest pastel dresses from Talbots and sensible kitten heels. It was like walking into a mixer for recently divorced sexagenarians, or a welcome reception for new timeshare owners. We knew out of the gate we should probably mingle and get a head start on cracking the case. But instead we headed straight to the buffet so we could load up on the carbs. Mama didn't raise no fool, 'cause when I'm back in the South, there's not a lot a vegan can eat. Just like back in the Poconos, my plate was a beacon of beige. A castle of carbs. A citadel of starches. Before I could ask the chef if they were gonna refill the mashed potatoes, a woman tapped on a microphone.

"Hello, everyone! And welcome to the Jekyll Island Murder Mystery." Everyone golf clapped and found a seat. "My name is Margot, and I am so excited you all decided to join us this weekend. Well, some of you decided . . ." A collective "ohhh" spread across the room as Margot continued, "Some of you here are not who you say you are. And it is your job this weekend to figure out who and why. And on Sunday, all will be revealed! Now, to get started, why don't we stand up table by table and introduce ourselves? Your name, what you do for a living . . . whether you're a murderer not. I'm kidding!" Margot really liked her own joke.

One by one, tables rose, and people gave their intros. For the most part, it was a lot of retired teachers or contractors. When it came time for Maegan and I to do our thing, I could feel eyes glaring at us. Sure, we weren't the usual crowd. Both young (in comparison) redheads, with Maegan covered in tattoos. But, damn, they were looking at us like we were holding bloody butcher knives and matching shirts that read "I ❤ Murder."

"Hi, my name is Maegan. I live in New York City, and I own

a vintage clothing company." Whispers weaved throughout the tables. She sat back down, gesturing that I now had the floor. "Hi, my name is Mamrie . . . and I'm an alcoholic." Blank faces from the crowd. This was not my audience. "I'm not, I'm kidding. I mean, maybe I am, but this isn't the place— Okay! Sorry. Again, I'm Mamrie. I live in Los Angeles, and I am a writer." Audible gasps. Go to iTunes right now and look up "shocked crowd of adults" and that is verbatim what we heard. No gasps off the alcoholic joke, but plenty from the actual facts of my life.

Now, most of the guests were so vanilla that I can't remember any of their names. But allow me to go down the roster of the key players who stood out to me.

THE LONG ISLAND SISTERS: The only siblings of the batch, these two were a straight-up *SNL* sketch, and I loved them despite the fact that they were clearly talking about us every time they went out on one of their *several* smoke breaks.

BUCKET HAT & HOTTIE: This girl in her late twenties was PDAing all over her dude in his late fifties. I am never one to judge a May–December romance, but I am one to judge a bucket hat. They're unforgivable. I don't care if you are Idris Elba in a three-piece suit holding a tray of warm cookies, if you throw a Gilligan hat on that dome, it's done. Parents, if you don't want your teenage son getting a girl pregnant, just convince him that bucket hats are in style.

DAGGER EYES & CHEESE: As soon as we walked in the door, this woman stared Maegan and me down. If for one second you think I'm paranoid, please know that she literally did the "I got my eyes on you" sign language with two fingers pointed toward me before she introduced herself. Her husband, on the other hand, was a lovable big dude with a wide smile and a kind face. Dagger Eyes clearly wore the pants and even introduced him:

"This is my husband, Cheese. Yes, that is his god-given name." Ya can't make this shit up.

REAL ESTATE DOUCHES: Other than us, this was the only younger duo. Both in their midtwenties, the young Guido-looking dude was wearing a suit, and his girlfriend donned a short red dress. Apparently they were both real estate agents in Atlanta. I was immediately suspicious.

As soon as we were done with intros and everyone went back to their meals, the doors to the ballroom burst open. In ran a woman (I could tell only by the lack of sports bra) with a mask over her head and a fake gun. I screamed. None of this "Oh my pearls!" feigned-surprise yelling that I pictured myself doing—I straight-up screamed bloody murder and was practically perched on top of Maegan's head like a spooked cat. Can't be sure if I yelled "oh shit!" or not, but based on the way Dagger Eyes was shaking her head at me, I'm gonna go with yes.

The masked woman got twenty yards in when we heard a man's voice yell, "FREEZE!" Back at the door was a man in a Hawaiian shirt and (yes, another) bucket hat, holding up a fake gun at the perp. "Put down the gun and back away slowly!" he yelled in a New York accent. But Titty Bandit was having none of it. She raised her gun and BANG BANG!* Shots were fired! When the smoke cleared (and not from the Long Island Sisters vaping at their table), the masked woman lay on the ground.

Hawaiian Shirt moved to the middle of the room, standing above the lifeless goon.† "Ladies and gentleman, there is no need to panic. My name is Rocky, and I am a professional detective. I was on my way to Disney World when I got tipped off about a

---

*   Titty Titty Bang Bang? . . . I'm sorry.
†   Lifeless except for scratching the mosquito bite on her ankle. Wasn't surprised she wasn't committed to this role considering she didn't even get a line.

hit that had been put out here on Jekyll Island. I immediately turned my car around and came straight here. . . . Except for those two stops at Chick-fil-A." Oh no, Rocky was a hoot. He reached down to the masked body and pulled a business card out of her shirt pocket.

"Looks like we have our first clue!" he said and began reading the card. "'He'll be on her right. Don't mess this up.'" Interesting. So the hit was for a couple, but the message was vague. Did someone want the man dead, or the woman? Our mission was to find out not only who the hit woman's target was but also who hired her to make the hit. I went to look at the corpse one last time to see if maybe there was a clue that Rocky missed, but that bitch had already sprung back to life and was scooping up alfredo sauce at the build-your-own-pasta bar. So much for staying in character until you've cleared the curtains!

"We've got a big weekend of crime-solving ahead of us, everyone! We will reconvene at breakfast. But for now, get some rest. I'd tell you to sleep with one eye open, but that's physically impossible. Good night!" Rocky declared with such bravado you'd think he was playing Jean Valjean in *Les Mis*, not a detective whose trip to Disney World had been thwarted. We all watched as he stormed out of the room. Once the sound of his waterproof khakis rubbing together cleared, everyone started to file out, eyeing one another suspiciously, the true MVPs landing back at the horseshoe-shaped bar. Maegan and I sat there with the Long Island Sisters, exchanging theories.

"What do we think about the guy in the bucket hat and his girlfriend? Something's fishy," Maegan said, sipping her martini.

"I agree!" Sister #1 piped in. "I watched them leave the party, and as soon as they rounded the corner, they quit holding hands."

"Forget the May–December romance!" I added. "What's

with the skeezy real estate guy? He gives me bad vibes. No one that young comes to one of these—"

"The same could be said for you." I looked over, and sure enough, it was Dagger Eyes walking past the bar. "A writer? From Los Angeles? Sounds made up . . ."

"Made up? You said your husband's name is *Cheese*. Perhaps we should call him Daiya, 'cause that shit is clearly fake." Another fantastic joke wasted on ears that had clearly never heard of soy cheese, let alone a specific name brand. I tried again. "Or maybe we call him Swiss, because your story has some holes in it!" Big, gentle Cheese spoke up from behind his wife. "Actually, it's short for Wanchese, who was the last ruler of the Roanoke Island Native American tribe. Very well-revered." I nodded and went back to my drink as Dagger Eyes snapped her fingers to get Cheese to follow her like she was Danny Zuko rallying the T-Birds.

Maegan and I kept the barstools warm for a while, even after the sisters ran out of vape juice and called it a night. Just when we were about to do the same, who rounds the corner but ol' douchey real estate guy! He sidled up to the opposite end of the bar and ordered a Mich Ultra. A man scared of carbohydrates? Extra suspicious.

"So, what's your deal? Real estate, huh? More like *get real* estate!" I whipped my head to Maegan, who nodded in approval of my wordplay.

"Yep, real estate in Atlanta. The market's very hot right now," he said with a smirk. "About how long is that drive from Atlanta?" I asked with an eyebrow raised.

"Wouldn't know. We decided to private jet down here—"

"PFFFFT!!" Maegan and I scoffed in his face. "Private jet? Yeah, right! Who takes a private jet for an hour flight? Besides a Kardashian."

"Like I said. The market is hot. Now, I'm gonna go meet my girl. You two ladies enjoy your drinks, and good luck, ya know, raping dudes or whatever."

Yes, you read that correctly. Take a moment. This mothafucka with his low-carb beer and high-and-mighty attitude wished us luck on *"raping dudes or whatever."* We sat there in shock as he walked away, each with a hand to our chest like a flabbergasted Southern belle. What had we ever done to him? And who uses rape as a punch line? What an asshole.

Maegan and I headed back to our probably haunted room in silence,* reeling from the night's events. I had no doubt in my mind that Real Estate Douche was a fraud, but who did he want to put a hit out on? And why?

"He told you to have fun vaping dudes?" Sister #2 asked me at breakfast the next morning, blowing a strawberry-scented chemical cloud away from the table. Before I could correct her, a pissed-off older woman came storming through the banquet doors.

"Where is that no-good cheating rat?!" she screamed. Homegirl was working those local theater chops as well as my nerves. It was too damn early for screaming. Her head turned Linda Blair–style to the young hottie.

"Oh, if it isn't the tramp that's sleeping with my husband!"

"Tramp?! He said you were divorced!" Someone yelled to look outside, and sure enough, there was Bucket Hat hopping over the handrail and making a getaway. "We aren't divorced yet!" the wife screeched. "Not until he agrees to give me the house!"

---

* Except for Maegan going so HARD on a bag of Kettle chips that it sounded like a gravel truck was parked in our room. Also, remember when Ke$ha said she had sex with a ghost? Ahhh, simpler times.

Before Wife and Hottie could claw each other's eyes out, Rocky got in between them. Apparently, Bucket Hat had been cheating on his wife while telling the mistress he was single. Things were starting to really heat up, so Rocky, of course, dismissed us till lunch.

We spent the afternoon lounging by the pool, drinking margaritas, and telling everyone within earshot about Raping-DudeGate. "You know, come to think of it, I've never seen him at one of these before, but what could he possibly have to do with the affair?" Sister #2 asked. Apparently, the LI girls attended murder-mystery weekends all over the East Coast several times a year. And they weren't the only ones. Over by the cabana, Dagger Eyes and Cheese were eating barbecue they had brought from home to give to Rocky. He'd been their murder-mystery host before, and they were old buds! It was like we became part of a whole community I'd never known existed.

Later, at dinner, I wasn't three bites in before Rocky burst through the doors once more. "There's been a murder! Everyone follow me!" I swear, this weekend was almost becoming a cleanse. The real victim of the weekend was my buzz, because I couldn't get a sip down without someone busting into the banquet hall.

We followed Rocky out of the ballroom and down a flight of stairs. Sure enough, a murdered Bucket Hat lay lifeless on the sidewalk, stabbed through the heart with a butter knife. Questions raced through my brain. Who killed Bucket Hat?! Why would they use a butter knife?! When was the buffet going to refill the goddamn mashed potatoes?!

At the bar later, I sat with Maegan and the Long Island Sisters discussing theories. Every time someone from the murder mystery walked past the bar, I convinced them to take a seat and tell me their theories, hoping they had a lead or could find the connection between Bucket Hat's murder and the original hit that was put out. One by one, Maegan and I told our tale of the night before and how odd it was, and soon everyone was intrigued with the Douche. Hell, even Dagger Eyes and Cheese finally caved and had a drink with us. I'd like to think it was because I had proved to them my innocence, but she told me, "Honey, I Wikipedia'd you last night, so I know you're telling the truth."

Several drinks later, I laid in bed, trying to put together the puzzle pieces. I just couldn't figure it out. And right before I drifted off, it hit me. "I got it!" I yelled, sitting straight up in bed. "Got what?" Maegan asked sleepily. "I got our motives," I said, pulling the covers tightly around me as I smiled from ear to ear.

The next morning, Maegan and I headed to breakfast, rocking matching shirts in solidarity.

Specifically Friends Forever 21.

I walked in confidently, feeling like we'd really *12 Angry Men*'d these retirees. Margot took her place as I made extended eye contact with the Douche while shoveling grits in my mouth.

"We have had *quite* the weekend, haven't we? Before all is revealed, let's go around and share our theories, hmm?" Then, just like we had introduced ourselves at the first dinner, table by table everyone stood up and regaled the room with their scenario. Most were tired old theories that the wife put the hit out on Bucket Hat because he was obviously cheating on her with that youngin', and after the hit woman got shot, the wife came down to do it herself. Seemed too obvious. Of course, Dagger Eyes's theory involved Maegan and me being a part of the crime, despite our olive branch from the night before. Finally, our table was called, the last one to go.

"Wait, what are we saying again?" Maegan asked.

"Don't worry, I got this," I reassured her, standing up. I cleared my throat dramatically. "Well, well, well. While I loved listening to everyone's simplistic finger-pointing . . ." I said, staring down Dagger Eyes.

"Your Wikipedia said you had an acting degree!" she said, as Cheese took her arm to sit her back down.

"I, however, have come to a different conclusion. You see, my friend here and I"—Maegan pointed to her shirt—"had such a vile interaction with this guy"—Maegan pointed to the Douche—"that we knew there is no way he can't be in on it. No one is *that* big of a dickhead, so he has to be an actor. So! My theory is that this [yes, I used actual air quotes] 'real estate agent' here took out the hit on Bucket Hat, because he is the wife's real estate agent and wants her to get the house they share so she can sell it and he can make that commission. When it didn't go as planned, he tipped off the wife to cause a diversion so he could kill Bucket Hat himself! Aha! Gotcha!" I said, pointing my finger at him. "How's that for raping a dude?" I mimed a mic drop, high-fived Maegan, and sat down. The room was dead silent. I leaned back in my chair, proud of cracking the case. That is until I felt a little tap on my shoulder, I looked up and there was the Douche holding a business card.

"John Doe Real Estate."

I tried to laugh like I was kidding as I scanned the room and all its shocked faces. Dagger Eyes was apalled. I slinked down into my seat as the silence grew to a dull roar. Finally, Margot cleared her throat. "Okay. Ummm, that was . . . interesting." She moved past it and brought everyone's attention back to her, like there was a gruesome car crash in the room and she didn't want anyone to look.

Turns out while Maegan and I had tried to think out of the box on what the answer could be, it was a classic case of "husband cheats on wife so the wife puts a hit on him but it goes awry and she comes down to do the dirty work herself." It was *textbook*. We had overthought the whole thing. I yearned for a bucket hat to pull down over my eyes.

Meanwhile, everyone else was celebrating their victory. Since so many people had it right, they ended up just drawing a name for the winner. The prize was a discount off their next murder-mystery weekend, which we knew they'd be attending as soon as possible. But not Maegan and me. The second after Margot wished everyone a safe trip back home, Maegan and I full-on sprinted out of there, cackling as we ran past the trees. I had somehow been a bigger disaster than the cast of *Southern Charm* . . . and, let me remind you, two of them dug a hole on the beach and slept under branches because their golf cart ran out of gas and they couldn't find their way home.

"Maegan, were we assholes? Did maybe that guy not deserve the smear campaign we brought against him?" I asked her as we drove over the bridge away from the club. Maegan thought about it for a second, twisting her face in confusion before finally saying, "NAH. That guy made a rape joke. What a douche!"

And she was right. I was happy to leave the murder mystery with zero mysteries still in my brain, no unanswered questions . . .

Except why in the *hell* Dagger Eyes friend requested me on Facebook three days later?! Pick a lane, woman!

Love at First Fight

My HETEROSEXUAL LIFE partner,* Melissa, uses a phrase that I love: "This is my life now." She busts this out whenever we are trying something new and she falls in love with it. The best part about this is that most of these activities are usually dumb as hell. Here are some actual moments where I've witnessed Melissa say this:

> Sitting in a Monster Jam audience as Grave Digger, the most famous monster truck from North Carolina, a vision of neon green and purple, flies through the air.
> ~*This is my life now!*~

---

* We've used this phrase since college. It basically means that she's my girl for life. My wifey. Although it doesn't mean we can't be with dudes. Just means we date guys who are older than us so when their shorter life span makes them kick the can, we have a solid fifteen years of living that *Golden Girls* life together.

Being stoned on a kayak in the marina and almost being attacked by a sea lion.

~*This is my life now!*~

And in text form: I just ate mushrooms on a boat then sailed to a little island and fell in love with some baby raccoons.

~*This is my life now!*~

Never have I felt more Melissa, aka more ready to dedicate my life to something super dumb, than the moment I first walked through the doors of a WWE wrestling match at the impressionable age of twenty-nine. It was in that moment four years ago that everything changed. I had been aware of wrestling as a kid but was never into it. And as an adult, my feelings were more like: *The WWE is ridiculous. A bunch of people chanting along to theme songs? Silly costumes and story lines? Over-the-top shit talk? That is so immature.*

That all changed when I got to see my first live performance. I can now proudly say as an educated, and I'd like to think smart, woman that . . .

I LOVE WRESTLING.

Here's how it went down. Somehow back in 2013, while I was visiting LA, Grace was gifted with free tickets to *WWE Raw.* We didn't have anything better to do, so we actually considered going. Grace was like me—she had been aware of wrestling when she was younger but didn't pay it a second thought as an adult. But as soon as we walked into the Staples Center that night in 2013 and felt the energy of that room, everything changed for the both of us. All those ways I used to pass off this phenomenon were now said in a different intonation. Go ahead and read my doubts from before, in the same exact words but in your best *stoked* Mamrie impression.

The WWE is ridiculous! A bunch of people chanting along to theme songs?! Silly costumes and story lines?! Over-the-top shit talk?! That is so immature!

This was my life now.

As someone who has a theater degree, wrestling is pure art. WWE is basically theater in the round, just like Shakespeare's Globe Theatre.* But what makes it even better is that there's no pretending that the audience can't see you. The audience is part of the show. Wrestlers aren't just navigating the narrative; they are also bouncing off the crowd's energy and off the turnbuckles as they do complicated moves. Romeo never had to deliver a soliloquy that ends in a pointed elbow drop, amirite?

Another reason why I love wrestling is because while there are a million story lines, they are relatively easy to follow. You could go in there with no prior knowledge of a character's long history of backstabbing and walk out an expert on how he was backstabbed by his BFF tag team partner and now he's going to seek vengeance on his former teammate. Seasons of history are often filtered down to a five-minute backstory, thanks to beautifully edited video packages of previous matches playing on the massive screens. Sometimes you'll even luck out and get dramatic monologues filled with tons of exposition, ideally delivered with a single spotlight and usually ending with their enemy bum-rushing the stage to hit them upside the head with a metal

---

* I know I'm eliciting some eye rolls even suggesting that WWE is like Shakespearean theater. However, I did see Kevin Owens give a very Hamlet-esque twenty-minute monologue to open *Monday Night Raw* once. He wasn't holding a skull, but he did get hit in the skull by a metal chair, so there's that.

chair. Bonus points if they accidentally knock out the ref. It's a total soap opera circus!

Now, some purists out there might say that since Grace and I haven't been watching wrestling since its beginning, that we are "fake fans." And I say, "Uhhh, duh, I'm a fake fan. Everything about wrestling is fake. I am *literally* a fake fan." That's why we love it so much. So much so that we decided to make the ultimate gesture and FUCKING PROVE IT. So in the spring of 2017, exactly one year after I wrestled my emotions in the streets of France, Grace and I invited Jarrett to join us in attending the biggest event of the year: WRESTLEMANIA 33, in gorgeous Orlando, Florida!

We got in late Saturday night and kept it chill, saving our energy for the next day, as if we were going to be the ones in the ring. While Grace had a lot of editing and napping to do, Jarrett and I struck out on our own that Sunday for food and drinks. The last time he and I were together, as you'll remember, we were gallivanting around Paris, drinking incredible Bordeaux and eating *pommes frites*. How were we going to top that culinary experience? Culture at its finest: DOWNTOWN DISNEY.

Neither of us had any interest in going to *actual* Disney World. I myself have never been a Disney person. It might stem back to the only time I went to Disney World, back in seventh grade. To this day, I'm not sure what exactly happened, but after snapping a pic of Dale, from the famed Rescue Rangers, I was wrongly accused of hitting him. I know, right?! I don't know if it was someone else, or he got swiped by a stroller, or he just had a vendetta against me because he had heard of my distaste for rodents, but that chipmunk wrongly snitched on me, and I've never forgotten. Since then, I have no real interest in being around mute mascots. I'd rather stay on the outskirts of the parks and hit up something that has never done me wrong . . . theme restaurants.

And oh, there were plenty of them there. We drank Cheetah Ritas at the Rainforest Cafe, and then Raptor Ritas at the T-Rex Cafe, which is my new favorite spot and future wedding venue if I ever bump my head hard enough that it kicks in some desire to get married. Seriously, though, this place is *incredible* and stokes every aspect of my obsession with comically large things. From its glacier room that had floor-to-thirty-foot-ceiling fake ice walls and animatronic woolly mammoths to the massive, prehistoric octopus that looms over the bar, it's cheesy heaven. And in classic theme-restaurant form, they lay the theme on real thick with the menu names. Some of their specialties include . . .

Tar Pit Fried Shrimp: I get it. Dinos got stuck in tar pits, yada yada. But with the Gulf oil spill of recent years, don't you think it's maybe not the best idea to conjure up the idea of tar when presenting diners with your seafood?

Lava Lasagna: 'Cause that doesn't immediately make you feel like you are going to burn the shit out of the roof of your mouth as soon as you dig in, right?

Pterosaur Wings: I get where they are going here, with pterodactyls being the only dinosaur with wings, but why do they have to add the "saur" at the end? If you don't read that as "tear a sore," then congrats, you are much classier than I am. Couldn't they just be "Ptero Wings"? They really should have gone for "Ptero'bly Tasty Wings" and saved us gross-minded folks the visual.

I decided to go for the menu item they gave up trying to cleverly name—the Kale & Red Quinoa Salad. But a little healthy salad was no match against those specialty drinks, so by the time we got to the stadium, we were pretty lit. And we needed to be, because, MY GOD, walking into the middle of a hundred thousand screaming wrestling fans is intense!

We met up with our WWE contact, a super-on-top-of-it woman who led us to our seats. I knew we'd be close, since my girl Tessa (aka Dark Orgasm) hooked it up, but we actually had no idea how good they were going to be. As we emerged from the tunnel, we trailed single file behind her, mouths agape like a line of shocked baby ducks as we got closer and closer to the ring. "Here are your seats," she said, gesturing to them. "And remember that you can take them with you as souvenirs at the end of the night." She power walked away, leaving the three of us standing silent in shock.

We were in the FOURTH row, ringside, aka the fifty-yard line of what was usually a massive football stadium. We took our seats as the sun set in that Orlando sky, military fighter jets flying overhead as Tinashe sang "America the Beautiful." I don't know if I've ever felt more ~~redneck~~ American and thankful of everything I'd done in my life to lead me to that moment.

The next five hours were pure INSANITY. More matches than an arsonist's wet dream. I felt like I was going to have whiplash from jerking my head around to the ramp every time another theme song started spontaneously blasting. There were comebacks of nineties tag teams (the Hardy Boyz), retirement matches from legends (the Undertaker), and even a proposal (John Cena and Nikki Bella)! But it was the bad guys who really brought their A game, including an insane taped segment where Randy Orton burned down the family compound of his opponent, Bray Wyatt. When this played, everyone went *NUTS*.

"That's super fucked up," I said, as screens showed the house engulfed in flames.

"Super fucked up." Grace nodded in agreement before snapping back into amped mode. "Good thing it's not real!"

Oh, yeah! I was so consumed by the energy of the night that I had momentarily forgotten these plotlines were written by paid professionals. Randy Orton and Bray Wyatt were probs besties in real life and hitting up the nearest Hooters after the match.

At the end of the night, we were thrilled but exhausted, and we headed to the area where our driver was supposed to be picking us up, recounting all the details of the night as we schlepped with our commemorative seats in tow.

"That was absolute madness," Jarrett said, still in shock. "Can you believe the Hardy Boyz made a comeback?"

"Or that we were three of only a hundred thousand of John

Cena's closest friends he chose to propose in front of?" Grace said, shaking her head, as she hopped into the Escalade.

"For reals. But what was up with the house-burning thing? Do we really need to promote arson to an audience with children present?" I asked with a disapproving squint that makes me look like I'm doing a bad De Niro impression. "I mean, a lot of impressionable kids watch this! Or even worse, Southerners who love blowing shit up."

Oh no! Was my love for this over-the-top, no-holds-barred entertainment taking a turn toward judgment? Was this no longer going to be my life?! But before I could get too into my own head, Jarrett snapped me out of it.

"Randy Orton," he said, stone-faced.

"Yes, Randy Orton," I agreed. "I wonder if he went too far."

"No," Jarrett said, looking past me. "Randy Orton is coming right for us." I looked behind me, and like a bull charging toward a matador, Randy Orton was at our window before I had time to react. He threw open the door, and we all screamed like little girls.

"You're in my car," he said, taking a moment to look each of us directly in the eyes. If that moment were a children's book, it would be titled *Orton Hears a Whodafuckisinmycar?!*, but it didn't register. We sat there, frozen. "You're in my—"

Then reality hit us. "Sorry, Randy Orton," I said.

"So sorry, sir," Grace said, equally terrified.

The next twenty seconds were composed of about forty more "sorry"s and "sir"s through shaking voices as we slid out of that car like flattened cartoon characters.

The Escalade with Orton in it peeled off, kicking up the slightest bit of dust onto three stunned idiots holding chairs.

Guys, I told you from the start of this book that I was going to always be honest with you, so here it is . . . I peed my pants a little in that moment. Not like a full, go-change-your-pants-before-we-go-out type of way, but I definitely had a momentarily loss of control of bodily fluids when I saw that six-five, 250-pound beast coming at us while I was talking shit about him.

People can talk about wrestling being fake all they want, but in that moment, the fear was real. And **really** fun. All in all, I urge you to attend all the silly events you can. Don't be a snob. What you might have cast off as being dumb or too lame or just straight up beneath you might be your new obsession waiting to happen. Go find reasons to say "This is my life now." I promise, it'll be worth it.

Somebody Rockin' Knockin' Da Boots

WHEN MY DEAR friend Kelly invited me to her wedding in the mountains of North Carolina, it was a no-brainer. Sometimes you get an invite to a wedding you would need to travel across the country for, and it's like, "No, thanks. Here's a toaster!" But this one was right up my alley. The wedding invite teased biscuits, barbecue, and blueberry moonshine, a service held under a giant oak tree, and the reception in a barn. Plus, all the guests could rent beautiful cabins on the property.

I had met Kelly briefly in college, but we became tight when we both lived in New York City. She was killing the game as a playwright while I was busy mastering the art of playing wrong. Although we didn't know each other until our twenties, we had grown up about thirty miles from each other, weirdly enough. There is something so lovely about sitting at brunch with a girl-friend, talking about rubbing elbows with a celeb at a fancy party the night before, knowing good and well that we both used to consider a Friday night at the Winston-Salem Ruby Tuesday to be the epitome of class.

It wasn't even a question of whether I would go. Not only would I be able to spend time during my favorite season in my home state, I had yet to go to a wedding as a now-single woman. I LOVE weddings: the open bar, the dancing, the rituals. I am in top form at a wedding, but I'd never had the infamous wedding hookup like you see in all the movies and/or the remnants of during brunch the morning after. I was ready to get tipsy at a wedding and not just flirt with the groom's grandma. I wanted real sparks. Plus, it was Kelly's wedding, so there were particular ~~targets~~ potential suitors I already had my eye on. . . .

Allow me to explain. Kelly has three brothers in the Marines, two still single. Though I had never met them in person, I had seen pictures of them on her blog and in her Facebook albums for years. These men looked like Marine Ken dolls. I had never pictured myself with a military man, but they were both hot as hell; plus, there would be the added bonus that, if all went well, I could potentially end up becoming Kelly's sister. Win all around!

Let me take this moment to say, with all my heart, family: KOHLRABI! I mean it. Don't say to yourself, *Well, I made it through her first book and was still able to look her in the eyes over Thanksgiving.* Close the book, or turn to the next chapter. . . .

Are they gone?

GOOD.

Because this chapter is about the first and only time I've ever had a threesome. Stick with me.

As the wedding drew closer, I was getting giddier and giddier. I had actually stayed put in LA for a month. I had finished my press tour for *Dirty 30* and been finishing some other deadlines, which kept me glued to my ancient Mac. Days were spent click-clacking on my keyboard while nights were spent hanging with my Pussy Posse. Oh, what's this Pussy Posse, you ask?

Well, in Hollywood it is sometimes the name given to the trio of Leo DiCaprio, David Blaine, and Tobey Maguire because they used to unabashedly go out and get so much pussy. *Fuck that*, I thought to myself. Pussy is Power. Not some descriptor for these dudes using their celebrity to bed women. When I decided post–Pity Party that I needed to just be surrounded by my women for a minute and not let myself get wrapped up in one dude, I found that my closest girlfriends were feeling the same way. So, I started calling my clique the Pussy Posse. I even got us all rose-gold bangle bracelets with "Pussy Posse 2017" engraved on them as little reminders throughout the day. They felt like Wonder Woman cuffs warding off bullshit.

Maybe it was something astrological. Maybe some moon was moving into its fifth house . . . or maybe I had just drank too many fifths, but we were over it. We all wanted to focus on our careers, our friendships, and ourselves. Guys were just meant to be a fun, no-strings-attached good time. Ya know, like seizing the opportunity to hang with a couple of hot brothers at a wedding. Pussy power, indeed.

With that mind-set in place, I couldn't wait to get away for a minute. Everyone was going to be staying in a little town called Ferguson, which had little to do and zero cell reception. Sure, as soon as the wedding was complete and my phone received a bar of service, work e-mails would rush in like people jamming into a rush hour subway car, but for those few days, all I would have was peace and quiet. I couldn't wait.

My cabinmate was going to be Kelly's friend Maggie, who is a magical creature from Iceland. She and I had hit it off after we spent a day together in LA when Kelly recommended that

Maggie take some photos of me. She will always hold a special place in my heart seeing as she took the first picture that I used for that first Raya dating profile.

Is this pic necessary to the story? Nope. Is it a hot pic of me and this is my book so I'm going to post it anyway? Ya damn right.

I was excited to catch up with her and chill with some of her friends, the other bunkmates who I had yet to meet. But, wouldn't ya know it, a week before the wedding I got a super apologetic e-mail from Mags.

"Mamrie! So sorry, but my travel visa wouldn't go through!!! However, CC'ed on this e-mail is Dustin. Dustin, this is Mamrie, she's wonderful. Mamrie, this is Dustin—he's wonderful and y'all will be staying in the cabin together. Go forth! Be best friends!" Was this ideal? No, but I trusted her recommendation.

Within five minutes, Dustin had reached out to introduce himself and offer a ride from the airport, since we were landing around the same time. Now, normally I would rather throw a cup of fire ants down my pants than take a ride with a stranger on a road trip, but I was still working out my license fiasco and the only thing that's worse than a couple of hours in a tiny rental car with a stranger is standing for hours at the DMV. Well, we all know there is something worse, and that's being *fake* hit on by a cop only to get a ticket for your expired license that ends up costing you tons of money in fees, but I'm trying to move past that.* So I took Dustin up on his offer and prayed for minimal amounts of awkward silence.

I landed in North Carolina after a red-eye and met Dustin at the Enterprise line. We immediately hit it off. "Sorry this is your first impression of me," I said, handing him the chai latte that I had offered to pick up for him from my terminal. "I'm literally on zero sleep. Couldn't get comfortable on the flight."

"I'm in the same boat. I stayed out till five last night and had an eight A.M. flight," Dustin told me, which explained why he was still wearing sunglasses inside.

In a rom-com, this moment would be called a "meet-cute," where a future romantic couple meets in an amusing way. However, there were no sparks between us. This was our meet-cute, new BFFs edition: Dustin and Mamrie! Aren't they adorbs?!

We gabbed the whole way up the mountain, whipping around the turns in our Kia Soul. I learned that Dustin and Kelly knew each other from grad school, when she was in the playwriting

---

* Fuckin' Marco, man. Like it isn't already difficult enough to trust cops in today's society. From now on, trust your vaj, not the badge!

program and he was an actor. Dustin grew up in Pennsylvania with a big family who owned and ran a local Italian restaurant. I made him regale me with tales of his sisters being waitresses and him and his brothers working the line and being busboys during high school. I was dying to know what their best dish was and just how long they let their marinara simmer.*

"I'm going to Italy in a few weeks. You should come!" I said, immediately regretting my words. Who does that? The lack of sleep must've been making me crazy, because inviting someone on a trip abroad after knowing them an hour is like asking a guy to move in with you on the first date. Luckily, we breezed past it and kept chatting.

As we drove, I blabbed about how much I love North Carolina in this weather and wouldn't shut up about how delicious Bojangles' biscuits are,† making him stop at the nearest one. And wouldn't you know it? They were out of biscuits. That's like KFC running out of chicken. But it was all good. We just laughed about it and continued down the road with Bo-Berry Biscuit blue balls.

We were having such a nice time shooting the shit as our car maneuvered through the mountain roads that I wasn't even concerned when our final bar of service disappeared, a moment that would normally be a "Pound the alarm! Mayday! Mayday!" moment for me. We stopped to get groceries, and I introduced him to his first Food Lion experience, where he was called out by a local for having trendy sweatpants that were hemmed a little shorter than normal. Honestly, you would've thought Dustin was wearing Gaga's meat dress by the way that old man was staring at his exposed ankles.

---

* I can only blame my jet-lagged investigative reporting on my hunger.
† Bojangles' is a southeastern fast-food chain that sells biscuits that are so buttery and flaky that whenever I see their sign, I black out and forget I'm a vegan.

Once we pulled into the grounds, we knew we were in for a treat when we saw the big, gorgeous cabins dotting the mountains. I couldn't wait to see which one Maggie had reserved for us.

"Do you care if our cabin is the party house?" I asked Dustin.

"It better be. I did not break out these revealing, fancy sweatpants to not be the party house."

I looked up to a house with a massive wraparound porch. "Get me drinking pumpkin beer up in some fall-ass foliage ASAP!" I exclaimed as our car rounded the corner and revealed the welcome center, stables, and barn. "The barn! That's where the reception is going to be right after the"—I looked to my left, there it was—"service under the old oak tree. God, this is perfect."

Inside the welcome center, Dustin checked in* as I perused the quaint gift shop. It was like a mini Cracker Barrel! Little wooden games, rock candy, fleeces, and small signs painted with uplifting, and somewhat Christian, quotes lined the store. I ran my hand along the wind chimes when something caught my eye on the top shelf.

There, shining down on me like a beacon of light from the heavens was a pair of cowboy boots unlike any I had ever seen. These beauties were white with shiny gold-and-silver leather stitching in the shape of a cowboy's silhouette and cactus, with metallic fringe accenting the sides. They were magnificent. It was like that moment in *Wayne's World* when Wayne first sees Cassandra. "Dream Weaver" was playing in my mind, and I uttered, "They will be mine. Oh yes, they will be mine." This was a lens flare moment.

"How much do you want for the boots?" I asked, carrying them

---

* BAHAHAHAHA. Dustin checked in. So close to *Dunston Checks In*. No doubt one of the top three films to ever feature an orangutan as an unruly hotel guest.

up to the sweet older woman at the check-in desk. "Those boots?" she asked, her twang in full force. "Well, I don't even know if those boots are for sale. Patty! Patty, is Debra selling her boots?"

Patty, another silver-haired honey, slowly made her way to the desk. "Those boots? Debra's boots?" Patty asked, as I wished there was a meter counting how many times the word "boots" was going to be said in the course of this conversation. Patty continued, "I think those boots were just up there for decoration. I don't think she's selling those boots. . . . But how much would you pay for them?"

Aha! This granny was trying to pull a fast one on me. Trying to sell me poor Debra's boots for probably way more than they cost because this vision from LA was asking about them. Hell, she might even pocket the money.

"I'll tell you what," I said, kicking off my rank tennis shoes. "I'll try them on, take them for a little spin, and when I come back, you tell me how much you want for them." I'm not sure if I've ever felt that smooth before in my life. As I started to slip them on, I questioned whether I really needed silver-and-gold metallic boots with fringe. But that doubt went out the window as soon as I stood up. They fit perfectly, like they were custom-made for me.

After a couple of figure eights and the Boot Scootin' Boogies, I twirled back to Patty. "How much for them?" I asked, squinting my eyes to try to intimidate the old broad.

She squinted right back. And then finally, "Fifty doll—"

"SOLD!" I screamed, attempting to fist bump her, to no avail. Dustin grabbed our keys, and I do-si-do'ed right out that front door.

We got back in our Kia Soul and plugged the address into the GPS, hoping the residual Wi-Fi from the welcome center would direct us to one of the palatial cabins up the mountain. Based on the website, the views overlooking the trees were straight off a postcard.

"That's funny—it says it's within a hundred yards," Dustin commented.

We followed the directions to our destination . . . only to reveal that our dream cabin was, no lie, the stable house behind the horse barns. It was a shack.

"Maybe it won't be that bad?" I squeaked, not even believing myself.

We approached it slowly, as if we were walking into a house on *Hoarders*. When we opened the door, what we found was a time capsule to the early nineties. Hey, I am all about that country-shabby chic, but this was shabby *chic*'ken house. Rooster art was everywhere: Rooster clock. Rooster dish towels. Rooster pillows. Massive decorative glass roosters. The sofas were overstuffed and brown, like the loaf of bread they serve you when you sit down at Outback Steakhouse that you say you aren't gonna eat so you can save room for a Bloomin' Onion, but you *always* end up eating.

I opened the closet, which led to a massive laundry room with six washers and dryers. Clearly, this was where all the stable stuff was washed. The screened-in back porch, a selling point in Maggie's pitch, was full of knickknacks, old furniture, and a weird miniature pool table with the felt so worn it had bald spots. Dustin pointed to what looked to be a rusty kennel for a fifty-plus-pound dog. He looked at me and said in a deadpan tone, "Yes, Mamrie. It's *that* bad."

He was right. But being the go-with-the-flow people we were, we did what anyone would do. . . . We called the front desk and begged Patty to find us another cabin. But they were all booked. Our dreams of running from room to room and claiming the best one for ourselves, a la the first episode of every *Real World* season, were crushed. "Well, you know what this means," I said, breaking into the wine we got from the Food Lion. "We are just going to have to get good and ripped to deal with our digs. Let's start now." And that was that.

A few hours later, we were gathered around the heat lamps at the welcome dinner. But we didn't just have burning propane to keep us warm; we had an internal heating system. And by that I mean that we had moonshine. Blueberry moonshine and apple pie moonshine, to be specific, which aren't like the real moonshine that could start a small engine, but they'll still get your aunt to bump and grind on the dance floor. I was in heaven.

"Mames, I have something for you," Kelly said, pulling me aside. She looked gorgeous in her cute dress and denim jacket. Not that she doesn't always look gorg, but she definitely had that inexplicable bride glow to her.

"From our local state trooper," she said, handing me a mason jar of clear liquid out of her tote bag. "It's the real stuff." That's right. The bride handed me a legit jar of white lightning as a thank-you for making it to the wedding. Ladies who are currently Pinterest'ing your perfect day, take note!

But before I could twist off the lid to make a lightning storm in my mouth, I spotted them. "Dream Weaver" kicked back in, but this time it wasn't for two boots; it was for two dudes who had been to boot *camp* . . . aka Kelly's brothers. They looked as if a witch had been walking through a Grecian statue garden, made two of the carved studs come to life, and then tossed fleece and khakis on them.

"Not too bad, right?" I whipped my head around and saw two of Kelly's bridesmaids, whom I'd met once or twice, and who (for the sake of anonymity) we'll call Ronnie and Bonnie.

"Get in line, girl," Ronnie said, holding her hands up to a heat lamp.

"Oh Jesus. We're all gunning for a brother, huh?" They nodded. "Well, just so you know. I have zero preference. I'll take whoever you don't want."

"Yeah, we feel the same way," Bonnie piped in. "I guess it's just every woman for herself," and with that, she strutted away to talk to the youngest one. Sonovabitch. I thought this was going to be like shooting fish in a barrel. Not only did I have competition, it was with two total hotties. Goddamnit.

I beelined it straight to Dustin. "We need more moonshine," I said, grabbing his arm and forcing him to the bar. Two more shots and I explained the situation. "Oh brother . . . literally," Dustin said with an eye roll I was already accustomed to from our brief time knowing each other. The rest of the evening got a little blurry, as I was (said like Larry David) *pretty, pretty, pretty* lit. But I do remember distinctly hanging out on a porch with the two bros and the competition. I don't remember one damn thing I said to them, though, nor do I remember a bunch of people coming back to our place to attempt to play pool, or eating an entire bag of Spicy Sweet Chili–flavored Doritos. But I do remember how bad my mouth hurt when I woke up. I must've dove into those treacherous triangles like I'd been stranded at sea for a week.

The next afternoon, Dustin and I took the Kia Soul up through the winding mountain roads dotted with mountain mansions we wished we were staying in. We happened upon a swing set a little ways off from a house with no cars in the driveway and decided to grab a seat and pop open some pumpkin beers.

"I can't believe everyone is going after the brothers," I said, gaining some real height as I pumped my legs. I looked down at Dustin, who was throwing me a "bitch, please" look a la Jackée from *227*.

"You know what you gotta do, right? You gotta wear your lucky boots."

"Lucky boots? Why are they lucky?" I asked, stopping my rocking.

"Because so far, on this trip, you've gotten exactly what you wanted."

"Not true. I am not currently perched on one of the brothers' faces."

"True, but besides that, you've been batting a thousand." I was caught off guard by Dustin dropping such a seamless baseball reference. "Think about it. You're drinking seasonal beer with some 'fall-ass foliage' as you so eloquently put it. AND we have the party house! Sure, it might just be because it's the closest place to party without having to drive drunk up a mountain, but still." I nodded. Our trash cabin was everyone's *getting* trashed cabin. I gave a little grin and started swinging again.

"Now, pound that, and let's go get ready in our super convenient little shit-shack back down the mountain. I am not driving once it starts getting dark!"

When it came to the wedding-day, Operation Brother Lover wardrobe, I was pulling no punches. I knew that Ronnie and Bonnie would be in classy yet sexy bridesmaids dresses (Kelly has great taste) and they were probably up in a fancy cabin getting their hair and makeup professionally done while drinking champagne. Meanwhile, Dustin and I got ready in our shack. I had taken for granted that the place would have a blow-dryer, so I roasted my roots over the radiator while pounding Bud Light Lime. I put on a short peach dress, despite it being frigid as hell, and a denim jacket, and I slid on those magical boots, aka my secret weapon. My new metallic kicks were made for walking and . . . I was ready to give Ronnie and Bonnie the boot.

I froze my ass off at the ceremony, which was gorgeous and under a big oak tree and Kelly was hilarious and beautiful and I'M SO SORRY THIS IS WHAT I'M WRITING ABOUT

REGARDING YOUR WEDDING. It was really lovely, though. Then, it was on to the reception. Everyone moseyed over to the barn, which was decorated in a way that can only be described as "fall as fuck." Big communal wood tables, little mason jars of wildflowers, burlap accents everywhere. Dustin and I made our way directly to the bar, where they were ladling out hot cider. "I'll take one of those," I said, breathing into my hands to warm them up. "Oh! Can you put some of that apple pie moonshine in there?"

"I don't see why not," the bartender said, and started making my drink.

"Hey, that's a great idea." I looked back and saw Kelly's oldest brother behind me in line.

"I thought so," I said, smiling over my shoulder, essentially doing an impression of the smirk emoji.

"Great boots by the way." Holy shit, it was working. Dustin and I took our spiked ciders and found our table—of course with him shaking his head at me. Mind you, we'd known each other twenty-four hours at this point, but it felt as though we'd been friends for ages.

The reception was thoughtful and wonderful, with little individual cobblers in tiny mason jars and a spread of NC barbecue, complete with a BBQ jackfruit option for us crazy, out-of-town vegans. By the time everyone was ready to rip it up on the dance floor, the wine and 'shine had been flowing, so we youngsters were ready to boogie.

I hit that parquet dance floor with a mission, busting out all my best moves. The brothers were busy doing their mandatory chatting with the great-aunts and friends of their parents whom they probably didn't know by name. I occasionally glanced over while shaking my ass in my short dress and flipping my hair in the wind, a stark contrast from Ronnie and Bonnie's tasteful navy floor-lengths and updos with baby's breath. Let me tell you, there is a *fine line* between shaking your ass to get someone's attention and going a little too sexy to Sam Cooke's greatest hits as several grandparents watch. That said, I was feeling good that night and having a blast. I kicked up my cowboy boots, did shots, then pulled off my ultimate "chill girl" move. All the ladies huddled on the dance floor, including Ronnie and Bonnie, as Kelly turned her beautiful low-back lace dress to us to throw the bouquet. As it left her hands and everyone did their slow-mo lunge toward it, I crossed my arms and ran in the opposite direction. "No thanks!" I said playfully, winking at the youngest brother. You could practically hear Dustin rolling his eyes.

After several songs, I took a breather. Dancing while sucking in a stomach full of jackfruit BBQ is exhausting! "I just heard them talking about how hot you are," Dustin said, nodding toward the bros. "Really?" I ~~squealed~~ asked nonchalantly.

Finally, the brothers went from from getting their cheeks pinched by elderly ladies while side-eyeing the dance floor to getting out there themselves. Now was my time to shine, and I went in for the kill. I would dance with one brother, then see the other one make his way over and saunter over to him for a minute. Both seemed to be into it. The only problem was, it was working for Ronnie and Bonnie, too. We would eye each other from across the room, trading between bros. It was like a fucked-up square dance meets that dance scene from *Mr. and Mrs. Smith*, when Brad's and Angie's characters are half tangoing/half about to shoot each other. Just when I thought one of the brothers was into it, he'd be dipping Ronnie and I'd start being spun by the other bro.

By the end of the night, all bets were off. The older folks had made their way to their cabins, and the barn belonged to all of

Kelly and her hubby's friends. Based on the super classy photo booth pic I took pretending a gray wig was a merkin, I'd say Mama was *feeling* the grain alcohol. Slowly but surely, couples and groups of non-singles started to peel off as well. But we three women stood strong, convincing the bartender to give us each one last drink as we watched the brothers take the final photo booth pics with their family. "Don't y'all have to go all the way back up the mountain?" I asked, sipping my now-straight 'shine. "I think the last shuttle is leaving in a second. Better hop in."

"We'll walk," Ronnie said, as Bonnie nodded. Goddamnit. No one was backing down. You know those "Hands on a Hard Body" competitions they used to have in the nineties? People would have to keep one hand on a car, without taking it off, and the last person standing wins the car? Sometimes it would take days, but you gotta do what you gotta do for a free Dodge Neon. This was just like that. It was a Hands on a Hard Body competition except, in this case, the hard bods were crafted to Marine standards.

Finally, the wedding party was done with their props and poses and started moseying our way. It was the moment of truth. We were the final five hanging on, under the warmth of a heat lamp, as the rest of the wedding party started getting into a van. I smiled at the older brother; he smiled back. As soon as he looked away, I smiled at the younger brother, who smiled, too, and cleared his throat. He opened his mouth with a grin and just as I think he's about to officially make a move, we hear one of those two-fingers-in-the-mouth type of whistles.

We looked over to see Kelly's dad motioning the brothers over to their van, Kelly in all her gowned gorgeousness beside him with her hands on her hips, yelling, "[Insert brother's name here]! [Insert other brother's name here]! Y'all can barely keep your eyes open. Let's roll!" And just like that, they were gone.

The three of us stood there in shock in the otherwise empty barn. There we were, just three girls who had thrown all their energy and time into claiming one of the brothers, all worked up from it, only to be left teeth-chatteringly cold and drunk in a barn. But all was not lost.

Remember when I said this was the story of the first time I had a threesome? Yep. It was that type of threesome. HAHA! GOTCHA! You thought I had slept with the brothers based on that brilliant setup. Sorry, darling reader, twist ending. You just got M. Night Shyamalan'ed! Now, I will stop gloating long enough to finish the tale.

I woke up the next morning with a hangover that could rival a Boston frat boy's on March 18. I looked down, totally butt naked . . . except those boots, sparkling in the morning sun. I wrapped a sheet around me and walked out into the living room to find Dustin lounging on the Outback bread couch. "Well, good morning, sunshine! Sounds like someone had fun last night. Wasn't expecting *that*!"

"That makes two of us," I said as he handed me a coffee. We stared at each other, shaking our heads, and then just started laughing. What was my life? A year ago, I felt like I was the crabby wife in every CBS sitcom, complaining that she has a headache or is too tired all while putting on hand cream from my side of the bed.* But not anymore! I had just slept with two bridesmaids. What? When did I become Owen Wilson in the opening credit sequence of *Wedding Crashers*?!

I stood there, sex hair and a look of bewilderment like I'd just

---

* Seriously, though, why are sitcom wives always putting on bedside table hand cream?! In any other scenario this would insinuate that it was about to be hand job central. But no, these wives must always have chapped hands from doing dishes. Resist, ladies. Resist!

survived the Hurricane Vagina of 2016, which is ironic considering that we were staying in the House of Cock. I mean, guys!!! The only thing I was wearing besides boots, was my rare gold bangle. Pussy Posse had taken on a *whole* new meaning.

"Get dressed," he said. "I still need to try Bojangles' biscuits." And that was that.

Three weeks later, I was sitting in a gondola in Venice, gliding through the canals with two of my closest girlfriends—and my new friend, Dustin. It was a perfect day. We took in the sights, sitting on the red velvet seats, huddled under blankets, as our driver navigated the boat through the bends.

Maybe my boots weren't just lucky because they brought me one of the top ten weirdest nights of my life. . . . They also brought me Dustin, my favorite kind of person. The type of person who will agree to meet you and your two girlfriends in a different country after knowing you for seventy-two hours.

"Dustin, you're Italian, right?" His head whipped to me, as he offered up an eye roll. The man grew up in rural Pennsylvania, but I had been asking him questions throughout the trip as if he spent his whole life in Italia.

"Yes, Mamrie. I am Italian."

"Then you'll know the answer to this: Where are we right now? Like, if Italy is a boot, where is Venice?"

"Northeast. Right at the top," he said, as the gondola got stuck under one of the tiny bridges. Within a few seconds, we were back in the sunshine, taking in all the heat we could get from its beams. "But while we're on the subject of boots . . ." Dustin said with a smirk on his face.

WHAP!

I kicked Dustin in the exposed ankle of his edgy sweatpants

before my friends could pick up on what he was saying. He laughed. It didn't matter that we had just met each other a few weeks before; it felt like I'd been friends with Dustin forever. He was what they call a keeper. . . . Mainly because he could keep (my) secrets.

Weirdest Day

HAVE YOU EVER heard someone ask, "What were you doing the day Kennedy was shot?" Anyone over the age of sixty knows exactly where they were and what they were doing when they found out the news. Now, I'm not old enough to have experienced that particular day in history, but there are other moments that feel this distinct and memorable to me. Like when 9/11 happened, I was in the middle of a small college class about ancient Pompeii. Why did a lazy college freshman theater major decide to take an intensive course on a first-century city? I asked myself that every class.*

 Another moment that will always stand out to me is finding out when Michael Jackson died. I was walking through Tompkins Square Park in New York, listening to music, when a text came in on my BlackBerry from Maegan.

Have you heard? Michael Jackson died. So sad. :-(

---

* In truth, it is because the description of the class said that each student would assume a role in the class. Naturally, I wanted to be a serf solely so I could say, "Serfs up!" at every chance I got.

I stopped in my tracks, and I must've had a look of total shock on my face because I heard a man say, "She just found out." I looked over to see two bums sitting on a bench, trash bags piled high beside them. I looked at them and nodded sadly. In retrospect, I find it kind of hilarious that two homeless men with zero access to the Internet knew before me; that's how wrapped up I was in the debut Lady Gaga album blasting from my iPod. Yes, kids, I'm *that* old.

But what I'm saying is that there are these moments in life where it feels like you are connected to everyone around you because you are all grieving. Never have I felt this camaraderie in sadness more distinctly than in November 2016, when Donald Trump was elected. This sobering moment was a lot of things for a lot of people, but for me and my girlfriends and a whirlwind trip abroad, it was the five stages of grief in twenty-four hours.*

Let me back up. A few weeks prior to election day, I got an e-mail asking if I'd be interested in moderating a panel about social media at a convention called Web Summit. While I had never been a moderator before, I figured it would be a breeze. Everyone just wants you to get through your short list of generic questions so you can turn the floor over to the audience for a Q&A. I would be "interviewing" two heartthrob-ish type vloggers so, Lord knows, the audience would be chomping at the bit for me to stop talking so they could ask the vloggers how their dogs are doing or if they can get a hug.

This conference was going to be in Lisbon, Portugal. Y'all

---

* I am going to go ahead and assume that since you are indeed literate, you probably agree with me that Trump is a terrible, unqualified, misogynistic pig. If not, you don't deserve this book. That's right! Take it to the Barnes & Noble counter, purchase it at full price, walk out of the store, and throw it in the trash.

remember how painless my panel was in Cannes. I basically got a free trip to talk for five minutes and then hang out and make MIP puns! But unlike Cannes, I wasn't part of a crew this time—this was a solo trip. As much as I like to travel alone, I wasn't feeling an unaccompanied adventure. Plus, I had popped by Lisbon post-Amsterdam trip for a couple of days, and it wasn't really a solo city based on the amount of discarded purses laying around. An idea started brewing. My travel buddy, Joselyn, and I had been talking the day before about how our next big trip together needed to be Italy. After that one afternoon in Pisa, specifically that one plate of pasta with cream sauce that will be my death-row last meal if my life goes really differently, fucked up all other pastas for me. And I LOVE pasta. But every time I ordered a plate of carby goodness, I knew it wasn't going to be as good as it was in Pisa.

So, I asked the convention if, in lieu of a first-class ticket, they could instead give me three round-trip coach tickets flying into Lisbon and out of Florence. That way, Joselyn and my other friend, Nata, could come with me. One night in Lisbon, then Italia! I knew it was a big ask, but they went for it.*

A few weeks of counting down the days and being tempted to do a #TBT of my pic of that pasta,† and we were on our way to the airport. It was election day, and we would be flying from LA to NYC to Lisbon. I had mailed in my ballot weeks earlier and was happy to get in the air, away from the Internet and the end-less scrolling of "I Voted" sticker pics on Instagram.

---

* Actually, it probably saved them money. I said it once, and I'll say it again: first class is a rip-off. Sure, do I enjoy boarding first and having the ability to fully recline and be-ing served a hot meal? Of course I do. But there is no amenity that would make me pay out of pocket for first class. If I'm spending three to five times as much on a ticket, then that meal better be prepared table side by Iron Chef Morimoto, okay?

† Instagramming your food is sad enough but doing a throwback Thursday of an entrée you miss is even too "fat kid" for me.

"Isn't it crazy that when we land in Lisbon, we'll have our first female president?" I asked my girls as we settled into our row.

"I am going to bawl my eyes out," Joselyn said, squeezing into the window seat.

"What if Trump wins?" Nata asked. We all laughed. In what world? I brushed it off. There was no need to give any thought to the idea of Trump being elected. That was like living in LA and just sitting around waiting for an earthquake to hit. It was a waste of energy.

"Okay, when we get there, I'm going to have to haul ass to get showered and head to my panel, which is annoying because I just want to hang out with you guys," I said, flipping my tiny seat TV to some mindless HGTV. "But it doesn't matter, because tomorrow night, we are going to be in the streets of Lisbon, toasting to Hillary and having a delicious dinner."

Here's the thing about me. I am known among my friends for my love of a "delicious dinner." I can get through any workday, any shoot, any bullshit, as long as I know that a relaxed, delicious dinner will close out my day. It is one of my sole motivations in life. Back when I did a travel show with my friend Grace, we were asked to do all sorts of insane activities: salmon fishing, spelunking, shooting guns, you name it. I could be freezing in a wet suit having white-water rafted all day, but by focusing on that "delicious dinner," I could get through it.* Being crammed into a tiny coach seat with nothing to eat but peanuts for half a day would be worth it as long as I got a good meal with a big glass of wine after the sun went down.

We landed at JFK for our three-hour layover around ten P.M.

---

* My other mantra to get me through anything is "hot showers, cold martinis," which I will often chant over and over to myself to get me through a tough day.

and immediately went to the closest bar with a TV, which turned out to be a little tapas place in the JetBlue terminal. I bopped up to that bar with a little kick in my step and ordered a glass of Rioja. But that kick in my step turned into a punch in the gut when I saw the screen. Trump was in the lead. It was unthinkable. "Actually, I'll go ahead and take a whole bottle," I said to the waiter, who gave me an understanding nod back. The three of us sat there, anxiously stress-eating our *patatas bravas*, barely talking as Trump clinched Florida and North Carolina.

That last one especially hurt because there was a chance for my home state to turn blue that year. Between their discriminatory laws restricting transgender public bathroom usage and other bigotry on display, North Carolina felt like that shitty boyfriend you're always making excuses for, claiming that their words and actions don't actually reflect their heart. Like, "Look, I know he called you a pansy-ass bitch, but pansies are a vibrant and lush flower. It was totes a compliment!" I felt betrayed by North Carolina and was glad I'd left that tumultuous relationship in my early twenties.

By the time we had to peel ourselves away from the bar to board, Trump was only thirty-something electoral votes away from sealing the deal. Despite the odds, there was still this hope in my head that it wasn't going to happen. This election had been so fraught with ratings and conspiracies; maybe all the news channels just needed viewers to stay tuned so they were reporting the Trump states before all the Hillary ones to keep people's attention.

We boarded our flight, saying good-bye to Internet for the next ten hours. "It'll be okay," Joselyn assured us from our aisle seats. "When we wake up, Hillary will be president and Donald Trump will be so embarrassed he'll just fade away. Let's just get some sleep."

But sleep I did not; I was *wide* awake that whole ten-hour

flight. Since we were flying over the ocean, we didn't have Wi-Fi or live TVs, so I opted to watch everything they had on demand. Not even the dull delivery of astrophysics jokes on *The Big Bang Theory* could lull me to slumber.*

After what felt like years, the waitresses started coming down the aisles with the breakfast snack carts. One by one, people's sleepy peepers were pried open by the smell of shitty coffee and the realization that wheels were rolling over their feet. Once we had our little snack and got our wits about us, the pilot started speaking on the microphone in Portuguese.

I pulled my seat up and put away my tray table. I don't speak Portuguese, but I do know the "we have started our initial descent" speech by heart. I was halfway through throwing my sneakers back on before the whole plane GASPED.

Jos and Nata and I looked at one another in terror, each grasping the other's thigh with a death grip. That kind of collective gasp could mean only one of two things:

1) A flock of birds have flown into the engine and the pilot is about to have to Sully this bitch to safety.
2) Trump had won.

We waited with bated breath for the pilot's message to be translated into English. "Ladies and gentleman, I would just like to inform you that Donald Trump has won the presidency of the United States of America. . . ." He kept talking, but in that moment, I blacked out. Immediately, the three of us started bawling.

---

* I don't know what it is about *The Big Bang Theory* that always makes me watch it on flights. I NEVER watch it on land. Same thing with drinking tomato juice on a flight. I have seen maybe two people in my *entire* life order a tomato juice at a restaurant, but put those motherfuckers thirty thousand feet in the air and it's like the red stuff is blood and they just got bit by Edward Cullen.

Questions swirled through my head. How could this happen? Why the fuck would the pilot tell us while we were still in the air? Did we actually ascend into the stratosphere? Because everything felt like it was in slow motion.

For that next hour, I tried to squelch my sobs and fight off a panic attack. I had seen the safety demonstration of when the oxygen masks fall from the overhead in case of cabin pressure change upward of eight million times, always hoping I would never have to see it in real life. Now, I was wishing those bags of oxygen would plop in our face, just so I could catch my breath.

"What if the pilot got the news wrong?" I said, with a glimmer of hope in my leaking eyes. "I mean, what if someone told him that as a joke and he took it seriously? Captains are known for kooky high jinks, right, guys?!" Ahh, there it was. The first stage of grief: **Denial**.

The three of us held hands as the plane started to land, which was the first time I had ever wanted a plane's wheels to hit the tarmac and take right back off again. Because once we landed, we were going to be reconnected with the world and have the nightmare confirmed.

We got off the plane as quickly as we could. Mainly because there was one old lady in our section who clapped during the Trump announcement and I didn't want to be responsible for accidentally pushing my carry-on near her and breaking the old broad's hip. How quickly I had moved on to stage 2: **Anger**.

I stormed through the terminal and out of the adult Disneyland that is Duty Free. My anger was bubbling inside me so furiously that I didn't even smile at the double cartons of Marlboros that they arranged to look like one giant box of cigarettes, normally an ace in the hole to make me cheer up. It took all I had not to just grab a three-foot-long Toblerone and go all Beyoncé

I took this photo as soon as I caught my breath from
bawling; in case you wanted to see what a woman
looks like after zero sleep, one emotional sucker punch
to the gut, and two bottles of wine. It was a low.

in the "Hold Up" video to work out some anger. But there was
no time. I had to get checked into the hotel and shellac my face
before heading to my panel. The thought of sitting and talking
about something as trivial as "The Legacy of Social Media" was
unfathomable to me.

After we checked into our rooms, I took the world's fastest
shower and hopped into an Uber to head straight to my panel.
The driver had the radio playing, and I understood nothing except the word "Trump" being said every thirty seconds. It was
driving me crazy not to know every little detail. But I blocked it
out and took the twenty-minute ride to scribble down some

questions in my little notebook. Sure, they were the same generic drivel you'd hear at any other panel, but I was planning on putting my own unique flair on them.*

"I cannot go any closer; I have to drop you off here," the driver said as we approached the bustling convention center. I hopped out of the car, immediately regretting wearing new shoes. Ten yards of walking and I could tell the sides of my ankle boots were scraping against my skin. Twenty yards and I already needed a Band-Aid. After checking into the center, I was guided to the room I would be speaking in by an adorable Portuguese man, Alberte, who looked all of eighteen years and was four-foot-nothing.

"This convention is a lot bigger than I thought it would be," I said, out of breath and hobbling a few feet behind.

"Yes, it's the biggest of its kind in Europe," he called back, bobbing and weaving between patrons in lanyards and barkers trying to get you over to their booth. I swear to God, at one point I ducked down to not be hit in the face with a drone. Three inches closer and it would've given me one hell of a mullet. Alberte cleared it by a foot.

We finally burst through doors to the outside only to reenter into a another massive expo hall . . . then another . . . and another . . . until Alberte flashed his badge to a giant security dude and dropped me off in a green room. Just in time, too, because I'm pretty sure at any moment my cute new tan Steve Maddens were going to be soaked crimson from blood.

"There's food, drinks, whatever you need. When you're twenty minutes out from your panel, someone will come brief you. And if there's nothing else you need, I'll be going. Enjoy Lisbon!"

---

* Curse words.

"Wait, Alberte! Do you know how big the room I'm speaking to is? Like, how many people will be in there?"

He cleared his throat. "Ah, yes, of course. The room is a thousand," he said. A thousand?! I didn't have the brain capacity to sound eloquent in front of a room of quadruple digits. Surely I had misheard.

"For a second there, I thought you said a thousand."

"Oh no," he said, as I started to maniacally laugh.

"Good, because my brain is way too crazy right now to get up in front of that many—"

"I said, *fifteen* thousand."

.

.

.

.

.

.

.

That space represents my blacking out for the next few minutes. I only came to with the use of smelling salts. Aka beelining it to the food and stuffing my face with anxiety fries.

No, no, no, no. This can't be happening, I thought to myself. I had done a million of these panels, and the largest room I had ever seen was six hundred. FIFTEEN THOUSAND PEO-PLE?! That was like a goddamn AC/DC arena show! I surveyed the room as I continued putting fries in my mouth like they'd just announced a potato famine and these were the last ones I was going to see for a while. The stage was massive, and the screens for close-ups were even bigger. I imagined my jet-lagged, puffy eyes from crying all morning projected thirty feet wide and shuddered at the thought.

When my debriefer came to meet me, I was already catapult-
ing face-first into stage 3: **Bargaining**. "I just had no idea the
room was going to be this big and I'm totally ill-prepared and
obviously this is a traumatic morning to be an American and—"
I kept rattling off reasons to try to get out of it to the nodding,
patient woman who was leading me onstage. Could I bail? No.
They flew me out here. Hell, they flew *three of us* out here. There
was no way out. I had to pull myself up by my bloody bootstraps,
block out the football arena worth of onlookers and the impend-
ing crumbling of America as a whole, and talk about the impor-
tance of Instagram, goddamnit! My name was announced, and I
walked out onto the stage. Let me tell you guys, the only thing
stranger than being cast out in front of an amphitheater full of
people is being cast out in front of an amphitheater of silent people. There might have been thousands of bodies in that room,
but you could've heard a mouse whisper a secret.

I pulled out my tiny notebook, saw my swollen face on the
monitor, attempted a Trump joke to the silent faces of the audience, and dove in. Guys, I am not exaggerating when I say that
I don't remember one goddamn thing that happened for the next
hour. I vaguely recall nodding and smiling while the two guys
talked, all while I was having my own internal conversation that
was a mix of fighting off a panic attack and internally screaming.
Like, I could hear what they were saying, but I was having a
completely different experience in my head.

By some grace of a God I don't believe in, I looked down, and
the countdown clock onstage to let us know how much time we
had left was down to thirty seconds. I thanked the two vloggers
for joining me, signed off to the up-snore-ious crowd, and hightailed it off the stage.

I was so relieved that I think the corners of my dehydrated fry mouth even upturned into a smile. "See, that wasn't that bad," the debriefer said as she led me back the green room. I had a fleeting moment where things were looking up—that is, until I looked up and saw a group of folks gathered around one of the monitors backstage.

I grabbed a white wine from the bar and edged my way closer to the screen. There she was. It was Hillary conceding. Enter Stage 4: **Depression**. I practically chugged my Vinho Verde as Hillary finished her eloquent and inspiring speech, making sure that little girls everywhere never gave up on their dreams. After the speech ended, I couldn't watch the commentary anymore; the depression was too real. I needed to get the hell out of this massive clusterfuck, get to my girls, and finally have that delicious dinner. It was as if I had been digging a tunnel with a spoon à la *Shawshank Redemption* and that delicious dinner was the light at the end. I was going to finally get to it and use that spoon to dig into something delicious.

"Fifteen thousand people?!" Joselyn shouted at me as I joined them at a cute table on a classic Lisbon tiled sidewalk.

"Yep, and my fifteen-minute Uber took an hour and fifteen minutes to get there, so it probably cost nine hundred dollars. Will you order me a double gin and tonic? I'm about to piss myself." I headed to the bathroom, clunking along in the still-very-painful Steve Maddens. After taking a piss longer than Tom Hanks in *A League of Their Own*, I attempted to leave the sliding-door bathroom and realized . . . I was stuck. I tried again. The door was still not moving. Of course. I banged on the door again and again, but no one could hear me in the bustling restaurant. I sat on the toilet, defeated. Tears started to well up in my eyes. All the previous stages of grief were taking a bonus lap through my body.

The Denial: *This can't be happening. I can't be stuck in this bathroom.*

The Anger: *Why the fuck can I not catch a break today?!*

The Bargaining: *Please just let me out and I'll never go to the bathroom again! Just let me have a drink!!*

The Depression: *Well, I live here now. This is my new home, this tiny bathroom in the back of a bar in Lisbon.*

But rather than accept it, I grabbed on to the anger and beat on the door and screamed my head off until, eventually, someone heard me. Three big waiters had to use all their might to let me out.

I drank a record two double gin and tonics and a glass of red in under thirty minutes, and then we took off to walk the small, cobblestoned streets of the Bairro Alto neighborhood to find a spot to eat. Since leaving LA, I had only eaten that tiny plate of *patatas bravas* at JFK and the anxiety fries at the convention center. My body was begging for something that wasn't a tater.

Eventually, we strolled up to a crowded alfresco place that looked appealing. Scanning the menu, I saw the three greatest words a girl can read. Nope, not "I love you" . . . I'm talking: "vegan vegetable sausage." It was as if choirs of angels were singing from the heavens. Here we were in meat-central Lisbon, and we finally found a place where my dinner could be something other than carbs. Maybe my day was turning around.

We went hard on the wine and kept attempting to talk about anything but the election, but we always circled back to it. Even on this beautiful old street, with a bottle of delicious red, surrounded by friends . . . we couldn't shake it off for a second. But my despair turned to hope as soon as that veggie brat hit the table. I was sleep deprived, and hungry, and mildly drunk, and ready to take it to the face.

"Fuck a knife and fork," I said. I picked up that sucker and bit right into it . . . or at least I tried. Turns out that Lisbon's idea of a veggie sausage was stuffing some ground-up vegetables into industrial-strength plastic. It was like trying to bite into a sleeve of saltines with the wrapper still on. My dreams of a delicious dinner clearly were dashed.

"I cannot believe this shitty wiener. What a disappointing, full of shit, piece of plastic wiener," I said, the weight of the past thirty-six hours coming to a head.

"You talking about your meal . . . or our new president? Hey-yo!" Joselyn said, nudging me and refilling my wine. And I finally laughed, the first time since before we boarded in LA. There it was . . . Stage 5: **Acceptance**.

The acceptance wasn't about the election results in any way, shape, or form, or being okay with what was happening back in the States. I don't mean that type of acceptance. But accepting that this was my reality: that I had gone from the hope of Hillary to the reality of Donald Trump in one plane flight, that I spoke to a room of fifteen thousand people but somehow didn't recall a single moment of it, that I got stuck in a bathroom for twenty minutes, and now I was eating this sorry excuse for a vegan meal. But I wasn't going to let it ruin this trip. So I asked for a sharper knife and dug right into that heavy-duty condom filled with vegetables. And wouldn't you know it, it tasted . . . terrible.

Fact is, it was a bad wiener. But twenty-four hours later, I would be in the presence of a different wiener. No, I didn't hook up with anyone in Italy. I mean the most famous of wieners: Michelangelo's *David*. I stood in front of that masterpiece, dwarfed by its wonder, in awe of its beauty. And then I positioned myself so it looked like I was cupping his junk for an Instagram post.

I didn't know if this shit show was going to be for the next four years, or four months, or the world was changing and it would be forever. . . . But I know that in that moment I was happy with my friends. And I, we, everybody needs to take those little moments when they come and not let them be tainted by the greater problems. Fact is, sometimes you're served a shitty wiener, but the only thing you can do is grab life by the balls, or David's, and try to laugh your way through it.

The Irish Hello

IF YOU DON'T know who Grace Helbig is, then I am assuming that you haven't logged on to the Internet since it was dial-up. Grace has been a major Web presence since 2008—she's an OG YouTuber, a Godfather of Jump Cuts, a proverbial Pilgrim of Putting Shit on the Web. She's also one of my closest friends.

"HOW CLOSE?" screams the audience reading this book.

So close we recently bought a vacation home together in Palm Springs and the cops came on the first night.*

Grace and I met at the Peoples Improv Theater in New York City in 2007. She was already performing on an improv team, but I had taken only one class there when we were put together on a house sketch team. On the night of our first show, I was nervous! But that all went away the second we got onstage, pretending to be a duo of party starters named Mitz and Fitz in our

---

* That story ain't in this book. Penguin, give me a third book, and give the readers what they want.

first sketch. I knew that if I went up on a line, it didn't matter because Grace could just think of something hilarious off the top of her head to get the laugh. She had my back, I had hers, and it's been like that onstage ever since.

I cannot tell you how many tours Grace and I have done together in the past decade. Along with Hannah Hart, we've performed our *No Filter Show* everywhere from basement rock clubs in Boston to gorgeous old theaters in Melbourne, Australia; and Grace and I have taken our two-person show, *This Might Get Weird, Y'all*, throughout the United States. I've watched her sing ballads about the French bulldogs she follows on Instagram and do interpretive dances about getting a toilet clogged at a party, but Grace's most impressive performance is always offstage, in her seamless, utterly perfect execution of an Irish good-bye.

Okay, so we all know what the Irish good-bye is, right? If you don't, congrats on being a person who has actual manners when leaving a social function. An Irish good-bye is when, instead of going around the room announcing that you are leaving a party or gathering, you just dip the fuck out without telling a soul.

Irish good-byes are great for getting out of the whole rigmarole of endlessly repeating "we have to get together soon" and hugging random people you had ten-second conversations with in line for the bathroom. They also come in handy when someone shows up that you want to avoid, or when you realize you are *definitely* the drunkest person at the party and you need to excuse yourself before you end up in unflattering Snapchats.

Now why is it called an Irish good-bye? No clue. I tried to officially research it and found no real results. In my experience, Irish people aren't particularly known to leave in that manner. In fact, I used to frequent the hell out of a true Irish bar in Brooklyn called the Irish Haven. The owner was a cop, and after last call at four A.M., they would just lock the doors and continue drinking. There weren't Irish good-byes at this bar. There weren't good-byes, period, because no one ever left.

Grace has elevated this curtain call to new heights. You can be having a deep convo with her, turn around for one second to get another mini quiche and BLAM. Bitch is gone by the time you turn around. I'm genuinely surprised she hasn't added elements like smoke bombs or lasers to jazz up her exits. But her illustrious career of Irish good-byes doesn't have shit on the one time we got Irish hello'd.

Picture this. It's November 2016. I had been back in the States after blocking out the election results for a week. As soon as my feet hit American soil from my Italian adventure, I was waist-deep in the depression of it all. I was watching the news nonstop, like that scene in *A Clockwork Orange* where the guy's eyes are strapped open and he's forced to watch all those terrible images, except I was the one forcing my eyes open so as to not miss anything. It got to the point where I started waking up in the middle of the night and refreshing CNN on my phone. Simply put, I couldn't handle it. Nothing felt funny. So, my antidote for not being able to laugh was to hopefully make someone else laugh. I needed to get onstage and ideally put another stamp in my passport.

Luckily, Grace felt the same way. "We can name the show *Adopt Us!* And frame the whole thing like we are trying to get adopted by our audience so we don't have to come back to America!" Grace said as I told her over one of our midday vodka-soda catch-ups in my kitchen. "I'll call the boys," I said, meaning our joint managers we've had since Grace and I were whippersnappers in Brooklyn.

You could hear the hesitation in their voices when we told

them the plan over speakerphone. It was as if we were their two teen daughters who had just turned eighteen. They knew we were going to do whatever we wanted, so they might as well grin through gritted teeth and say, "Sounds like a plan!" Within the week we had two shows booked, one on Thanksgiving Day in London and the other two days later in Dublin. It was ON.

It's also worth mentioning that this was the first time in our nine-year friendship that Grace and I were both single. And let me tell you, there's a whole new layer of friendship that is formed when neither of you is constantly texting with a boyfriend. You know that YouTube video of the two babies who are just laughing like hyenas in their diapers, trying to get to the bathroom but continuing to fall? That was us, but in our early thirties. Our managers had reason to be worried. But hell, they both had kids in private school and this was bizzznass, so they booked the shows. A few weeks of being glued to MSNBC later, and it was time to go.

Grace had to be in New York the week before tour, so rather than just meet her in London, I headed out a day early to meet her in NYC. The plan was to put on our sweats, lock ourselves in our hotel room, and wake up that Sunday morning with a fully fleshed-out show before our flight to London. That way, we could relax when we got there for a few days and not have the monkey on our backs of planning a show. It was the perfect plan. We never did things that far in advance. Every single time we booked a tour, we said it was going to be different, that we'd prep ahead of time, and yet every single time, we ended up drinking till three in the morning thirty-six hours before our first set, creating lyrics to an opening number and Photoshopping ridiculous pictures, e.g., this Rest in Peace Dick Bicycle image that went up on the big screens during this very tour.

You know it's a classy tour when this is projected on
a movie-theater-size screen behind you.

While our plan to prep in NYC had great intentions behind it,
we were now living in the era of single Grace and Mamrie. "We
work better with a buzz," we rationalized. "It's like gasoline to start
the engine of our brains. Let's go out to a bar." One drink turned
into two, two turned into too many, and lo and behold both of us
ended up getting white-girl wasted, high-fiving each other as we
parted ways to reunite with boys we knew from our past.

"I'll text you when I get up," I said, slurring as I entered a cab
headfirst. "What hotel are you in again?" Grace replied, and I
nodded like I had heard anything over the subway rushing under
the grates below her ankle boots. I got myself in and rolled down
the window as the yellow cab drove off: "Mace is getting laid!!!"*

The next morning, I woke up freaking out. *What time is it?
Goddamnit! I fell asleep in my contacts again.* I painfully squinted
to see the time on the TV. It was ten fifty. My stomach dropped.

---

* "Mace" is our "ship" name, the combo of our first names together. It also has an extra
layer because, just like mace spray, when we get together, that shit can be dangerous.

I had missed my nine thirty flight. Who knew how many times Grace had called, wondering where I was, and not knowing the name of my hotel?! *She must be livid*, I thought. *Livid, and an hour over the Atlantic en route to London without me.*

Why hadn't I woken up from the alarm on my phone? Had I even set an alarm? And most important, WHERE WAS MY PHONE?!

I destroyed my room looking for it. I straight-up picked the mattress off the bed like I was performing a drug raid. No luck. I got on my laptop to find the number for the bar we'd last been to, then went all nineties reenactor and used the landline to call them. I was hopeful, until an annoyed morning-shift bartender who probably takes five of these calls a day replied they didn't have it.

I didn't know Grace's hotel, either, so the only thing left was e-mail. I typed in a panic. . . .

"GRACE! HOLY SHIT DUDE, I AM SO SORRY! I think my phone must've dropped in my cab last night but I was too drunk to notice. I just woke up! I am so sorrrrrrry. I'll find another flight ASAP!!!!!!"

I sat there anxiously hitting refresh until an e-mail from Grace popped into my in-box. I clicked it to be greeted by a very chill "All good dude, I'm just waking up, too." We had *both* over-slept. What a relief! Misery might love company, but fucking up welcomes a whole guest list.

Our hangover fever-dreamed us through an endless after-noon at an AT&T store, spending WAY too much on new flights going out that night, and trying to ward off our pulsing headaches. Come seven o'clock and we finally had our butts in coach, ready to turn off our new phones (Grace upgraded, too!) and pass the hell out.

We woke up in England ready to rock. And by that I mean we went to an awards show, got drunk with our SORTEDfood boys,* and once again creating our show in the twenty-four hours leading up to it. We might be procrastinators, but at least we have consistency going for us! *Adopt Us!* existed, and no one asked for a refund. So, with the London show under our belt, we headed to the land of Guinness.

"Welcome to Dublin!" our dapper Irish driver said as he took the carry-ons from our shaky, hungover hands. We got the rest of our luggage from the baggage carousel and trudged slowly behind him as he pushed the cart with all our suitcases full of dirty clothes and ridiculous props. Honestly, if you think airport security is a pain in the ass, try getting your carry-ons full of props through an X-ray machine. There's nothing like holding up the line as an unamused TSA agent pulls a blow-up doll out of your bag. This is an actual thing that happened to me in Chicago after a show. No regrets.

As we walked through the enclosed overpass to the parking garage, we came up behind a group of four dudes. I don't mean to help strengthen the Irish stereotype but it was ten A.M., and these guys were WRECKED. They were wobbling harder than Tara Reid at the 1999 MTV Beach House.

We passed them with a good few feet of distance so as to not draw any attention to ourselves, heads down into our phones, soaking up the last little bit of airport Wi-Fi. We were almost past these ogres when one came straight toward Grace.

---

* For those of you who've read the first book, you will remember these British blokes as the dudes who saved Grace's and Jos's and my butts by giving us a ride home from Vegas after Britney Spears's show. Don't know this story? I'm sure that book is cheaper on Amazon right now than one decent glass of wine. You're almost done with this one; Prime Now it for backup!

"I like your hat," he said, referring to Grace's classic knit cap with a pom-pom on top.

"Thank you," she said nervously, and kept walking. And then, this Irish asshole reaches his baseball mitt of a hand and roughly pats Grace on the head five times. It was like he momentarily forgot what personal space meant and decided to play Whack-a-Mole with a human. Grace's eyes went as wide as dinner plates. I knew my Queen of Hating Confrontation didn't want to yell at him like he deserved. I had an "if you touch her again, I will punch you in the penis" lined up in my throat, but I knew the best thing to do was to keep walking. These guys were wasted, and if they casually bonk a girl on the head as a means of morning "flirting," I didn't want to see what they would do when they were pissed off.

We picked up our speed and didn't say anything till we were safely in the back of the car. We were flabbergasted. "I can't believe that guy touched you!" I said, as our car looped around to the exit.

"I didn't know what to do. How did he think that's okay?" Our driver paid the parking attendant, and as we drove under the gate, the sound of tires screeching emerged from behind us.

"Those tinkers just got through on our parking pass and nearly rear-ended us," the driver said, his brow furrowed. For those of you not familiar with the term "tinker," allow me to explain. Knowing this Irish slang is one of the many things I learned from hanging out in that aforementioned Irish bar in Brooklyn. A tinker is a word to describe a traveler, also known as a Gypsy. You might have seen them on the TLC masterpiece *My Big Fat American Gypsy Wedding*. It's basically *Jersey Shore* meets *Teen Mom*, but with trashy youngsters spending too much on weddings that always end in fistfights. It's essentially the equivalent of European white trash culture. And I'm allowed to say that because I've been arrested for being too drunk at a Lynyrd Skynyrd concert in Alabama.

Anyway, back in the car, our driver was gripping the wheel for dear life. It was clear that these guys were drunk driving, swerving a few cars behind us. As a person with car anxiety, my whole body was clenched. They then straight-up *Fast and Furious*'ed around other cars to make their way right beside us. The head bopper rolled down the window, leaned his head back, and SPIT on our window.

You could've driven a train through our mouth with how wide our jaws dropped. And with one quick "Fucking Americans!" they sped off. We cracked up as soon as the shock passed. We hadn't been in Ireland for more than fifteen minutes, and this is what we were greeted with.

"Welcome to Dublin!" our driver said again. "Welcome to Dublin!" we repeated, laughing hysterically. And off in the distance we watched karma do its job as their car slammed through the side railing of an overpass and crash-landed on the ground below.*

The rest of the day went smoothly. We got our naps in and then had an awesome show despite being a little nervous, since Dublin is the only town we've ever been heckled on a previous tour. I was feeling celebratory and ready to go at it.

"I think we should go out tonight," I said, sipping on a perfectly poured Guinness that the stage manager had left for me in our dressing room. Grace popped her head out of the bathroom, her face covered in neon paint.

"I don't know. Hasn't this day been, like, nine years long?"

---

* That did NOT happen. Karma doesn't work like that. But how hilarious is it that people who aren't reading these footnotes think I'm an awful person?

We ended every show by breaking up with audience members onstage and then covering our faces with paint to Gotye's "Somebody That I Used to Know." Don't make me explain our art.

There she was. Old-school Grace. The Grace who would need to go back and check in with a boyfriend via WhatsApp before the time change got weird, the one who would rather stay in her hotel than go out. But there was no boyfriend this time, damnit! We needed to rally.

"Grace, the last time we were here, we were heckled and then got into that ridiculous fight.* Then ol' Spit Take this morning? Come on. We have to have an Irish memory that's good besides being onstage."

---

* Yeah, you wish I'd write about that, don't you?? Some friendship stories must remain among friends.

I saw a little glimmer in her eyes. "Okay, we'll go out for *two* drinks. That's it. We don't need to be losing phones or missing flights tomorrow." I pumped my fist in the air. I got her! Single Grace was coming out!

We dropped our stuff off in our rooms, did a Superman-in-a-phone-booth speed change of clothes (not that our super flattering onesies wouldn't have been a hit) and headed out. Luckily we didn't have to go far because our hotel was just a couple of blocks off Temple Bar, the Irish equivalent of Bourbon Street. We walked our already-tipsy asses straight into the first place we saw and sidled up to the bar. There was a band playing, and the whole place was in full swing.

"What can I get you ladies?" asked the cute older bartender. "Do you have Fireball?" we asked in unison. They did not. In fact, in the land of Jameson, even asking for it was probably blasphemous. But they did have something exactly like it, so spicy cinnamon whiskey shots and Guinness it was! After about a half hour of chatting with the bartenders and listening to the band playing the traditional Irish tunes of the Red Hot Chili Peppers and the Eagles, two dudes approached us.

"Mametown and Smellbig, is it?" the one who looked like a poor man's Keanu Reeves asked. *OH GOD*, I thought. *They're fans.* I was debating in my head just how inappropriate it would be to hook up with fans before I remembered we were wearing soccer jerseys with our names on the back that we'd been given by the sweetest girl at our preshow meet-and-greet. "Oh. Hi, I'm Mamrie, this is Grace." We explained the shirts and that we had just done a comedy show and were in town for only one night.

"Us, too!" said his friend, who, considering his blond curls, could have been the Bill to Keanu's Ted. "We're here doing business for one night."

"What do you do?" Grace asked, motioning the eavesdropping older bartender and the hot younger bartender for another round.

"We're in finance. We work for ING out of Amsterdam. Just had to come in for a meeting today." Grace and I shot each other looks. Bankers out of Amsterdam were not our style, and their boot-cut jeans were definitely not our (or anyone with taste after 2007) style, either. But then again, we were ready to make a memory, and this was presenting itself as an interesting possibility.

The younger bartender set down the shots. "Do y'all want one, too?" Grace asked. They agreed, and we took down some Flameballz (or whatever it was called) and chatted. We had to admit, they were kind of douchey. And the bartenders definitely thought we were lowering our standards by the way they were cutting eyes at us. Just then, a cute girl came over and handed the dudes a shot, winked, and walked off.

"Who was that?" Grace asked.

"Ohhh." Keanu shook his head. "She's one of our coworkers. She's actually super annoying. I think she thinks we're definitely going to hook up, but I am *so* not into that."

Grace and I shot each other a suspicious look, as the coworker kept motioning the guys to come join their group.

"Ugh, we'll be back in just a sec," and with that the Dutch Bill and Ted went over to their coworkers to join them for a shot.

This is when Grace and I used our powers of being longtime friends and began communicating telepathically. Not an actual word was uttered between us, but this convo happened through our eyes. . . .

GRACE: Something is up with these dudes.
MAME: Yeah, that was totally *not* a coworker.

GRACE: Also, they haven't offered to buy us a drink.

MAME: We bought *them* a drink. And that girl did, too.

GRACE: Something's fishy, and it's not just this Guinness.

MAME: What do you mean?

GRACE: Don't they use some kind of fish guts in the beer-making process?

MAME: Fuck my life. I'm going to pretend I didn't hear that.

GRACE: BTW, why are we speaking telepathically when those dudes left and we can just use real voices?

I cleared my throat, which was already a little scratchy from all the travel and shows and debauchery. It felt like losing my phone in New York had been eighty-four years earlier. "Maybe we should just pack it in for the evening," I said, barely believing the words coming out of my own mouth. "I mean, I know we are in the country of luck, but it does not look like we are getting lucky tonight."

"No, let's wait. These dudes don't deserve an Irish good-bye." I was shocked. Grace, the QUEEN of Irish good-byes, was refusing to leave that old wooden bar, like a hippie chained to a tree. I didn't know what was about to happen, but I knew I could trust her.

Bill and Ted came back, and Grace popped into full girl-flirt mode. I followed her lead. I cannot deny or confirm if I twirled my hair with my finger. You could tell between their exchanged looks that they thought it was a done deal. A pair of shoo-ins, one might say; meanwhile, we were about to put a metaphorical shoe-in their ass.

"So, tell us about your job," Grace said, adding on a little LA vocal fry for effect. "It must be super stressful. Freddie Mac is a big company."

Ted smiled. "It is. But we make time for fun," he said, placing his arm around my shoulder.

"Oh really?" Grace said with a smile that then fell flatter than my sixth-grade chest. "You said you worked at ING. You guys are full of shit."

Ted looked to Bill, his eyes wide. "Wait, what did we say?"

I picked up Ted's hand from my shoulder with two fingers like it was a piece of litter and handed it back to him. "Oh my god! You two could've been plumbers and we wouldn't have cared. You blew it." We hopped off our barstools and breezed past them as they trailed behind.

"You two are obviously lying, too!" Keanu shouted. "You aren't comedians! You haven't made us laugh once."

"Yeah, well, that's our job and you're not paying us. I'd say buy a ticket, but it sounds like you don't have any money." We kept walking toward the door, but right before we got there, Grace turned on a dime. She walked right up to their female "coworkers" and pulled the smiley one to the side. "Just so you know, these dudes aren't bankers, and they said you all were annoying." Girl comically GASPED. Bet Bill and Ted wished they had a time-traveling phone booth then!

The only people smiling harder than us were the two bartenders, who had been watching this spectacle the whole time. We changed directions and smiled right back.

Turns out, despite confronting these two jerks on their terrible game, there actually was an Irish good-bye that night. And by this I mean that those two bartenders hopped right out of the bar and left with Grace and me during the middle of their shift. Our luck had changed.

Frasierween

WHEN IT COMES to doing outrageous, fun shit, a lot of people talk the talk but never walk the walk. In fact, forget walking; some people simply *crawl* through life, staying low and close to the ground, careful not to get hurt or, worse, embarrass themselves. Not me! I don't want to just walk the walk; I want to throw on moon shoes and bounce my way through life! When it comes to the type of dumb, outrageous ideas that become legend, New Year's Eve 2016 takes the cake.

Despite my general love of drinks and debauchery, I've never been a big New Year's person. There's always so much hype and expectation for things to be crazy, which to me feels like an awkward cloud of forced fun hanging above your head all night. I've had some fun ones—you might recall the mushrooms, catching myself on fire, shallow champagne tub story of New Year's '05. But nine times out of ten, it's a whole lot of work with not that great of a payoff. Personally, I am a bigger fan of Halloween, my absolute favorite holiday. Besides the ability to make anything "slutty"—I have been a slutty Tetris piece before—I also love that it's the one day out of the year that you can scare the shit out of kids and no one bats an eye. If you rolled up on a neighbor's house any other day of the year, and the front yard was covered with fake dismembered hands and feet, and a man pretended to be a scarecrow only to terrify the living hell out of your kids and then try to make nice with them with a mini Snickers, that shit would not fly. But on Halloween? Sure, why not? Throw in a chain saw while you're at it to really solidify some nightmares.

In September of 2016, I met up with my friends Scotty and Flula to get some drinks. Scotty is a friend I've known about eight years since back in the Brooklyn days. He is a hilarious comedy writer, an even better drinker, and is always down for a weird time. We share the same mentality when it comes to doing something for the sake of randomness. Flula is one of the funniest motherfuckers on the planet. He looks like he might've been an experiment by the German government because he is tall and perfectly built. With his thick accent and affinity for fanny packs and dancing, he's basically a Bavarian Party Ken doll.

So, there we were, sitting in our swivel chairs at our go-to bar, Taix. Taix is one of those rare places that hasn't changed at all since it opened in 1972, with its plaid carpeting and its menu full of things like coq au vin and escargot. Sure, there are your standard hipsters who filter through the bar on a nightly basis, but for the most part, you are delightfully surrounded by old people slurping on mussels and croque madams. My favorite sighting I've ever had there was Ron Jeremy, the godfather of porn actors, sitting by himself, eating a big bowl of soup, with a napkin tucked into the neck of his shirt, while watching the news on the bar's TV. Just goes to show ya, you can have sex with more than two thousand people on camera and still end up eating your minestrone alone.

Anyway, Scotty and Flula and I were shooting the shit over some cocktails and got around to talking about Halloween. "I don't remember what I've done once for Halloween since I moved here," I admitted.

"I went to a party last year, but I don't really want to go to one this year," Scotty said.

"But I used to LOVE Halloween," I said, beginning to get really bummed about a love that was once so passionate. At one point in my life, I had started planning my costumes months in advance, and now I would just ask my friends what they were up to the day before and half-heartedly do whatever was easiest, like a lover planning intricate dates for their partner, then years later just saying, "Meh, let's order Domino's."

"Let's do something very weird this year. Very strange," Flula said after his third Bulleit on the rocks.

Now, I don't remember what sparked this idea, but by our fifth round, we had decided that the funniest thing alive would be if we, along with some other recruits, went out for Halloween in Seattle dressed as the cast of *Frasier*.

In case you aren't well versed in Kelsey Grammer's catalog, *Frasier* was a TV show that took place in Seattle. It was 100 percent silly sitcom antics at its finest, involving two uppity brothers whose crotchety, masculine dad comes to live with them and hijinks ensue. When I watched it as a youngin', I don't think I even understood most of the jokes, but I still loved it. They spoke so eloquently and were always drinking sherry and quoting old plays. I felt classier just watching it, despite being a kid in Bumfuck, North Carolina, sitting on a tie-dyed beanbag, eating veggie nuggets.

"I would want to be the dad's recliner and make people sit on me," I said, having no fucking clue how someone would even pull off making a recliner costume.

"I would be the Space Needle!" Flula said, his eyes getting as big as Ping-Pong balls.

"You would both be inanimate objects?" Scotty asked as we nodded. "Well, I would be Frasier. I think if I grew my hair out for a couple of weeks, I could pull it off." The night progressed, and our ideas for the event got more and more specific. We would have to have a solid crew of eight to round out other characters and prop pieces. Seemed doable. And then someone had the genius idea that we could rent a party bus and do a bar crawl, blasting the *Frasier* theme song each time we rolled up to the bar.

"We can call it Frasierween," I said, knee-deep in vodka at this point. "Frasierween!" we all said in unison. We kept on brainstorming till the place closed, which wasn't that late, because, as I said, the majority of the clientele are well into their seventies.

The next day we all texted about what a fun idea it was. We were fired up and wanted to pull it off. But days turned into weeks, and all our schedules becoming insane, and, sure enough, Halloween was right on our heels and we hadn't done any planning. We found ourselves back at Taix.

"We really dropped the ball on that one," I said. "I guess we can always do it next Halloween. Frasier is timeless, after all." I looked over to see Scotty scheming. I can tell when he has an idea that he's excited to share but is still gathering his thoughts, because his eyes squint a little and his upper lip curls in like Fire Marshall Bill, displaying his front teeth.

"It doesn't necessarily have to be on Halloween," he said. Flula and I leaned in, ready to hear what dumb shit was about to follow. "What if we went up there for New Year's? It would almost be *more* fun because people would be so confused why we're all in costumes."

Flula and I looked at each other. It was taking an already weird event and making it even stranger. "But everything is so packed on New Year's Eve. Do we really want to go out in big costumes to packed bars?" Flula asked, concern in his eyes.

"True. Last year I wanted to avoid crowds so bad that I literally went and ate Chinese food three blocks from my place, drank a couple of glasses of champagne on my couch, and was asleep by eleven," I said.

"What if we went out on December thirtieth?" Flula said with a mischievous look. We all sat there thinking about it for a second; then one by one we grinned like silent idiots. "That is perfect," I said. Scotty leaned back in his swivel chair, folding his hands and nodding at the ceiling. A modern-day equivalent of Auguste Rodin's *The Thinker.*

"This could work," he said, still nodding. "That way the bars aren't super crowded and then when we are all hungover on New Year's Day, everybody can do whatever they want. There's no pressure."

IT WAS DECIDED. THIS WAS HAPPENING.

Despite my doubts, I knew it was locked in when Scotty sent his flight info to Flula and me, a move more official than tagging someone you've just started dating in a pic on Instagram. We needed to invite more folks, but who would be willing to travel to Seattle? Luckily for us, we had a few friends from New York City who were going to be there anyway. Scotty invited his girlfriend, and Flula had a friend who lived there who was also down. It was all coming together. We had a solid eight folks, and we were off and running.

Anticipation grew with the coming months, until, finally, I was on my flight to Seattle. My heart was filled with excitement, and my checked luggage was filled with the recliner costume that I had made with foam core, hot glue, striped fabric, a nude onesie, and a lot of hope that it wouldn't fall apart immediately.

I got checked into my hotel, which was a corner suite, *ooh la la*, and waited for the rest of the crew to trickle in throughout the day. That night we sat at the hotel bar, drinking too many rounds and figuring out our bar route for the next night's festivities. We were all going to do our thing during the day and then meet downstairs at five for a drink. The party bus would be arriving at six.

To say the next night was epic is an understatement. To say it was very drunk is a lie. It was BEYOND. Here we all are before the tsunami of mayhem and Jägermeister kicked in.

Yep, we had a fake Eddie the dog and a REAL dog. Then later I had a stuffed dog to attach to my seat. We did not come to play.

As you can see, we had our classic Frasier, brother Niles, dad Marty, producer Roz, a recliner, the Space Needle, a piano, and Eddie the Dog. The real dog was just a temporary loaner. Despite Seattle being all cool and weird, they wouldn't let a canine come on the bar crawls.

The rest of the night became a blur of bars, doing as we promised and blaring the *Frasier* theme song from a portable speaker we carried with us. In fact, that is the only thing we played in the party bus, too. If I had to guess, I would say that we played that theme song four hundred times.

Every time we entered a bar, we were met with two reactions. People would ask us what we were doing, and one of us would say, in our own variation, "We are celebrating Frasierween, a holiday we made up where you go on a bar crawl dressed as the cast of *Frasier*. The only rule being that it can't be on an actual holiday."

People either went, "Ohhhh, got it," and nodded, clearly confused, or said, "That's amazing! Can I get a pic?" By the time we were all very inebriated and got to our fourth bar, a tiki-themed spot with karaoke, our group started dropping like flies. My friend dressed as Niles got to the point where she was just housing pizza at the bar, looking so upset you would've thought Daphne had just dumped her.

"Excuse me?" A lady with a sweet face approached me, holding her boyfriend's hand. He looked nervous, perhaps because he was watching a striped recliner do the Dougie. "Excuse me, I hate to bother you, but my boyfriend and I saw you all and we were wondering . . . Are you the cast of *Frasier*?"

"You know it!" I said, still dancing. At this point, the boyfriend face-palmed his forehead and started shaking his head and grinning ear to ear. "I told you. Oh my god, this is amazing."

He was in awe. The girlfriend piped in: "You don't understand. That is his favorite show. He's obsessed, so when he saw you guys walk in, he freaked out."

"With good reason! It's an amazing show," I said, taking a seat in a chair beside me. I went on to explain to them at length what Frasierween was. I mean it when I say that the boyfriend's eyes were lit up and he was open-mouthed smiling like he was in sex ed and just learning about the glory of doing it. When I finished, the girlfriend chimed in again: "Would it be okay if he—"

He cut her off, looking bashful. "No, it's okay."

"Don't act embarrassed. I'm drunk as a skunk dancing in a recliner costume. What do you want?"

Girlfriend continued, "Can he take a picture with you?"

"Only if he sits on my lap." I patted my seat cushion, and he approached me with the excitement and hesitation that is usually only seen when a four-year-old is next up to see Santa Claus. He plopped down on my lap, his girlfriend snapped a few pics, and then he hopped right up. "Thank you so much. This . . . this . . . this is incredible." He smiled and started to walk away. His girlfriend lingered for a second and then leaned in when he was out of earshot, which wasn't hard because someone was wailing on some Radiohead* on the karaoke mic. "Seriously, thank you. We got engaged over Thanksgiving, and this moment is probably the highlight of his year." That alone made this entire spectacle worth it.

After that bar, the night got blurry. The next morning I woke up, and it looked like someone had hired a set designer to make my suite look like a drunk girl had come home to it. It was

---

* No. Just no. Please don't sing Radiohead on karaoke. Or Tool. Or Live. Or Pearl Jam. Or anything else that won an MTV VMA in the nineties for the alternative category.

textbook: My purse was dropped right at the door with all its contents sprawled everywhere. My bodysuit was crumpled right in front of the toilet, indicating I had pulled it down to urinate and just kicked it off right there. An entire bottle of minibar wine was opened, of which I drank two sips before passing out but definitely forgot to recork, so that forty-dollar bottle was ruined. Twenty dollars a sip!

Fun fact: We got so drunk that Flula woke up in my recliner outfit and I woke up as the Space Needle. Not even together. We just randomly switched costumes at some point and don't remember it.

I spent a good part of that day recovering before dragging myself out to explore. Our hotel was a block from a pier with a Ferris wheel on it. I trudged my crazy-brained self down there, grabbing a snack on the way. That snack being a pack of candy cigarettes that allowed for this official Ferris wheel pic.

The rest of the day was perfectly lazy. Everyone came over to my suite to receive their surprise satin baseball jackets complete with the official "Frasierween #1" patch Scotty had designed. We got Thai food. We all piled back in my suite wearing robes and watched some New Year's Eve coverage. We were zonked and so happy to not be out in the madness.

When the clock struck midnight, I found myself sitting in a hot bath with a glass of wine. Ringing in the New Year in a tub . . . sound familiar? It's exactly how I ended my first book. But unlike a decade earlier, I wasn't on mushrooms and sitting in six inches of room-temp champagne. I was submerged in hot bubbles and drinking a classy red. I was a mature woman in my thirties now, and times were changing faster than ever.

Ashleigh, the girl I used to drink bottles of Popov vodka with, would soon be giving bottles to a little baby. I was dating for the first time in my adult life. My friendships with women had grown stronger and more supportive. I could focus on my career and pursue opportunities unabashedly. And I was *happy*.

I heard once that with the rate that your body regenerates its cells, you are basically a new person every seven years. I felt like my heart and brain had been on a regenerating fast track those past twelve months, learning who I was on my own. Truly independent, not just an independent mind with someone to seal in all the cracks. I was proud of myself. Proud of the boozy, solo-dancing adult I'd become. Proud of my Southern accent that I still clung to. Proud that I was unabashedly driven by work, which allowed me this ridiculous life that I was so thankful to carve out. I was proud of this new brain and heart. . . . But I was also exhausted.

Perhaps I should take a few months when I get back to LA and take it easy, I thought as I turned on the shower because I'm no animal that just sits in their own stew without a rinse afterward. *Buckle down and get my adult on for a minute.*

And that's exactly what I did. I boarded my flight to LA the next morning, content with my adventures from the year before and ready to drop anchor.

When my plane started taxiing that next morning and the pilot came on the intercom, he greeted us with a "Happy New Year, everybody, this is your pilot speaking. Our flight time to Los Angeles today is about four hours and twenty-five minutes." I snuggled into my window seat and looked out as we ascended into the clouds, knowing that when we touched down, I would be taxiing into a calmer, more mature year ahead of me. . . .

GUYS. Come on, we've been together a couple hundred pages here. You should know that there's no damn way I was going out like that. Instead, the captain came on and let us know that it would be a smooth and easy flight to New Orleans.

Remember that first guy from Raya, who caught my attention by complimenting my dog? Well, after I got out of the tub that night, we texted about how fun it would be to spend the first few days of the new year ripping it up in the Big Easy. Naturally, I changed my flight.

. . . After all, I don't want to be telling the same stories over and over again. It was time to go make some more!

Until next time—

XOXO, Mamrie*

---

* Can you imagine if I earnestly ended my book with an "XOXO" like I'm Gossip Girl or something?! LOLZ. See you next time, suckas.

Acknowledgments

The acknowledgments page kind of feels like an acceptance speech at an awards show. Except this time, it's like, "Thank you to all these people for actually accepting me." So, here goes . . .

First of all, a massive thanks and hug to Kate Napolitano, my editor extraordinaire for both my first book and this one. That woman knows more about my vagina and inner thoughts than I do. I will gladly pay for your inevitable therapy, Kate.

A huge thanks to all my friends who have not only put up with me the past couple of years but also threw caution to the wind and went on so many adventures with me. And then, so lovingly agreed to let me write about it once I had them good and liquored up. Maegan, Ashleigh, Melissa, Veronica, Hannah, Renata, Renee, Tess, Jess, Hayley, and, of course, some honorary dudes as well . . . Jarrett, Frasierween crew, and Dustin.

Special shout-out to Grace Helbig for being on the maniac train with me, but also for being a constant source of inspiration and creativity and an overall badass comedy partner who I can't wait to *Golden Girls* with in Palm Springs.

And biggest thanks to Joselyn Hughes who, these past two years, has not only been my travel partner and absolute rock (yes, both supportive and very Dwayne Johnson–esque) but has also stepped in to so many roles. Which include but are not limited to: roommate, ledge-talker-off'er, personal chef, dance partner, dog aunt, spiritual guide, sister, and so much more.

I'd like to thank my family, obvs. Thanks for letting me let it all out there and still supporting me . . . or at least doing a great job of pretending to but secretly cringing. Especially my brother, Dave, who lived with me during the summer of single mayhem and is always ready for tacos, a drink, and a bitch fest. And to Seth, who isn't family but feels like it. Wouldn't be here doing all these wonderful things without you being in my corner for a decade.

My team of professional peoples who might have freaked me out at that Rockefeller Center lunch but pushed me because they believe in me, even when I'm having doubts. C.C. Hirsch, Cait Hoyt, all the folks at CAA. Tess Finkle (and Duff) for being not only an idea machine and cheerleader but also helping me make these adventures happen logistically and then giving the best performance the Red Light District has ever seen. And, of course, Vincent Nastri, manager and friend, who always has my back and an available pack of mints.

31901061054344